The Future

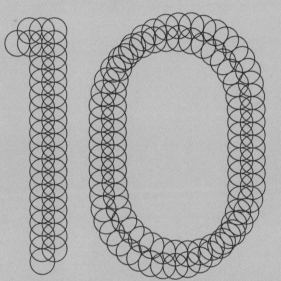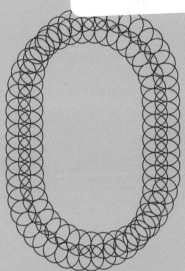

改變未來的 100 件事

2021 年全球百大趨勢

+WUNDERMAN
THOMPSON

2021 The Future 100
Writer / Wunderman Thompson Intelligence

Editor-in-chief / Emma Chiu
Editor / Emily Safian-Demers
Writers / Chen May Yee, Marie Stafford, Elizabeth Cherian, Sarah Tilley, Maeve Prendergast, Nina Jones, Jessica Rapp
Sub editors / Hester Lacey, Katie Myers

Creative director / Shazia Chaudhry

Assistant editor / Jill Chang, Ophelia Lee, Yafan Chang, Vik Liu, Yongyan Jiang, Pin Hsu, Zola Wu, Emily Wu, Kevin Huang, Tina Chen, Chia Huang, Wei Huang, Sandra Tsai, Cloud Kao

Chinese version contributor / Wunderman Thompson Taipei

Translator / Rye Lin Ting-Ru

Publisher / Wunderman Thompson Taipei
Address / 13F - 5, No.8, Sec. 7, Civic Boulevard, Nangang District, Taipei City, 115, Taiwan
Tel / (02) 3766-1000
Fax / (02) 2788-0260

Agent / China Times Publishing Company
Tel / (02) 2306-6842
Address / No.351, Sec.2, Wanshou Rd., Guisha District., Taoyuan City, 333, Taiwan

Retail price / NTD 500
ISBN / 978-986-98992-1-5

+
WUNDERMAN
THOMPSON
A REPORT BY WUNDERMAN THOMPSON INTELLIGENCE

Introduction

Cautious optimism sets the pace for 2021 as the world reflects on the challenges of 2020 and enters a hopeful year of economic rebound and societal healing. Big change is already in motion. The United Kingdom exits the European Union, a Biden-Harris administration assumes leadership, and multiple promising COVID-19 vaccines roll out around the world—offering a glimpse of a post-pandemic era.

The need for brands to plan ahead, understand consumer behaviors that will stick, and employ creative innovation is more important than ever. "The Future 100: 2021" previews 100 bitesize trends and changes to track this year.

Tech's influence on culture and economies accelerates. Conferences, festivals and brand launches turn to gaming as the chosen third space to reach existing and new audiences (New gaming frontiers, page 9). Retailers merge entertainment and ecommerce into engaging live digital experiences (Live commerce, page 145). But amid the opportunities, new cautions arise, as issues such as data sustainability (page 37) and deepfakes (page 42) dominate conversations around how to create a safe and durable digital ecosystem.

Brand purpose goes mainstream, driven by ethical consumers who continue to turn to businesses that reflect their values. This is being propelled by companies like Did They Help? keeping tabs on brands' efforts—or failure—to do good (Ethical scoreboard, page 81). Businesses are also looking at the bigger picture, choosing to collaborate to tackle social and environmental challenges (Branding together, page 73).

Health is elevated and now extends into every business. Expect to see brands designing business plans and marketing around public health, and the appointment of chief health officers (page 164) to the C-suite leadership team.

The report also includes 21 predictions from industry experts, weighing in on their one big projection for 2021.

The road to recovery begins this year. Brands, leaders and individuals are guiding us towards a hopeful journey that requires collaboration and resilience in order to achieve restoration and betterment.

Emma Chiu
Global Director, Wunderman Thompson Intelligence
intelligence.wundermanthompson.com

Introduction

This will be the fourth year publishing the Chinese edition of *The Future 100* in Taiwan. I am glad to have received a lot of positive feedback about the content. Some said it is the essential tool book for their annual strategy brainstorm meeting; others have shared how it has inspired new business ideas. Some even expressed gratitude towards me because they felt like this book brought them on a journey, showed them snippets of things happening around the world.

Yet no future forecast could've predicted the pandemic. Because of the pandemic, people have changed their lifestyle.

Due to the pandemic, people started social distancing. Desires to be in the outdoors have increased because of it.

We see the business of food delivery services skyrocketed as people are trying to avoid contact with others. As a result, new restaurant concepts like the ghost kitchen(page 107) were born.

Live events were forced to cancel due to the pandemic. Game industry has bloomed since people need something to do when they are home. Even some of the conferences and corporate events lie in gaming. Gaming is no longer just for gameplay(page 13). It will set to emerge as the next dominant technology platform—much the way search engines, mobile phones and social networks redefined industries in previous decades, the *Wall Street Journal* reported.

The work from home model, used to be considered a rare luxury in conventional companies, became the norm for many people. When you stay at home for too long, you are eager to go out. As a result, new concepts such as "touchless travel"(page 44) and "isolationist travel"(page 76) have been introduced. What even more, workcation—a new kind of travel that blends work and play (page 168).

The pandemic has made the past irreversible, and the future unfathomable. People are still finding ways to live with it. Social connectivity, environment protection, clicks and mortar, nostalgic formats, auto organisms, decarbonized aviation, climate-friendly diets, circular market, suitability and morality, brand safety, upending deepfakes, space exploration, stratospheric cloud service, dark store, social media credit, digital nutrition, transformation of ewallet, universal income experiments… etc, the pandemic didn't stop revolutionary ideas from happening.

Therefore, we believe in ourselves. We will get over this pandemic with more technologies, understanding and care for everyone. We have faith in not being separated from each other, but even closer.

Why do we believe? Because all these trends revealed in this book gave us strong faith and confidence, let us hope for a bright tomorrow.

Evan Teng
Managing Director, Wunderman Thompson Taipei

Culture

01

Outdoor redesigned

The prioritization of open-air experiences is driving innovation and investment in outdoor public spaces.

From spring 2021, Manhattan will have a new floating island park, located in the Hudson River. Designed by Heatherwick Studio and conceived by billionaire couple Barry Diller and Diane von Furstenberg, the two-acre Little Island will expand New York's limited green space and will feature lawns, gardens, meadows and an amphitheater hosting artists, bands and entertainers as part of a program of waterfront performances.

Copenhagen residents will also have a new venue where they can hang out on the water. Plans for Copenhagen Islands were unveiled in April 2020 by Australian architect Marshall Blecher and Danish firm Studio Fokstrot. The "parkipelago" will comprise a cluster of floating "islands" in the city's harbor where people can relax, swim, fish and even watch the stars. The move comes after the success of a similar island prototype, CPH-Ø1, in 2018. Made with sustainability in mind,

Little Island at Pier 55. Image courtesy of Heatherwick Studio

Copenhagen Islands are being constructed from steel and recycled flotation materials, covered in lush trees and greenery and anchored to the sea floor. The underside of each island will provide space where aquatic life can flourish.

Precht has designed Parc de la Distance, a maze-like park in a vacant green space in Vienna. Tall hedges separate the many routes in the park, allowing people to explore the green space while adhering to social distancing guidelines. The design aims to overcome the challenge posed when public parks closed their gates during the pandemic.

In England, engineering firm Arup is creating new seating areas for public spaces that allow for social distancing, as part of Liverpool Without Walls. This project, devised in collaboration with Meristem Design and Liverpool City Council, will see adaptable modular units, referred to as "hybrid street furniture," installed around the city.

Why it's interesting
Green spaces are shaping up to be the future of city planning. Outdoor urban spots have long been attractive assets for city-dwellers around the world, and with the outbreak of COVID-19, the desire for fresh air and open space has intensified. Urban designers are pointing the way forward to more permanent solutions, creating new cultural spaces backed by hefty investments.

01

02

New gaming frontiers

The stage is set for a gaming revolution.

The consumer gaming industry is expected to reach a value of $198 billion by 2024, not including sales from hardware and devices, augmented reality, virtual reality and advertising, research from consulting firm Activate revealed. This growth is likely due in part to the fact that digital games are increasingly serving as the backdrop for a variety of activities, from going to a concert to celebrating a graduation to staging a protest.

More and more traditional gaming spaces are transforming into cultural centers where people can virtually gather for community, entertainment and business.

Game payments firm Xsolla thinks the future of conferences and corporate events lies in gaming. In October 2020, it launched Unconventional, a platform for holding virtual events with 3D avatars inside virtual worlds, for the game industry. The company explains the pivot into events as a logical next step for the industry and says the project is aimed at relieving Zoom fatigue. "With in-person events sidelined due to the

pandemic, there is a tremendous need for virtual event and entertainment platforms offering turnkey solutions for custom experiences," says Chris Hewish, president of Xsolla.

Teooh has experienced this first-hand. The avatar-based virtual event platform has exploded in popularity since launching in April 2020; as of December, the metaverse had amassed an overall population of 50,000 users across 10,000 active rooms, with a total of 12,500 hours spent in the virtual space, Teooh CEO Don Stein tells Wunderman Thompson Intelligence.

The platform has been used for everything from business meetings to birthday parties. Think Global School, the world's first traveling high school, gathers all its students and teachers together on Teooh for its weekly assembly meeting; the platform hosted an 800-person film festival by Animayo in May 2020; Reebok founder Joe Foster launched his memoir there with a virtual meet and greet; Jay-Z's Roc Nation held a record release party in the metaverse; and it has served as a gathering space for support groups like Alcoholics Anonymous.

Epic Games' *Fortnite* is also becoming a new gathering point. In May 2020, the game launched its nonviolent Party Royale mode, which serves as a virtual space for performances and socializing. "This is a tour stop," explains Nate Nanzer, head of global partnerships at Epic Games.

The game is also serving as a stage for cultural events. In July 2020, it hosted We the People, a series of in-game conversations about race in America. Led by CNN's Van Jones, the event featured journalists Elaine Welteroth and Jemele Hill, and musicians Killer Mike and Lil Baby in discussion about systemic racism in media, culture and entertainment.

Why it's interesting
Gaming is no longer just for gameplay. According to Michael Wolf, cofounder and chief executive of Activate, gaming is set to emerge as the next dominant technology platform—much the way search engines, mobile phones and social networks redefined industries in previous decades, the *Wall Street Journal* reported in October 2020.

Left: Reebok founder Joe Foster hosts his virtual book launch.
Image courtesy of Teooh
Right: a virtual event with Twitter cofounder Biz Stone. Image courtesy of Teooh

03

Rooted reassurance

People are turning to nature-inspired design to create a sense of comfort and stability.

Feeling unsettled during a period of unprecedented health threats, social unrest and political turmoil, people are hunkering down and searching out steadying elements that offer a feeling of grounding and security.

In particularly stressful times, the practice of nature immersion—an emerging treatment prescribed by doctors for patients suffering from anxiety, depression and high blood pressure—is carrying over into interior spaces, which are being cocooned in warm, earthy tones to evoke a connection to nature in a calming, soothing environment.

Shutterstock's color trend predictions for 2021, released in November 2020, feature an organic-looking palette of soft whites, rich golds and deep blue-greens. Shutterstock users' recent download choices "are reflecting a shift in creative thought," says creative director Flo Lau. "They're leaving behind the bright, saturated hues that defined 2020 and moving toward 2021 with a rich, natural palette that speaks to new opportunities and, more simply, a desire to get outside."

03

Shutterstock's color predictions for 2021 include Tidewater Green.
Image courtesy of About Life and Shutterstock

In September 2020, paint brand Dulux chose its "reassuring" earthy beige hue Brave Ground as its 2021 Color of the Year. Brave Ground was selected as an "elemental" shade that reflects "the strength we can draw from nature," the brand explains.

The PPG 2021 Palette of the Year, also announced in September 2020, features three nature-inspired colors to "improve mindfulness and intention, with an emphasis on compassion and optimism," says the brand. The palette offers cozy neutrals, calming blues and warm, silty browns. PPG describes one of the featured colors, Big Cypress, as "a shaded ginger with persimmon undertones; the equivalent of a big, comforting hug for your home."

Dee Schlotter, a senior color marketing manager at PPG, says that this "organic and hopeful palette represents what we have been longing for after decades of overstimulation and overconsumption—simplicity and restfulness."

Why it's interesting

Interiors are becoming sanctuaries as never before, and as people are seeking stability, they're gravitating toward colors and spaces that evoke feelings of warmth and security. The softness, dependability, and versatility of neutrals "create interiors that soothe, comfort and protect," Gemma Riberti, head of interiors at WGS, told *Refinery29*.

04
Animation resurgence

The entertainment industry is propelling animation into the go-to format for storytelling.

The demand for animated TV shows for adults is on the rise as a result of quarantine grinding live-action filming to a halt. This has provided much-needed time in which animators have been able to flourish and, even as filming resumes, the medium's renaissance continues.

From CBS's *Tooning Out the News* to Hulu's *Solar Opposites*, 2020 was a ripe year for debuting animated shows aimed at grown-ups. Even live-action programs *Black-ish* and *One Day at a Time* introduced animated episodes.

One of animation's attractions is the appearance of provocative guests. *Black-ish's* animated episode, which aired in October 2020, features Stacey Abrams, founder of voting rights advocacy group Fair Fight. *Tooning Out the News* includes Alan Dershowitz, the Harvard Law School professor and lawyer who was part of Jeffrey Epstein's defense team.

Trekkies were able to take a break from revisiting classic episodes with the launch of an animated series, *Star Trek: Lower Decks*, which debuted in August 2020. This new addition to the Star Trek universe dialed up on humor and included a sprinkling of in-jokes for fans of *The Next Generation* and *Deep Space Nine*.

There are plenty of animations in the works too. Fox is developing an animated spin-off series of 90s cult show *The X-Files*, perhaps hoping to tug at the nostalgia strings of gen Xers and revive the X-philes movement. Netflix announced in September 2020 that it is set to revisit Norman Lear's 1970s sitcom *Good Times* in the form of an animated series. Disney is banking on its Marvel franchise with an animated TV series *What If…?* Airing on Disney+ it will debut in summer 2021, consist of 10 episodes and is rumored to have a star-studded cast.

Why it's interesting

The future of television will be animation. The global animation market is projected to reach $473.7 million by 2026, up from $272.1 million in 2020, and audience appetite for adult cartoons has strengthened over the years, with veterans such as *The Simpsons* and *South Park* still going strong, alongside newer arrivals that include *Big Mouth* and *BoJack Horseman*. Make way for more.

> **"**
> The global animation market
> is projected to reach $473.7 million by 2026,
> up from $272.1 million in 2020
> **"**

05
Rewilding

The rising rewilding movement aims to restore nature, for the benefit of wildlife, the planet— and people too.

"Rewild the world" is the rallying cry issued by naturalist David Attenborough in his 2020 Netflix documentary *A Life on our Planet*, in which he calls attention to nature ravaged by human exploitation.

Rewilding describes a process of restoring ecosystems to the point where nature can take over and look after itself. Humans have an active role in driving regeneration, nurturing natural processes and even reintroducing species.

The approach has benefits for biodiversity and supports the fight against climate change. According to scientific research published in the journal *Nature* in October 2020, rewilding can have a significant impact on greenhouse gas emissions by absorbing and storing carbon, while also protecting wildlife habitats.

Perhaps the most celebrated example of rewilding to date can be seen at Knepp Castle Estate in West Sussex, England. Once intensively farmed, the land was given over to a pioneering project in 2001 to help nature thrive. Over time, the site—which still produces food—has seen dramatic increases in wildlife, including the return of rare species such

Image courtesy of Durrell Wildlife Conservation Trust

"

Our vision is to heal the land, heal nature and heal ourselves

"

Jan Stannard, chair, Heal

Rewilding by Heal: the marmalade hoverfly. Image courtesy of Chris Towler

as the peregrine falcon and the purple emperor butterfly. Thus far, many early rewilding initiatives, like Knepp, have been on private land. Launched in 2020, Heal is a UK-based charity that hopes to use crowdfunding to convert ecologically depleted land, including former farms and green belt areas. The aim is for these sites to become sanctuaries not just for wildlife, but also for people. Speaking to the *Guardian*, Heal's chair Jan Stannard said, "Our vision is to heal the land, heal nature and heal ourselves."

Foundation Conservation Carpathia is taking a different approach, buying up parcels of privately owned land to combat illegal logging and create a protected wilderness in Romania, which in 2020 saw the reintroduction of grazing bison.

Urban rewilding projects aim to bring benefits to cities too. Trinity College Dublin replaced its closely mowed lawns with wildflower meadows. Wildlife charity Plantlife wants to transform Britain's roadside verges into wildlife corridors, having completed a successful pilot in Dorset in 2020.

Why it's interesting

There are growing opportunities for brands that want to tackle climate change to partner with rewilding initiatives. Volvo Cars UK is supporting some of the Durrell Wildlife Conservation Trust's restoration projects, including Recover the Atlantic Forest, which will see 17,000 trees planted in the Brazilian rainforest. Luxury watchmaker Audemars Piguet has helped to fund the world's first rewilding center, under construction for Scottish charity Trees for Life in the Highlands and due to open in 2022. Wunderman Thompson Data finds that 58% say they value the outdoors and the environment more as a result of the pandemic crisis.

05

06

The future of live events

Promoters and businesses are devoting extraordinary energy to crafting safe in-person experiences for 2021.

Event organizers demonstrated creativity, resilience and technological prowess to pull off innovative virtual events throughout 2020. Various events that took place last year set the stage for at least the near future of live music, given the unclear timeline for vaccine distribution. In August 2020, Virgin Money Unity Arena, which claimed to be the first dedicated socially distanced music venue in the United Kingdom, hosted its first concert. The venue features 500 elevated "personal platforms," distanced six feet apart, each holding up to five attendees for a total capacity of 2,500.

Similar concepts are being tested around the world, from Finland's Suvilahti Summer music and film festival to an open-air theater in the Netherlands. The Flaming Lips took social distancing to new heights in October 2020 by playing a concert in which the entire audience and band members were ensconced in inflatable plastic bubbles.

Music promoters are itching to bring back large-scale concerts both indoors and outside, including Glastonbury festival in the United Kingdom. Plans are afoot for the world's

Virgin Money Unity Arena. Image courtesy of Bennett Media

biggest festival to go ahead as normal in June 2021, with acts such as Kendrick Lamar, Taylor Swift and Paul McCartney to be rebooked from the canceled 2020 edition. Founder Michael Eavis said large-scale testing facilities could be set up to prevent COVID-19 transmission and protect attendees.

Even with a virtual pivot, live event organizers have faced major revenue-stream setbacks due to the pandemic, and the industry's fate rests on their ability to bring back pre-pandemic crowds. The incentives for doing this safely could be twofold. "Festivals could be utilized by governments to trial certain safety products or procedures, as they are, in effect, temporary cities," Gordon Masson, the editor of live music business magazine *IQ* told the *Guardian*, citing technologies such as wristbands that vibrate if concertgoers get too close to one another.

Justin Bolognino, founder and CEO of experience product company Meta, sums it up neatly to Wunderman Thompson Intelligence, explaining that there is "no way" this is the end of physical gatherings. "It's going to be a rocky road to get there, but we're going to get back to that. We have to. You can put that on my headstone." He adds that, for the time being, we can learn how to augment in-person experiences in safer ways.

Why it's interesting

Although circumstances dictate that many events, including institutions such as CES and SXSW, will deliver all-virtual packages in the coming months, other organizers are planning "phased returns" for concerts and conferences that will give all attendees the VIP treatment.

07

Mobilizing fandom

Fandoms are taking on a life of their own.

Members are moving on from simply consuming pop culture to becoming amplifiers and content creators for their idols, online and en masse.

Around the world, social media has connected the fans of hit TV series, movies, books and musicians to the objects of their adoration and, crucially, to each other. In the United States, Taylor Swift has her Swifties, Beyoncé has the Beyhive and Lady Gaga the Little Monsters. With a single social media post, these fans can rise as a group to boost music sales, defend their heroes against detractors and, increasingly, throw their weight behind social and political causes.

The South Korean pop industry has applied new technology to fan engagement to a degree not seen elsewhere.

There are special content channels, personalized messaging platforms, and, during the pandemic, streamed concerts enhanced with augmented and virtual reality. Fans identify as a community and will buy and stream songs continuously on multiple devices to push them up the charts, as well as creating and sharing fan fiction, artwork and compilation videos.

BTS fans. Images courtesy of MTV and YouTube

> **"**
> Social media has
> overturned the rules of
> the music industry
> and elevated the power
> of the fan
> **"**
>
> Eun-Young Jeong, reporter,
> Wall Street Journal

ARMY, the global fan base of boy band BTS, exemplifies this breed of digitally savvy, content-sharing admirers who are ready to mobilize at any time. When *The Tonight Show Starring Jimmy Fallon* held BTS Week in autumn 2020, the group's fans made it the show's most social week ever, generating 10.5 million interactions on Facebook, Twitter and Instagram, a jump of 1,300%.

"Social media has overturned the rules of the music industry and elevated the power of the fan, with BTS' ARMY leading the way," reporter Eun-Young Jeong wrote in November 2020 in the *Wall Street Journal*, after BTS won the newspaper's 2020 Music Innovator award.

The influence of the K-pop fan base has spread beyond entertainment. In 2020, they supported Black Lives Matter in the United States, sabotaged a Trump rally by booking seats they never meant to use, and raised money to buy helmets and goggles for pro-democracy protesters in Thailand.

Why it's interesting
Devoted, digital and global, fandoms are moving from being boosters of their idols to becoming a force in their own right. Brands that align with fans, consumers and people who support specific causes will gain their own loyal fandom.

CULTURE

WUNDERMAN
THOMPSON It's OK Bluetooth cassette player

08

Nostalgic formats

Consumers are seeking comfort in throwback
entertainment formats, especially now that
portability and on-the-go access aren't top priorities.

The humble audio cassette, much maligned for poor audio
quality, continues the unlikely revival we first noted in "The
Future 100 2020" trend *Analog Renaissance*. UK cassette
sales doubled in the first half of 2020 compared to 2019,
according to the Official Charts Company, hitting a 15-year
high. Pop acts such as 5 Seconds of Summer, Lady Gaga
and Dua Lipa dominate sales, pointing to a new, young
audience for the format. K-pop legend BTS is also a convert;
the group's US web store sold out of its last two singles
"Dynamite" and "Life Goes On" in both cassette and vinyl
formats.

Industry experts have theorized that the cassette comeback
is driven purely by the memorabilia market, yet we're also
seeing compatible audio devices hit the market. Hong
Kong-based NINM Lab has launched the It's OK Bluetooth
cassette player, a modern-day version of the classic
Walkman. In summer 2020, French startup We Are Rewind
unveiled its prototypes for a Bluetooth cassette mini-deck,
reimagined as a sleek, stylish device for the home.

The vinyl revival is well established by now, but it too has seen a boost during 2020, with sales outpacing CDs in the United States for the first time since the 1980s, according to the Recording Industry Association of America. In the United Kingdom, too, sales are up, with 2020 on track to be the best year for the format since 1990, according to a November 2020 report in the *Guardian*. Popular vinyl artists suggest a slightly different audience to the cassette crew, with classic albums from the Beatles and Oasis leading the sales in the United States and the United Kingdom, respectively.

The nostalgia is extending beyond music. In the same year that the much-hyped short-form mobile entertainment streaming platform Quibi bit the dust, we've seen the renaissance of that old-time favorite, the drive-in cinema (see trend #10, Elevated drive-in experiences, page 29). In September 2020, the BBC reported on a wave of openings from Russia to Germany, the United Kingdom and South Korea, also noting plans for the world's largest drive-in cinema, The Lighthouse 5, slated to launch in Florida in 2023.

Why it's interesting

In an age where almost every experience is now mediated via a screen, some entertainment fans are opting for tangibility over immediacy and convenience. The reassuring physicality of analog formats speaks to a need for a sense of ceremony, coupled with the desire for sensory engagement in a zero-touch age.

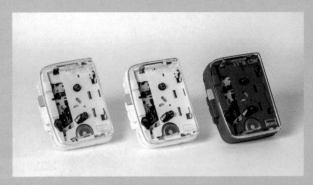

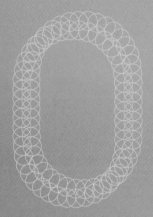

we
are
rewind

Primetime game-tainment
Is gaming the new Hollywood?

The entertainment industry is turning its attention to game-tainment, setting the stage for a new breed of gaming cinema.

Gaming is drawing record numbers—not just among players, but also among spectators. *The Sims 4*, for example, hit a peak of almost 10 million unique visitors in the second quarter of 2020, with 2.5 million joining in May and June. On July 1, more than 160,000 viewers tuned in to watch popular gamer Ninja play *Fortnite* on YouTube.

Tribeca Film Festival is bridging the gap between entertainment and gaming. The festival's advisory board announced in September 2020 that it would be adding video games to its official lineup, starting in 2021, along with the inaugural Tribeca Games Award. "Where there was once a clear delineation between media, there is now a blurring of the lines—stories have become games and games have become stories," says Jane Rosenthal, cofounder of Tribeca Film Festival and Tribeca Enterprises.

Other leaders in entertainment agree. In July 2020, Sony announced a massive investment in Epic Games, the creator of *Fortnite*. The $250 million investment gives the entertainment kingpin a 1.4% stake in the gaming company—and foretells a growing crossover between the silver screen

The Sims Spark'd. Images courtesy of Electronic Arts and ELeague

and the computer screen. "Sony and Epic have both built businesses at the intersection of creativity and technology, and we share a vision of real-time 3D social experiences leading to a convergence of gaming, film and music," says Tim Sweeney, founder and CEO of Epic Games. Bringing this vision to life, Sony and Epic jointly announced a new "immersive reality" concert experience at CES 2021, debuting on PlayStation VR and Oculus VR later this year.

Cable channel TBS is tapping into game-tainment with its new *Sims* reality television show, *The Sims Spark'd*, presented by ELeague, the gaming arm of Turner. "While competitive esports have long been broadcast around the globe, *Spark'd* is poised to become the first mainstream reality show based on an electronic game," the *New York Times* observed. The four-episode miniseries, which debuted on July 17, 2020, features 12 contestants competing in timed challenges to create the most unique characters, worlds and storylines within the popular life simulation game, in a format echoing that of *Project Runway* and the *Great British Bake Off*. The show is a collaboration between *Sims* creator Electronic Arts, WarnerMedia subsidiary Turner Sports, and Buzzfeed's gaming channel Multiplayer.

Why it's interesting
Gaming has been steadily growing in popularity and influence over the past few years, with far-reaching impact: it has spurred a new league of gamefluencers, informed luxury retail, served as an outlet for wanderlust and wellness, and even as a platform for activism. Now, with playership skyrocketing, big brand investments are elevating game-tainment to a primetime attraction.

"
Where there was once a clear delineation between media, there is now a blurring of the lines—stories have become games and games have become stories
"

Jane Rosenthal, cofounder, Tribeca Film Festival and Tribeca Enterprises

10

Elevated drive-in experiences

From raves and art shows to performances and gourmet dinners, the drive-in is getting a modern-day makeover to offer an eclectic mix of live entertainment.

Automakers are embracing consumers' demand for in-person, in-car collective events. Ahead of the 2021 launch of its Rogue Routes car, from November 2020 to January 2021 Nissan partnered with travel company Atlas Obscura on a drive-in performance series. Rogue Routes experiences took audiences to "hidden gem" locations where they were entertained with live music, presentations by scientists, artist and innovators, drone light shows and daredevil stunts. "It's our hope that the Rogue Routes campaign inspires families to seek out new experiences in a vehicle design with their every need in mind," said Allyson Witherspoon, vice president and chief marketing officer at Nissan US.

Lexus is another company refreshing the drive-in. During November 2020, the luxury car manufacturer hosted a three-day branded Culinary Cinema, a drive-in theater in Los Angeles including a gourmet three-course meal. The events sold out, showing people's appetite for such experiences.

Rogue Routes drive-in series by Nissan and Atlas Obscura

Event organizers are also banking on super-charged drive-in attractions. In Germany, Club Index hosted Autodisco in spring 2020. Each of the three drive-in raves catered for 250 cars and switched the usual enthusiastic screams from the crowd with horns honking to the beat. In the summer, the UK's Pub in the Park series of events was adapted into a drive-in Garden Party with live music, food and convivial vibes "designed for these unusual times."

Art exhibitions are also making necessary changes. The biennial art festival Dallas Aurora has converted a 100,000-square-foot parking lot into an immersive drive-through exhibition, Area 3, which ran from October 2020 to January 2021. In Toronto, a 35-minute drive-in art installation, Gogh by Car, showcased Vincent Van Gogh's work with the help of light, sound and projectors inside a warehouse.

Experiences can extend beyond cars. In Paris, a floating cinema sponsored by Häagen-Dazs during summer 2020 on the Villette canal basin made 38 small boats available for hire to customers. The ice-cream brand also partnered with Openaire to deliver a floating cinema experience in London which ran for four weeks.

Why it's interesting

Audiences are craving in-person group experiences but equally want COVID-secure options. The car provides an obvious safe haven. Now car brands and event organizers are expanding the traditional drive-in movie theater into innovative live performances which have reinvigorated the car experience entirely.

10

11

Tech & Innovation

20

Virtual athletics

Traditional sports and esports are converging, with at-home amateur athletes now able to compete against top-level professionals.

The unprecedented shutdown of live sports in 2020 has driven rapid innovation throughout the sector, giving rise to a growing crossover between virtual sports and esports. "Suddenly many began to discover esports can be as entertaining as traditional sports," Robert Rippee, director of the Hospitality Lab and Esports Lab at the University of Nevada Las Vegas's International Gaming Institute, tells Wunderman Thompson Intelligence. "The pandemic accelerated the convergence of the two."

Motor sport, where pro athletes already use racing simulators for training, is seeing new brands enter the market to provide tech for virtual racing enthusiasts. Targeting the luxury esports player, Aston Martin announced its AMR-C01 racing simulator in September 2020. Retailing for around $76,300, the simulator takes its design cues from Aston Martin's classic aesthetic, with sleek lines and seat positioning that reflect the brand's racing vehicles. For those who can afford the hefty price tag, the AMR-C01 offers an experience as close to a real Aston Martin hypercar as possible.

Aston Martin AMR-C01 racing simulator

Amateurs have long enjoyed competing as their favorite players in the virtual realm. Now, with the pros themselves hitting the online world, competition has reached a new level. Zwift, the online cycling and running training platform, hosted the first Virtual Tour de France in July 2020, allowing professional and non-professional riders to compete on the same course to see how they measured up.

In March 2020, Adidas launched its GMR smart insole, which allows amateur soccer athletes to record and merge their training skills with the EA Sports FIFA Mobile game. Kicks, shot power, distance and speed are measured in real life, with players able to translate their stats into digital rewards.

Why it's interesting
The blurring of esports and traditional sports looks set to continue as the virtual increasingly merges with real-life experiences.

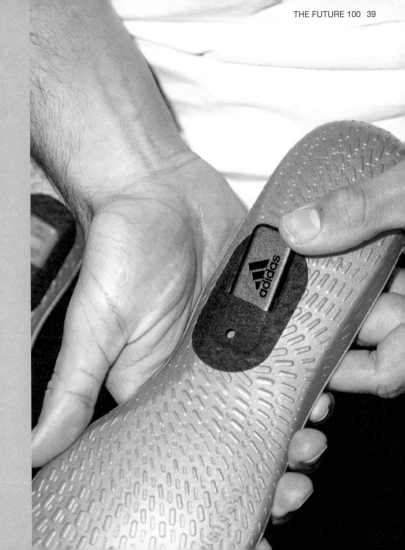

12

Auto organisms

Automotive design gets a biophilic makeover.

Mercedes-Benz is taking a radical new approach to the smart car. At the Consumer Electronics Show (CES) 2020, the German manufacturer unveiled an avatar-inspired concept car that is meant to feel more like a living creature than an automobile. "We didn't want to create a car," Mercedes-Benz chief design officer Gordon Wagener said of the Vision AVTR concept in a keynote speech at CES 2020, "we wanted to create something like a living organism."

The far-future concept, intended to "blend harmoniously into its environment and communicate with it," includes a number of features inspired by nature. The car has a distinctly reptilian appearance, from its frog-like shape to its scaled roof to its crab-like sideways mobility. The interiors are constructed using sustainable and recycled materials, with colors that evoke the sea. And the intuitive and gestural controls, such as palm-powered startup and biometric measurement, are designed to help the car operate as an extension of the human body.

" The ultimate luxury is the fusion of human and nature with the help of technology "

Mercedes-Benz

Hyundai is also embracing biophilic design. In March 2020, the South Korean carmaker unveiled the Prophecy, an electric vehicle concept designed with soft, rounded edges to look like a "perfectly weathered stone." The concept car aims "to forge an emotional connection between humans and automobiles."

The Polestar Precept boasts a natural and sustainable interior. Materials include seat covers made from recycled plastic bottles, cork-based vinyl for head rests and carpets made from reclaimed fishing nets. Polestar, which is owned by Volvo and its Chinese parent Geely, began production of the Precept in September 2020. And at CES 2021, Cadillac introduced a concept car with integrated biometric sensors that monitor passengers' vital signs and adjust the car's temperature, humidity, lighting, ambient noise and aromatics accordingly.

Why it's interesting

The past couple of years have seen an ongoing shift in the technology industry towards more organic, human-centric designs. Now the auto industry is following suit, marking biophilic and biological cars as the emerging standard for luxury vehicles. "In the ecosystem of the future," Mercedes-Benz predicts, "the ultimate luxury is the fusion of human and nature with the help of technology."

13

Data sustainability

There's growing recognition of the impact of humans' digital footprint on the environment.

Climate-change conversations tend to fixate on physical waste, but digital activities also have a significant effect. The volume of digital information stored at data centers is swelling, accounting for 2% of global electricity consumption, and that figure could quadruple to 8% by 2030, according to figures cited by Bloomberg.

Every email sent and every Google search performed, whether on a computer or on a mobile phone, has an environmental cost. In an increasingly online world, that burden mounts up like waste in landfill. According to a March 2019 report by the Shift Project think tank, digital technologies are responsible for 3.7% of global greenhouse gas emissions—a similar amount to those generated by the airline industry (see trend #25, Decarbonized aviation, page 59). Console waste is a related issue, due to the minerals used in the manufacture of gaming systems and the difficulties around safe and eco-friendly disposal.

Cloud computing and content streaming are poised to further transform the way consumers work and play, with the arrival of 5G. Tech giants and gaming platforms are increasingly faced with concerns about the infrastructure required to support these technologies at remote data centers processing vast quantities of information. A 2020 study by researchers at Lancaster University in the United Kingdom forecast that a large-scale switch to streaming games rather than using consoles could prompt a 30% increase in carbon emissions caused by gaming by 2030.

Microsoft and Google are addressing this issue, both claiming their data centers are carbon neutral. Microsoft is working towards renewable energy solutions in its Azure data centers, citing a 2018 in-house study that showed cloud computing "can be up to 98% more carbon efficient than on-premises solutions."

Sony has added an improved energy-saving low-power mode to its PlayStation 5, and the new Xbox Series S and X models offer a similar feature.

Why it's interesting
Digital is accelerating to accommodate remote work, online shopping and an expanding gaming landscape, which means the environmental implications of data usage are more urgent than ever for brands. Expect data sustainability to be a major keystone in companies' climate-change goals over the next decade.

> "
> Expect data sustainability to be a major keystone in companies' climate-change goals over the next decade
> "

14

Touchless travel

Airlines and airports are working to minimize contact and maximize hygiene standards across the travel experience.

From check-in and baggage drop to bathrooms and in-flight entertainment systems, all aspects of air travel are being reimagined in an effort to rebuild consumer confidence in a sector greatly affected by COVID-19.

Passengers traveling through Norwegian airports operated by Avinor can experience an end-to-end touchless process, with technology from travel tech company Amadeus. The system offers a complete absence of interpersonal contact, with passengers using a phone app instead of touch-screen machines. Lufthansa is enhancing its self-service offering with an initiative that sends text messages to customers affected by baggage delays, cutting down on queuing and crowding. The airline is also developing contactless processes for managing flight delays and cancellations.

Airlines are taking steps to maximize hygiene standards at every touchpoint of the journey. As well as touch-free check-in and baggage tag printing, Alaska Airlines is introducing socially distanced boarding, with airline staff able to scan boarding passes from six feet away. Passengers on selected flights can also pre-order meals from the Alaska app

or website, and store payment methods for contactless in-flight transactions. Designers are focusing on "less-touch" and "fewer-touch" approaches for cabin facilities where contactless methods are not possible—such as in-flight entertainment systems and bathrooms—with everything from soap dispensers to locks on doors ripe for reimagining.

While new travel patterns add a measure of health protection, they also threaten to further complicate the debate around data privacy. Airlines and airports will rely on a greater use of biometric data to facilitate developments such as touch-free security screening, which has been introduced at Nashville International Airport. The US Transportation Security Administration is also testing facial recognition technology.

Why it's interesting

New touch-free technology solutions to keep travelers safe will be key to the travel industry's comeback. Matt Round, chief creative officer at design consultancy Tangerine, tells Wunderman Thompson that, despite privacy concerns, he predicts these technologies will be met with "an increasing amount of acceptance," in the same way that travelers adapted to stricter airport security following 9/11. "It could be similar with COVID-19 that people will recognize the need for change, and they'll adopt it quickly," he says.

15

Mixed realities

Step aside, virtual reality and augmented reality—
mixed reality is the next big thing in gaming.

Unlike augmented reality (AR) and virtual reality (VR), mixed reality (MR) integrates real-world objects within a virtual world to create new environments for gameplay. Limitations such as VR's bulky and expensive equipment and AR's reliance on mobile devices have cleared a path for MR, with its ability to blur the lines between online and offline spaces. Its adaptability and ease of
use are quickly making it a rising star in the gaming world. The MR market was valued at $382.6 million in 2019, according to Mordor Intelligence, and is set to grow at a rapid pace, thanks to improvements in hardware and software.

The *League of Legends* World Championship has taken place in arenas around the world since 2011, with massive in-person audiences as well as those watching online. For the 2020 tournament, however—along with most things last year—the live event had to adapt due to the pandemic. Riot Games, the developer of *League of Legends*, created a high-tech MR stage to provide an immersive live experience for audiences at home. Using a set built from massive LED screens, Riot Games was able to make virtual elements of the gameplay come alive.

In October 2020, Nintendo launched its new MR game, *Mario Kart Live: Home Circuit*, to much fanfare. Designed for the Nintendo Switch, the game allows players to race remote-controlled vehicles around their homes, interacting with both virtual and real-world elements.

MR is also attracting the attention—and investments—of Big Tech. In July 2020, Indian company Jio Platforms unveiled its new Jio Glass MR glasses, backed by Google and Facebook. Facebook invested $5.7 billion in Jio in April 2020, while Google announced an additional $4.5 billion investment in the company in July the same year. Patents filed by Apple in 2020 led many to predict that the company would soon launch its own MR glasses.

Why it's interesting

MR's seamless bridging of the virtual and physical worlds makes it a compelling solution for enhanced experiences. "Most events and spaces will be equipped with augmented and mixed reality 'layers,'" Justin Bolognino, founder and CEO of digital experience company Meta, tells Wunderman Thompson Intelligence. He believes that using extended and mixed realities "to layer more nuanced and sharable dimensions to a space" will become the norm.

16

Upending deepfakes

Artificial intelligence is increasingly being deployed to fight back against deepfake images and videos.

Whether they're disseminated by pranksters and trolls or political operatives and propagandists, deepfakes can be confusing to the public and corrosive to the social fabric. These tools of disinformation are a downside of today's highly sophisticated applications of artificial intelligence (AI), but AI itself is the main weapon being used to disable them.

When it comes to deepfakes of famous people, AI technology can "learn" a person's typical movements and gestures, and compare these with the suspected deepfake to identify inconsistencies. In September 2020, Microsoft launched Microsoft Video Authenticator, a new AI-powered tool that scans an image or video and gives the viewer a percentage estimate of how likely it is that the content is a deepfake. The technology identifies signs of deepfakery that may not be discernible to the viewer, detecting grayscale elements or blurred boundaries between two images that have been blended.

Authentication tools are also becoming prevalent. Microsoft's Azure now allows content creators to embed certificates and hashes within content, which can then be read and authenticated. Blockchain timestamps are another emerging application. These act as "digital fingerprints," allowing users to trace and verify the origin of the content and any subsequent modifications.

However, Facebook's June 2020 Deepfake Detection Challenge, a competition that invited participants to test their models against real-world examples, suggests AI still leaves much to be desired when it comes to accurately picking out deepfakes. The winning algorithm managed an accuracy rate of just over 65%.

South Park creators Trey Parker and Matt Stone struck their own blow against deepfakes by satirizing the genre. Their YouTube "Sassy Justice" series, released in October 2020, uses manipulated images of Donald Trump, Ivanka Trump, Jared Kushner, Michael Caine and Mark Zuckerberg to tell a story about a local news reporter (with Donald Trump's face) investigating—you guessed it—deepfakes. "We just wanted to make fun of it because it makes it less scary," Stone told the *New York Times*.

Why it's interesting

Misinformation surrounding COVID-19 and the 2020 US presidential election has heightened the need for robust solutions around maintaining a trustworthy digital ecosystem. However, dealing with synthetic media raises new questions and challenges around the appropriate boundaries between free expression and censorship.

17

Stratospheric tech

The tech industry is going into orbit as leading brands set their sights on outer space.

In October 2020, NASA and Nokia announced a new partnership to put a 4G network on the moon. The initial objective is to improve data transmission to help astronauts control lunar rovers, navigate lunar geography in real time and stream videos. Ultimately, however, the mission aims to "validate the potential for human habitation on the moon," according to Bell Labs, Nokia's research arm.

Some analysts have projected that overall revenue from space-related cloud services could total around $15 billion by the end of the decade, the *Wall Street Journal* reported. Microsoft and Amazon are battling it out to lead the way in developing this new frontier.

Microsoft is teaming up with SpaceX to target interstellar cloud services. The collaboration, announced in October 2020, plans to deploy new cloud-computing services using fleets of low-orbit spacecraft proposed by SpaceX, as well as traditional higher-altitude satellites. The initiative targets both government and commercial space businesses.

WUNDERMAN
THOMPSON   NASA

Amazon Web Services announced the launch of its new Aerospace and Satellite Solutions segment, led by former United States Space Force director Major General Clint Crosier, in June 2020. "The aerospace and satellite industry needs the agility, speed, and flexibility that cloud offers. It's one of the first things I heard from a lot of my defense and intelligence customers in the space arena," Amazon Web Services vice president Teresa Carlson told CNBC.

"Eventually we're all going to want the Hulu or Netflix experience when we're in space," Carlson predicted. "So, you need that same kind of technology as you're developing and creating these programs."

Why it's interesting

With investment in the space technology industry rapidly increasing, companies are looking to develop commercial opportunities and become leaders in the field.

Left: Microsoft Azure Space
Right: NASA

18

Cloud gaming

Big Tech battles it out in the cloud gaming arena. Game on.

The Netflix of games has arrived in the form of cloud gaming. Players can do away with physical discs or hefty downloads and instead stream high-quality games direct from the cloud.

Major players are betting big on cloud gaming, including Amazon, Google, Tencent, Microsoft, Sony and the latest contender, Facebook. In October 2020, the social media company announced the addition of free-to-play cloud-streamed games to its existing Facebook Gaming platform. The initial launch featured a limited number of titles, but Facebook intends to expand on its game variety and scale its cloud technology capabilities. "The expansion will start in 2021 with the addition of action and adventure games," said Jason Rubin, Facebook's vice president of Play. "Games will launch with in-app purchases and ads enabled, depending on game format and developer choice."

In September 2020, Amazon promised to "help shape the future of gaming" with the announcement of Luna, its new cloud gaming service. Unlike Amazon's established competitors—Google's Stadia, Microsoft's xCloud and Sony's PlayStation Now—which all require bespoke hardware, Luna allows players to stream games from existing devices.

Chinese tech giant Tencent is working to quickly upgrade its cloud gaming tech capabilities with collaborations. In March 2020, Reuters reported that Tencent had teamed up with telecom company Huawei on an innovation lab to develop a cloud gaming platform. Tencent Games' Start cloud gaming service previously partnered with American-based tech company Nvidia.

Much like the competitive trends in over-the-top (OTT) entertainment platforms, these companies are acknowledging that content is king and are battling it out for more game releases. Google's Stadia launched in November 2019 with only 22 titles, and offered over 100 by the end of 2020. And Microsoft's Xbox Game Pass Ultimate service announced over 150 games for players to stream when it launched on September 14, 2020.

Why it's interesting

These disruptions in the gaming industry mirror the evolution of the entertainment industry, which is shifting from broadcast television to OTT service platforms. The shift is drawing the attention of tech giants, which are investing heavily in cloud-streamed games as on-demand play emerges as the future of gaming.

Remaking Silicon Valley

Next-generation startups are striving to reimagine
entrepreneurial tech as a force for good.

An increasingly disillusioned and suspicious public attitude
toward Big Tech is emerging. The *New York Times* pointed out
in October 2020 that the United States could be "on the cusp of
a new era of trustbusting," with the US Justice Department
having filed a lawsuit against Google, accusing it of "holding an
illegal monopoly over internet search and search advertising."
Facebook and Amazon were also under investigation by federal
and state officials. The newspaper noted that the "common
thread in these investigations is a concern that big companies
have become so powerful that they're bad for the country."

In step with this mood, young entrepreneurs are taking a more
altruistic, ethical and inclusive approach to the products and
brands they conceive. Gen Z Mafia calls itself "a community of
young builders" who create apps and games in line with its
young members' values. These include MegaBlock, which lets
the user "block a bad tweet, its author, and every single person
who liked it—in one click," and Vibes.fyi, a platform that allows
users to "share the good that happened to you today," and is
billed as a "gentle reminder of our human connection."

In June 2020, young employees at a swath of Big Tech
companies generated buzz around the "eye mouth eye" emojis.
Styled as a startup, it was in fact a vehicle to donate to

organizations supporting criminal justice reform and mental
health services for the Black and trans communities. While
the method used did garner some criticism, the group said in
a statement on its site: "We're a diverse, ragtag group of
young technologists tired of the status quo tech industry, and
thought that we could make the industry think a bit more
about its actions," adding that "most of the industry still stays
obsessed with exclusive social apps that regularly ignore—or
even silence—real needs faced by marginalized people all
over the world, and exclude these folks from the building
process. As an industry, we need to do better."

In the climate tech field, Peter Reinhardt, who sold data
company Segment.io for $3.2 billion in late 2020, has created
the Charm Industrial startup, which converts waste biomass
(plant and animal material) into bio-oil. The bio-oil is then
either injected deep underground as negative emissions, or
reformed into green hydrogen that can be used as a fuel or an
industrial chemical (see trend #25, Decarbonizing aviation,
page 59).

In stories charting Silicon Valley interest in climate tech,
Quartz notes that startup accelerator Y Combinator put a
callout for carbon removal technology startups, and that there
was a fresh wave of interest towards the end of 2020.

Why it's interesting
The unfettered growth of Big Tech is no longer so readily
tolerated by governments or people. According to research by
Accountable Tech, published in July 2020, 85% of Americans
believe Big Tech has too much power. But a new generation
are still inspired by tech's promise of shaping the future, and
are now seeking to do this through a more altruistic lens.

20

Protecting generation alpha

Having a digital presence has become ubiquitous and increasingly unavoidable—what does this mean for the youngest generation?

As more and more aspects of daily life take place online, the idea of data as a cold and impersonal series of zeroes and ones is falling away. Instead, it is being acknowledged as a deeply personal pillar of digital identity.

This is especially true for parents trying to manage their child's digital presence. Fifty-three percent of American parents (57% of moms, 48% of dads) with children under 18 years old are "very concerned" about the privacy and security of pictures of their children, while 58% of moms wish there were more security and privacy options built into kids' devices, according to research from Wunderman Thompson Data.

Tech giants are still navigating how to put parents at ease when it comes to their child's digital footprint. Amazon's answer has been to create a "safe space in a walled garden" across the kid-friendly versions of its smart devices, as *Fast*

Company reported in September 2020. Facebook's Messenger Kids tweaked its parental controls in February 2020 to help adults manage their child's privacy on the app more easily, and updated its privacy policy to include more kid-friendly language and illustrations.

Other companies have built their entire concepts around privacy-first services. In November 2020, Rego Payments introduced Mazoola, a new digital wallet app that is compliant with COPPA (Children's Online Privacy Protection Act) rules. As well as teaching financial literacy, the app allows children to make purchases from parent-approved retailers and deliver peer-to-peer payments, while protecting their identity.

London-based Yoto teamed up with design studio Pentagram to release an audio player that promises to put "kids in control." The Yoto Player foregoes a camera, microphone and ads altogether, instead using tactile smartcards, loaded with audiobooks, podcasts and music, enabled with near-field communication technology.

Why it's interesting
The risks to online privacy start almost from birth. In the United States, 92% of children have an online presence by the time they are two, according to security company AVG, thanks in large part to "sharenting," which sees millennial parents sharing pictures of their children on social media. As parents address the issues of privacy for children, brands are starting to consider the implications for kids' data.

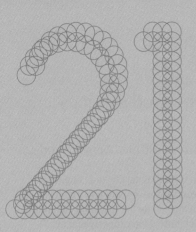

21

Travel & Hospitality

30

21

Member-based services

Luxury travel embraces the membership model.

In July 2020, famed Los Angeles hotel Chateau Marmont—
a favorite among Hollywood stars—announced that it would
become a members-only hotel over the following 12 months.
Members will purchase shares of the property and in
exchange, they get access to the hotel, use of a private
dining area, a personal butler, as well as the right to store
their belongings and book extended stays. Following Chateau
Marmont, the hotel's owner André Balazs plans to roll out the
membership model at other properties in Milan, Paris, Tokyo,
London and New York.

Luxury travel club Manifest, which opened in August 2020,
offers "escapes"—curated, small-group trips and private air
travel for its members.

Existing high-end travel clubs have experienced
unprecedented surges in demand following the COVID-19
outbreak. Inspirato, a luxury travel club whose membership
dues start at $600 per month, rents hotels and private homes
on behalf of clients. The company experienced its "highest
occupancy ever—near 90%" in July 2020, cofounder Brad
Handler told the *New York Times*.

Another members' club, Exclusive Resorts, "saw the highest
level of demand since 2013" in August 2020, chief executive
James Henderson told the *New York Times*. "We signed
members in August that have been in our database as
prospects 10 years ago and decided now, at this time,
they wanted the security and trust that we can offer."

Why it's interesting

Exclusive destinations and private transport are nothing new
in the world of luxury travel, but these upgraded initiatives
point to the growing popularity of the membership model for
clients who seek elite, private travel solutions.

22

Multigenerational travel

After months of separation, extended families are now opting to holiday together.

As households have reduced their social circles due to COVID-19 and some travel restrictions ease, a multigenerational holiday with children and grandparents has become a viable, less risky option for many families, Christie Hudson, senior public relations manager at Expedia, told *USA Today*. As a result, private vacation home rentals—popular with large groups—are rebounding more quickly than other types of accommodation.

"While some are only socializing with their own household or immediate family, others—myself included—have expanded that circle to include the grandparents," Hudson said. "The natural extension is to take it on the road and travel together as well."

A survey of 440 North American travel advisors, conducted between August 24 and September 8, 2020, by MMGY Myriad and Travel Market Report, found that 40% of client queries were for domestic destinations and only 20% for international.

> **A multigenerational holiday with children and grandparents has become a viable, less risky option for many families**

Around four in 10 clients were extremely or very interested in multigenerational travel, about the same proportion as for nuclear family travel.

Arlene Rowe, a law librarian in Washington DC, told *Condé Nast Traveler* that she and her husband had initially dreamed of an international trip for their first family holiday with their infant son. In the light of the pandemic, however, their plans inevitably changed and instead they ended up organizing an extended family gathering with her parents and in-laws at a rental in Lake Anna, Virginia. After family members undertook virus testing and self-quarantined, the group was able to meet and celebrate two wedding anniversaries, and the grandparents could hug the baby for the first time in many months.

"It was really just about taking the time to be with each other because that time is so precious," Rowe said. "We basically needed to cram a year's worth of holidays into one vacation."

Why it's interesting
In Asia, the trend of traveling with kids and grandparents has been apparent in recent years, often as an alternative to Lunar New Year reunions in hometowns. Now, as international travel remains constrained and family time takes priority, travel brands beyond Asia may also do well to tap into multigenerational groups.

23

Hospitality redesigned

With consumers looking for safe, socially distanced stays while also yearning for connection, many hotels are rethinking their offerings.

Cocooning, self-contained pods, venues that make the most of outside spaces, and expansive yet welcoming shared public areas are among the features that could characterize hotel and hospitality design in the COVID-19 era.

Integrated architecture, design, planning, and consulting firm Gensler stated in a September 2020 website article that "historically, the symbiotic relationship between cities, architecture and epidemics has always been complicated; diseases have prompted our cities to morph and progress." It noted that "COVID-19 has accelerated the need for a morphological change. The hospitality industry is among the most affected segments impacted by this pandemic."

One change that Gensler called out is the need for spaces such as guestrooms and common areas to be multipurpose.

"
Guestrooms need to be flexible enough to allow people to realize multiple activities within the same space
"

Gensler

"Guestrooms need to be flexible enough to allow people to realize multiple activities within the same space—from working to resting, eating, exercising, or gathering with friends and family. Common spaces will also need to transform to mitigate risks but still bring people together."

Jerry Tate, a partner at London architecture practice Tate Harmer, pointed out to *Sleeper* magazine in June 2020 that the company's hospitality projects frequently featured "self-sufficient accommodation." He cited Tate Harmer's Upland Park project, in the United Kingdom's South Downs National Park, that will create self-catering eco lodges to replace a "large, unsightly" hotel. "The key trend here is that guests now expect to be able to do more than just make a cup of tea in their room," said Tate. "The more facilities you can create in a space to allow them to be reasonably self-sufficient, the more choice you can give them about whether or not they will join in with the busier areas of the hotel."

The concept of the hotel as an escape has been cemented by the outbreak of COVID-19. Alina Roytberg and Lev Glazman, founders of beauty brand Fresh, launched The Maker hotel in Hudson, New York, in July 2020. Speaking to *Glossy* in August 2020, Roytberg said the hotel's concept was inspired by "the idea of creating an escape—but a reachable escape," which "has become even more important now."

Birch, set in 55 acres of parkland in Hertfordshire, just outside London, won the *Sunday Times* Hotel of the Year award in 2020. Centered around the idea of reconnecting, the former stately home has a laid-back luxe aesthetic and the rooms have no phones or TVs. The hotel is also designed to make the most of its surroundings, with a lido that will open in spring 2021 and the house's stables renovated to create a gourmet restaurant. The *Sunday Times* called the hotel "a breath of fresh air in our muffled, nervy times."

Why it's interesting

Guests' desire to capture a sense of freedom—and their hyper-awareness around contracting coronavirus—is likely to influence hotel design in coming years. The rise in popularity of self-contained accommodation is also accelerating a trend that began with hotels instilling more of a "home away from home" feel to their offerings, in a response to platforms such as Airbnb.

24

Incentivized travel

Eager to reignite the tourism industry, some countries are now paying travelers to take a break.

The Italian government is banking on national tourism to stimulate the country's economy, designating €2.4 billion for its "holiday bonus" scheme that launched in June 2020. The initiative offers low-income households up to €500 to holiday in Italy, rather than go abroad. Sicily hopes to attract tourists with the See Sicily voucher, which can be redeemed at the island's hotels and attractions, with the program currently due to be extended until December 2021. The Japanese government launched the Go To Travel campaign in July 2020, offering citizens up to 50% off across transport, accommodation, attractions, retailers and restaurants.

A loyalty program has been set up by Maldives Immigration, the Ministry of Tourism Maldives, Maldives Marketing & Public Relations Corporation and Maldives Airports to reward frequent travelers to the country. The Maldives Border Miles program was launched in December 2020 and has three tiers. Visitors earn points based on the number of visits they make and the duration of their stay to access exclusive benefits, services and rewards.

Destinations are also offering pandemic insurance coverage as an incentive. In early August 2020, the Canary Islands' Department of Tourism, Industry and Commerce partnered with French insurer Axa to give visitors free insurance covering coronavirus-related incidents. Airlines are using free COVID-19 insurance as a perk to encourage travelers to take to the skies again. On July 23, 2020, Emirates became the first airline to cover COVID-19 expenses and quarantine costs. Others have quickly followed suit, with Air Canada and WestJet also launching free COVID-19 travel insurance. WestJet will provide this coverage until August 31, 2021. Virgin Atlantic is offering complimentary COVID-19 global insurance cover for all customers until March 31, 2021.

Why it's interesting

From country loyalty programs and subsidized travel perks to free pandemic insurance coverage, the travel industry is reinvigorating tourism with new initiatives aimed at both domestic and international travelers.

25

Decarbonized aviation

Can the hydrogen-powered aviation dream become a reality?

Aviation accounts for over 3% of total global carbon emissions, according to a comprehensive international analysis published in *Atmospheric Environment* journal in January 2021. Long-term impact shows no signs of slowing, despite 2020's enforced hiatus; the International Air Transport Authority currently expects air travel to return to its pre-pandemic level by 2024.

The push to decarbonize air travel has seen hydrogen, which has little to no carbon footprint, emerge as an alternative to fossil fuels. The European Union's Clean Sky initiative reported in June 2020 that the use of hydrogen energy and technologies could mitigate the global warming impact of aviation "by 50% to 90%."

The world saw the first commercial aircraft flight powered by hydrogen fuel cells in September 2020 when ZeroAvia, the British/American innovator in zero-emission aviation, successfully completed an eight-minute flight in a retrofitted Piper M-Class six-seater plane. With more tests in the pipeline to prepare the technology for commercial use, the

firm's CEO Val Miftakhov believes it will be passenger-ready by 2023.

For hydrogen to succeed, a number of challenges such as safe storage must be addressed, and significant investment in transport and refueling infrastructure is required. Here too, innovation is under way. Norsk e-Fuel, a European renewable energy consortium based in Oslo, has announced plans to make Europe's first commercial plant for hydrogen-based renewable aviation fuel operational by 2023.

While there is still skepticism that hydrogen could be a realistic option for commercial aviation in the near future, leading aircraft manufacturer Airbus has signaled its commitment to the technology, announcing three hydrogen-powered concepts under the codename ZEROe in September 2020. The company believes commercial flights could enter service as early as 2025. Rival Boeing has also signaled its interest in the hydrogen opportunity.

Why it's interesting

Although hydrogen-powered travel is still in its infancy, major players from the aviation and energy sectors are investing in hydrogen technology, recognizing the environmental cost of fossil fuel. The cost of the climate damage caused by aviation's emissions was estimated at $100 billion for 2018 alone, according to research published in the journal *Global Environmental Change*. As the commitment to offset these costs grows and research into hydrogen power gains momentum, more opportunities to commercialize the effort will present themselves. Forward-thinking businesses should already be thinking about how to capitalize on the decarbonization opportunity.

26
Subterranean resorts

Hotels are being designed to seamlessly integrate into the landscape, maintaining the natural beauty and tranquility of their surroundings.

This increasingly popular hospitality experience centers on respecting a location's surroundings and helping guests feel more connected to nature. Casa na Terra, meaning house in the land, is a small building embedded in the ground in Portugal's Monsaraz area. Part of boutique hotel group Silent Living, the property was designed by architect Manuel Aires Mateus and includes three en-suite rooms and a grand patio overlooking Alqueva lake. "The house is located in an area where construction is not allowed," Aires Mateus told *Wallpaper.* "Our ecological responsibility was also to make the house disappear into the landscape."

Sharaan is a subterranean concept hotel by French architect Jean Nouvel, due to be completed by 2024. Designs were unveiled in October 2020 for the 40-room resort, which will be built into sandstone cliffs in Saudi Arabia's AlUla desert without compromising its history, heritage and landscape. "Our project should not jeopardize what humanity and time have consecrated," says Nouvel.

In the United States, those looking to get away from it all could literally live under a rock. In late 2020, Hotels.com gave travelers the opportunity to stay in a rustic, man-made cave in New Mexico, 50 feet below ground. This unique experience was exclusively offered by the booking site as an off-grid, long-weekend stay during the November 2020 US presidential elections, for those wanting to alleviate "election stress disorder."

Why it's interesting
Travel experiences are increasingly centering on protecting and preserving the environment. Architects are designing hotels that blend into the landscape, offering guests the chance to enjoy beautiful and unspoiled natural surroundings.

27

Travel bubbles

Would-be travelers are staying closer to home, driving local revivals.

Travelers are looking local as the tourism industry constricts. Various countries have selectively opened up their borders to admit regional travelers from neighboring areas. Australia and New Zealand were among the first to publicize plans for a "corona corridor," although the corridor didn't open until October 2020. Even then, it was only one way, with Australia admitting New Zealanders, but Australians not allowed to enter New Zealand.

Airbnb reported an increase in local holidays as the COVID-19 pandemic continued. The percentage of Airbnb bookings within 200 miles of renters' homes shot up from a third in February 2020 to over 50% in May, and local US listings had more bookings between May 17 and June 3 than the same period in 2019, without the company injecting any marketing support. The company reported a similar increase in domestic bookings in Germany, Portugal, South Korea and New Zealand.

Vacations "will probably look more like they did in the 1970s, before deregulation made air travel more affordable," the *New York Times* predicted in June 2020. "Think of highways with cars packed full of gear and children in the back asking, 'Are we there yet?'"

Why it's interesting

As travel in a pandemic world shifts "from airplane to car, big city to small location, hotel to home," as Airbnb CEO Brian Chesky noted in a June 2020 interview on CNBC, travelers are rediscovering destinations in their own backyards in place of exotic trips to far-flung locales.

> "
> Travelers are rediscovering destinations in their own backyards in place of exotic trips to far-flung locales
> "

28
Subscribed stays

Hotels are reimagining the subscription model to attract customers and appeal to a growing clientele of digital nomads.

Luxury US hospitality brand Inspirato charges a flat fee of $2,500 per month for its Inspirato Pass subscription, which allows members to book unlimited stays at its selection of homes and hotels with no nightly charges, taxes or fees. The $600 per month Inspirato Club subscription offers access to Inspirato's accommodation portfolio, with nightly rates for members as they travel. The company says its subscription model "encourages you to vacation more," and founder and CEO Brent Handler told *Bloomberg* that Inspirato enables its partner hotels to fill unbooked rooms without publicly discounting and damaging their brand. "We're buying inventory from the hotel, and we're paying for it, and the consumer is never seeing the price," Handler said.

Selina, based in Panama, is a global hospitality platform offering accommodation for extended stays and coworking. In October 2020, the company acquired the Remote Year brand, which organizes work and travel abroad programs. Travel industry intelligence platform Skift reported that the deal offers Selina "a new path to a promising segment of demand for its hotels and hostels." In August 2020, Selina also launched subscription passes that allow members to buy travel credits for lower rates, or stay in a property for one, three or six months, with coworking facilities included. "The rise of digital nomads is going to be one of the biggest movements hospitality has ever seen," Selina cofounder and CEO Rafael Museri told Skift.

Travel company Oasis is also tapping into remote workers' desire to explore and stay in destinations for long periods, now that they might not be tethered to an office. In October 2020, it launched the Oasis Passport, which allows users to pay a monthly fee to stay in different residences around the world over a three- to six-month period. A three-month pass for Latin America starts at $1,625 per month, while passes for Europe start at $2,150 per month. The company says, "why stay in NYC year-round if you can spend three to six months between Barcelona, Paris and Buenos Aires?"

Why it's interesting

The events of 2020 have both accelerated the trend in remote working and stymied international travel. Travel subscriptions are a way for both hotels and residences to attract much-needed custom, and for these businesses to pivot to offer accommodation that's targeted to remote workers, rather than traditional vacationers. This trend could be poised to cement itself after the pandemic if, as the results of a May 2020 Upwork survey predict, one-fifth of the US workforce could be entirely remote after COVID-19.

"

One-fifth of the US workforce could be entirely remote after COVID-19

"

29

Informed journeys

Transportation apps are giving users information on making their journeys as safe and sustainable as possible.

Transportation apps have long been a staple on smartphones, and now they are going beyond simply giving directions. Using newly added functionality, they are advising people on how to make the smartest choices for physical and planetary health.

Looking to help commuters travel in healthier, safer ways, Google Maps introduced information on COVID-19 cases in September 2020. Available via the layers function within the Maps app, the data shows as an overlay with the seven-day average number of confirmed cases of COVID-19 in each area.

Transport for London included health-focused capabilities in its Go app, which launched in August 2020. The app includes information to help people avoid packed trains to prevent virus spread, and offers walking and cycling options.

Launched in 2019, the Float mobility app allows users in cities across the United States and in Singapore to find the most cost-effective, safe and sustainable ways to travel. In October 2020, the platform announced a partnership with health and safety-focused Yellow Cab of San Francisco, to allow Californians to choose safer, convenient travel options.

Why it's interesting

As conscious consumers grow more aware of the impact of their transportation choices not only on their own health but also on that of the planet, they will expect mobility brands to help them make informed decisions.

30

Isolationist travel

For 2021, think remote destinations, private lands, and no other tourists in sight.

Travel hotspots in 2021 will be less about dense big cities and more about spacious immersions in the great outdoors.

"Even once a vaccine is available, the allure of the outdoors is evergreen, and a year of being pent up will make the desire to be in nature even greater," Gareth Chisholm, creative director at Tentrr, tells Wunderman Thompson Intelligence. Tentrr is the Airbnb of campsites, working with private landowners across the United States to provide unique glamping retreats. The company was growing rapidly prior to the pandemic, according to Chisholm, and has introduced stringent COVID-19 precautions.

Tentrr lists more than 800 glampsites. Examples include an abandoned zoo in New York's Catskill Mountains, with access to miles of hiking trails, and a furnished site in the rugged Steinaker State Park in Utah, with water activities in a nearby reservoir. Chisholm notes that people are looking for secluded

destinations with a "wow factor"—this could range from on-site waterfalls to epic vistas from forested mountains. "People are not only looking for a getaway, they are also looking for some adventure."

Interest in campsite bookings and equipment has spiked too. The United Kingdom's Cool Camping booking agency saw a five-fold increase in bookings when the lifting of lockdown restrictions was announced in May 2020. British retailers John Lewis & Partners, Asda and Halfords all reported an uptick in camping equipment sales over summer 2020.

Pitching up in the wilderness has also led to a surge in overlanding—off-road camping on grounds less trodden. In the United States, Google searches for overlanding have approximately doubled in the past year, peaking during the

summer as restless adventurers took to Jeeps, caravans and RVs to experience new territories accessible by road.

More thoughtful and conscious escapes are part of isolationist travel. As Chisholm observes, "While we all do enjoy distant and exotic lands, there has been a greater awareness regarding the impact of air travel, or giant cruises. Some of that thinking will definitely filter down to the more mindful traveler, and they'll consider local or more drivable destinations."

Why it's interesting
As the travel industry starts to pick up, preference for destinations that include nature, adventure and solitude will rise for those who desire a mindful, truly socially distant escape.

Brands & Marketing

31

Branding together

A new class of leadership means that brands are putting aside competition and instead collaborating to tackle social and environmental challenges.

Generation Z are setting a new standard for brand purpose. In an October 2020 survey by Wunderman Thompson Data, 80% of US gen Zers say that brands should help make people's lives better and 82% believe brands should leave aside their differences and work together for the greater good. Brands are listening.

In response to the climate crisis, Microsoft launched the Transform to Net Zero initiative in July and teamed up with eight corporations including Nike, Mercedes-Benz, Unilever and Danone to become carbon-negative businesses by 2030. In late 2019, Gucci's CEO Marco Bizzarri debuted the CEO Carbon Neutral Challenge urging companies to join him in reducing their greenhouse gas emissions. Those joining Bizzarri include the RealReal, Lavazza and software company SAP.

Banding together in the face of the pandemic made for swifter research and innovation. In April 2020, British pharmaceutical multinational GSK and the French drugmaker Sanofi joined forces to develop a COVID-19 vaccine. Similarly, American

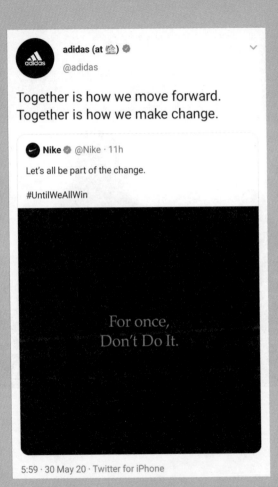

adidas (at 🫣) ✓
@adidas

Together is how we move forward.
Together is how we make change.

● Nike ✓ @Nike · 11h

Let's all be part of the change.

#UntilWeAllWin

For once,
Don't Do It.

5:59 · 30 May 20 · Twitter for iPhone

" 82% of US gen Zers believe brands should leave aside their differences and work together for the greater good "

pharmaceutical company Pfizer collaborated with German biotechnology company BioNTech for a vaccine which has shown swift success, with the United Kingdom being the first country to approve the vaccine for use in early December 2020.

In the United States, the death of George Floyd on May 25, 2020 under police arrest set off global protests and anger concerning systemic racism. Many brands were quick to respond. Nike released a tweet on May 29 saying "Let's all be part of the change" along with a video standing against racism with the message "For once, Don't Do It." The next day Adidas replied with "Together is how we move forward. Together is how we make change," in solidarity with Nike's messaging.

Tackling unemployment among those who are under-represented in jobs, 27 firms including JPMorgan Chase, Amazon and IBM banded together to create the New York Jobs CEO Council in August 2020. The Council aims to hire 100,000 people from low-income Black, Latino and Asian communities by 2030.

Why it's interesting
The cultural shift from "me" to "we" is extending to brands, demonstrating that change requires collaborative effort.

32

The visual language of connectivity

How can advertisers and brands convey togetherness without seeming irresponsible?

Scenes of clustered crowds and large gatherings will continue to appear inappropriate as 2021 unfolds. So how are advertisers and brands visualizing togetherness?

"Showing 360-degree life in the home is the dominant approach because it can convey safe social distancing practices, and a wide variety of lifestyles and activities," Brenda Milis, principal of creative and consumer insights at Adobe Stock, tells Wunderman Thompson Intelligence. Milis explains that brands are dialing up key themes as a result of the pandemic: connection, support and wellbeing. They are using visuals of families, partners and quarantine pods spending time together in different scenarios to express these themes.

Airbnb has community at the heart of its messaging. In June 2020, the company launched its "Go Near" campaign supporting local travel and economic growth. The imagery selected for the campaign shows small intimate groups on vacation, portrayed informally.

Amazon's "The Show Must Go On" campaign launched in November 2020 and tells the story of a young dancer who conquers the setbacks of 2020 by performing for her family, friends and neighbors. "Our TV ad is inspired by, and pays tribute to, the unbeatable human spirit and the power of community that we have witnessed so often this year," says Simon Morris, vice president of global creative at Amazon.

Forget the compilation of faces via a Zoom call depicting togetherness (so 2020)—brands and advertisers are opting for smaller group settings and capturing intimate moments to convey a feeling of community in 2021.

Why it's interesting
The message of community is being reframed, as Milis notes: "I've been extremely happy to see a scaling focus on building a sense of community through compassion as well as a growing understanding that we don't have to occupy the same physical space to build community, to support one another."

Left: The Show Must Go On commercial by Amazon
Right: Go Near campaign by Airbnb. Image courtesy of Airbnb

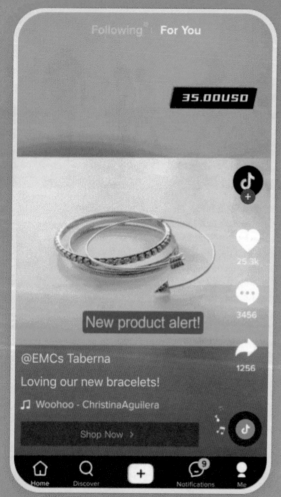

33

TikTok ads

The promise of the gen Z market is changing the face of advertising campaigns and brand messaging, and TikTok is well-poised to capitalize on this in a major way in 2021.

The favorite gen Z platform is the main driver of an uptick in short-form video advertising, but fellow social video app Triller is also entering the fray (the two companies happen to be engaged in a legal dispute about a patent). In October 2020, Triller announced a partnership with digital advertising platform Consumable to insert ads between Triller's video content.

TikTok is also drawing on lessons from its Chinese sister app Douyin. The platform helps users to monetize content, rather than focusing on big-brand advertising in the vein of Instagram and Facebook. "In China last year they helped 22 million creators make over $7 billion," Fabian Ouwehand, founder and growth director at Uplab, tells Wunderman Thompson Intelligence.

" TikTok is clearing a path that will see the platform mature into a powerful social commerce tool as well as an epoch-defining creative hub "

The platform also launched TikTok for Business in June 2020, essentially an in-house marketing agency following the example of Douyin. A Shopify integration was announced in October to bring e-commerce into the app's offerings.

The result of these developments is an ecosystem that is friendly to brands, but places the creator very much at the center. "The most important asset of TikTok is their own creators," Ouwehand says. "So they always try to leverage the creator, because if you look at all the trends which have come out of TikTok and how they got very popular, it's thanks to its creators."

Why it's interesting

By building these advertising and ecommerce functionalities, TikTok is clearing a path that will see the platform mature into a powerful social commerce tool as well as an epoch-defining creative hub. Having a rival like Triller snapping at its heels is not a bad thing either.

34

Big brands go circular

From Gucci to Uniqlo, fashion brands are getting into the second-hand business.

The trend is driven by sustainability concerns and by the fact that wallets are slimmer in a global recession. For luxury brands, it's also a way to police knock-offs.

Gucci announced a partnership with Nasdaq-listed luxury consignment store the RealReal in October 2020, following in the footsteps of Stella McCartney and Burberry. The Gucci x TRR eshop stocks items from consigners as well as products directly from the Italian fashion house. This came soon after Gucci launched its first circular collection, Gucci Off the Grid—a unisex capsule collection using fabrics that are organic, recycled or biobased.

"One garbage truck's worth of textiles is landfilled or burned every second," Julie Wainwright, the RealReal's founder and CEO, told *Vogue*. "Fashion can't continue being disposable— we have to buy things that are well made and resell [them]

> **"**
> The resale market grew
> 25 times faster
> than the overall retail
> market in 2019
> **"**

when we're done with them. Partnering and collaborating directly with brands, as we are with Gucci, is a meaningful way for us to harness their influence to increase exposure to the importance of circular fashion."The second-hand clothing market is forecast to grow from $28 billion today to $64 billion in 2024, according to San Francisco-based ThredUp, which calls itself "the world's largest online thrift store." The resale market grew 25 times faster than the overall retail market in 2019, powered by 64 million shoppers, ThredUp said in its annual report.

Uniqlo is recycling its own used down jackets into new down jackets under its Re.Uniqlo initiative. The project started in Japan in 2019 and launched in Singapore in October 2020,

with plans to expand the idea to 27 markets. Uniqlo has been collecting used clothes since 2006 and sorting and donating items to people who need them through the United Nations Refugee Agency and other organizations. In Japan, the fast-fashion retailer also turns clothing that cannot be donated into fuel or soundproofing material.

Why it's interesting

Brands are acknowledging that the second-hand market is becoming a key cog in the circular economy. Playing an active role in the fashion recycling business is also a way for brands to weed out fakes and keep resale values buoyant, which in turn shores up first-sale prices.

+ WUNDERMAN THOMPSON The RealReal and Gucci's Circular Economy partnership.
Image courtesy of the RealReal

35

Ethical scoreboard

How brands behave matters more than ever to consumers.

According to an IBM survey published in 2020, 40% of consumers are purpose-driven in their purchases, while *Forbes* mused whether 2020 "was the year that 'purpose' went mainstream."

Responding to this growing ethical motivation among consumers, platforms that monitor corporate behavior are popping up, while brands are putting their values front and center, even when this raises difficult issues. In October 2020, Disney began placing a warning ahead of its older films streamed on Disney+, including *The Jungle Book*, *Lady and the Tramp* and *Dumbo*, warning that they "include negative depictions and/or mistreatment of people or culture." The disclaimer adds: "Rather than remove this content, we want to acknowledge its harmful impact, learn from it, and spark conversation to create a more inclusive future together."

Did They Help? is a platform that launched in 2020 as an online record of companies' and public figures' "good and bad deeds," which it then scores. Visitors to the site can look up those that performed well or badly in response to events such as COVID-19 and Black Lives Matter. As founder Pooj Morjaria

tells Wunderman Thompson Intelligence, "While brands may not have had a moral or ethical responsibility in the past, they absolutely do now."

And to help companies avoid their ads appearing next to content that doesn't align with their values—a potential pitfall of automated, programmatic ad buying—Nandini Jammi and Claire Atkin founded brand safety consultancy Check My Ads in 2020. "If you juxtapose your media buy with one of your values and it's not aligned, then that's a problem. It's a message that you're sending to your entire universe of stakeholders when you either choose to uphold your values or to undermine them through your advertising budget," Jammi explains to Wunderman Thompson Intelligence.

Against this values-driven backdrop, brands are proactively highlighting their ethics. Riccardo Bellini, CEO of luxury fashion house Chloé, said in November 2020 that the house is placing purpose at its core, with initiatives such as a social profit and loss account, establishing a fund dedicated to girls' education, and incorporating social entrepreneurs into its supply chain. "What a brand stands for, its beliefs and values, will become as relevant as products and aesthetics," Bellini said in *WWD*.

Why it's interesting

Amid the COVID-19 crisis, the Black Lives Matter movement and a fraught political atmosphere, a sense of collective social responsibility has been pushed to the top of the agenda in 2020. Consumers are taking strong stances in terms of their values, and are demanding that brands do the same. Brands themselves and independent platforms are now making a company's ethics ever-more transparent.

> "
> While brands may not have had a moral or ethical responsibility in the past, they absolutely do now
> "

Pooj Morjaria, founder, Did They Help?

36

Flexperiences

Innovative companies are finding new ways to repurpose empty venues and assets, creating hybrid and adaptable experiences.

Thai Airways repurposed its airplane seats and first-class menus for grounded customers. At a pop-up restaurant at its company headquarters in Bangkok in September 2020, guests were served in-flight meals by cabin crew. The restaurant was kitted out with unused airplane seats and furniture made from recycled plane parts. (See trend #44, Plane dining, on page 98 for more on aviation-themed eating.)

In April 2020, the pandemic not only halted the airline industry, but the leisure industry too, as movie theaters closed across much of the world. Lithuania's Vilnius airport teamed up with the organizers of the Vilnius International Film Festival to transform the airport runway into a drive-in-style movie theater called the Aerocinema.

In China, a cinema changed its function entirely, opening as a fresh food market in attempt to survive economically. A video

circulated online of the cinema in Beijing's Chaoyang district, showing queues of people waiting to get in, the *Global Times* reported.

Why it's interesting

Not only do these examples show how brands and businesses can spark joy in tough times, they also highlight the powerful role agility and collaboration can play in adjusting to change. These creative responses point the way forward to a new genre of experiences that champion adaptive spaces.

37

Brand safety

Brand safety is the latest consideration when communicating brand values—and context is king.

What is brand safety? Broadly speaking, it's the protection of a brand's reputation. Practically speaking, that translates into monitoring the environment in which a brand's content or advertising appears. Increasingly this is a critical consideration for brands to appeal to a rising class of vigilant consumers.

"Customers just aren't responding to advertising the way they used to," Nandini Jammi, cofounder of brand safety consultancy Check My Ads, tells Wunderman Thompson Intelligence. Modern consumers are looking beyond messaging, diving into a brand's ethics, actions and values—and, most recently, are looking at where ads appear as an indication of those values.

Jammi and cofounder Claire Atkin launched their brand safety consultancy in June 2020 to address a flaw they observed in brand strategy amid the shifting consumer landscape: while a brand's messaging may align with its values, the places where its advertising appears can damage it.

"We're at a time where, in advertising, the environment in which you advertise is as important as the message itself. Where you advertise actually sometimes matters more than the brand's message—it either reinforces your brand message or it undermines it," Jammi says.

Popular social media platforms are ramping up their brand safety protections, giving companies more control over the context in which their ads appear. TikTok partnered with brand safety platform OpenSlate in October 2020 to ensure that businesses advertising on TikTok won't have their ads and branded content placed alongside material that is deemed questionable. "Content and context have never mattered more," says Mike Henry, CEO of OpenSlate.

In the same month, YouTube named Zefr as a brand safety reporting partner, with plans to develop and roll out brand safety measures in 2021.

Why it's interesting

"Brands are starting to wake up to the realization that in order to be brand safe, they must do good by their communities," Jammi says. The communication of a brand's values goes far beyond its products; it includes everything from brand actions to treatment of employees to the context in which its ads appear.

Check My Ads

Take back control of your ads.

Keep your brand away from fake news, disinformation, and hate speech.

38

Campaign: uplift

In a year of sickness, poverty and hardship, brands and marketers are trying to uplift people, particularly around major holidays.

During Ramadan 2020 in Indonesia, Telkomsel's "Continue Doing Good" campaign showed subscribers video calling relatives and friends to stay in touch. The country's biggest mobile service provider also reminded consumers they could transfer unused phone minutes and data to those who needed it, donate money, and stream religious content— in short, doing good while staying home.

In the United Kingdom, TikTok ran its first TV ad in May 2020, showing how people stuck at home were using its short-video platform to stay upbeat. It featured girl band Little Mix, rapper Tinie Tempah and chef Gordon Ramsay as well as members of the public (and their cats), and was part of a wider digital campaign, "A Little Brighter Inside," showing celebrities and creators sharing their lockdown routines on TikTok.

Also in the United Kingdom, John Lewis & Partners and Waitrose & Partners produced a feelgood Christmas 2020 campaign. The group's much-anticipated Christmas ad is known for tugging heartstrings each year, and the 2020 creation was especially poignant. In "Give A Little Love,"

A Little Brighter Inside campaign by TikTok. Images courtesy of TikTok

eight artists created vignettes connected by everyday acts of kindness, showing how a chain of good deeds can lift the spirits of those around us. Through the Christmas ad, the John Lewis & Partners and Waitrose & Partners group aimed to raise £4 million ($5.3 million) for charity.

Boots, the UK drugstore chain, also created a Christmas 2020 ad around kindness. With a series of singing bars of soap, loofahs and bubbles, and a soaring rendition of the song "What the world needs now is love sweet love," the ad solicited donations for soap and other hygiene products for those in need. At the end of the ad Boots announced it was donating £1 million ($1.3 million) to the Hygiene Bank charity.

In India, in November 2020 mosquito repellent brand Goodknight commemorated World Children's Day with an ad that looked almost like normal times. A boy feeds his toddler brother, pretending the approaching spoon is an airplane. A young girl pulls her father's sleeve away from the flame of the prayer candle he's lighting. A daughter reminds her father to apply mosquito repellent before leaving the house. The face mask he dons is the only clue to the pandemic.

The message is that everyone has a role in keeping everyone else safe, even the little ones, says Rishabh Parikh, Mumbai-based Wunderman Thompson planning director.

Why it's interesting

With the development of several promising COVID-19 vaccines, there could now be light at the end of the pandemic tunnel. But many still need help and the campaigns highlight how in uplifting others, we are ourselves uplifted.

> "The message is that everyone has a role in keeping everyone else safe"

WUNDERMAN THOMPSON

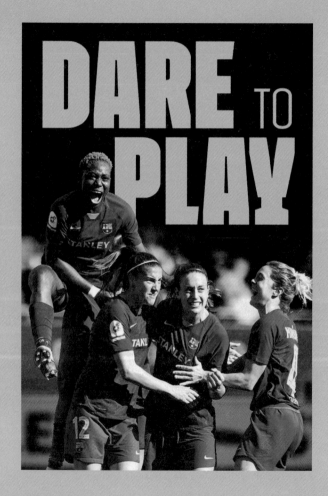

39

Fan fidelity

Sports are laying the groundwork for enhanced digital consumer engagement.

The pandemic-induced hiatus in the public attending live sports has given rights holders a renewed appreciation for the value of engaging fans digitally. Moving forward, digital fan engagement will become indispensable—and could offer a roadmap for up-leveling brand loyalty.

Even before the pandemic, digital innovation for sports fans was ripe for development. Blockchain-based company Chiliz, for example, launched Socios.com in November 2019 as a fan engagement app. At the time, Chiliz CEO Alexandre Drefus noted that "99% of sports fans are not in the stadium," pointing out that sport had become a global phenomenon, propelled "by social media, global TV rights, and the attraction of superstar players." Socios.com addresses this by giving fans the opportunity to earn rewards and incentives for engaging with their favorite club. By hunting, buying or earning fan tokens, supporters get to influence club matters by voting in polls and surveys. Tokens act as a virtual membership, entitling the holder to rewards, merchandise and one-of-a-kind experiences.

The COVID-19 outbreak has seen the trend reach new heights. In September 2020, the Mumbai Indians cricket club launched a number of virtual innovations to unite and engage its army of fans, known as the Paltan. Among them is *Paltan Play*, launched in association with Samsung. The second-screen experience for matchdays allows fans to compete against one another by predicting events in the game, such as runs scored or wickets per over.

La Liga North America is taking an exclusive approach, tapping the growing trend of watch parties to deliver a VIP experience for a group of Spanish soccer superfans. It is hosting a series of five exclusive watch parties on the LiveLike platform, presented by legends of La Liga such as Samuel Eto'o and Diego Forlán, and featuring streaming Q&As with the players and a live chat room throughout the game.

Alongside fun digital matchday experiences like these, fans want 24/7 content that gets them closer to the athletes and the action. That's why legendary soccer club FC Barcelona is now building a pedigree in entertainment. In summer 2020, the organization launched its dedicated streaming platform Barça TV+, a treasure trove of content for fans, featuring more than 1,000 hours of content from live matches and replays, behind the scenes exclusives and gems from the archive. The club also boasts its own production house that is creating content for the platform, including original documentaries and series, and even a soccer-based original drama.

The Barça TV+ launch is linked to the Culers premium membership program. An evolution of an existing

"
Digital fan engagement will become indispensable—and could offer a roadmap for up-leveling brand loyalty
"

membership scheme, it offers full access to all digital fan services alongside eligibility for a range of discounts, special offers and prize-draw opportunities.

Why it's interesting

A rich new era of fan engagement that prioritizes experience and immersion across multiple digital touchpoints offers brands a new playbook for consumer engagement—and could hold the key to long-term loyalty. As Stephanie McMahon, chief brand officer for WWE, said in a CES 2021 panel about the future fan experience: "Where the intersection of tech [and sports] really becomes successful is when it creates an emotional experience, an emotional connection for the audience."

40

Brand academy

Are cobranded diplomas the future of education?

With education systems in a time of transition, brands are stepping in. In 2020, lockdowns forced 1.5 billion students around the world home from school, as UNESCO reported. This created devastating barriers to learning for many education systems—and an opportunity for brands to come to the aid of teachers and students.

In November 2020, HSBC UK announced a partnership with financial education charity Young Money to launch Money Heroes, a financial literacy platform for children aged 3 to 11. Its program includes resources for parents and teachers, and covers everything from managing a budget to preventing fraud.

Facebook has been providing help for students and teachers around a variety of topics not traditionally covered in the classroom. In August 2020, it launched the Educator Hub, which includes courses for students on anti-racism, digital literacy and wellbeing, as well as resources for teachers, such as courses on supervising online learning.

Looking to help children learn more about environmentally friendly living, Beyond Meat teamed up with social education platform EVERFI to make sustainability education freely available to students and teachers in the United States. The online courses launched for the 2020-2021 school year, covering topics such as climate change and biodiversity, and new activities will be added throughout 2021 to reinforce the curriculum.

Why it's interesting

The concept of branded education is not new—McDonald's established its Hamburger University in 1961. However, companies are now looking to get involved in deeper, more impactful ways, training not just their current or future employees, but future generations.

Food & Drink

41

Adventure dining

Diners are seeking out unforgettable gourmet experiences in a new era of social distancing.

Restaurateurs are bringing high-end, socially distanced dining to unique locales for customers in search of a one-of-a-kind meal.

In Budapest, Michelin-starred eatery Costes is taking fine dining to new heights. On October 17, 2020, the restaurant served a four-course dinner on the Budapest Eye Ferris wheel, which offered guests stunning views of the city from the four-person cabins. A decline in visitor numbers due to COVID-19 travel restrictions gave Costes owner Karoly Gerendai the opportunity to implement his vision of creating a restaurant at the attraction. Tickets for the $155 meal sold out in days, *Reuters* reported, and, following the success of the event, Gerendai announced plans to repeat the event in spring 2021.

Luxury Parisian hotel Les Bains drained and repurposed its underground swimming pool—which dates back to 1885

when the hotel was originally built as a bathhouse—to create a unique private dining room in September 2020. It is part of the Les Bains Confidentiels series, showcasing exclusive and unusual spaces at the hotel. Options also include a private table in the hotel's iconic nightclub, which has hosted figures such as Mick Jagger, Naomi Campbell and Kate Moss.

At Little Palm Island Resort and Spa, restaurant reservation times are set by the tides. Located on Little Torch Key in Florida, the resort's Dinner on the Sandbar is a five-course meal for two, served at a private table in shallow water in the ocean. Introduced in September 2020, the gourmet experience costs $1,000.

Why it's interesting

The ritual of eating out is evolving. High-end dining destinations are getting creative, offering exclusivity and unparalleled experiences in an effort to comply with social distancing measures without compromising on ambience.

41

42

Climate-friendly diets

Healthy eating takes on a whole new meaning for "climatarian" diners.

A quarter of global carbon emissions are related to food production—and consumers are taking action. One in five millennials are changing their diet to reduce their impact on the environment, according to January 2020 findings from YouGov. To cater to consumers eating for planetary health, brands and platforms are introducing new offerings to help consumers better understand the impact that their food choices have on the environment.

In October 2020, Panera Bread introduced carbon footprint labeling on its menus. The bakery-café chain worked with the World Resources Institute to determine which of its meals qualify as low carbon and to identify its most climate-friendly options.

"Understanding the impact of what we eat on the environment is one way we can all take a small step toward combating climate change," said Panera CEO Niren Chaudhary. "So as a food company, we feel a strong responsibility to share this information and empower our guests to help make a difference."

In the same month, Chipotle launched a sustainability impact tracker to help customers analyze the sustainability of their lunch. The Real Foodprint tracker analyzes Chipotle's ingredients on key metrics like carbon emissions and gallons of water saved. The company teamed up with millennial favorite Bill Nye the Science Guy to demonstrate how Real Foodprint works with a TikTok video.

Just Salad anticipates that health-conscious diners will calculate carbon footprints the same way they count calories. The salad chain's new carbon labeling program, implemented in September 2020, lists the carbon emissions of each menu item.

These new programs are "contributing to a social shift where people do really start thinking about budgeting their carbon in the way they think about budgeting calories, money, steps on their iPhone," said Sandra Noonan, Just Salad's chief sustainability officer.

In November 2020, an alliance of health professionals in the United Kingdom called for a climate tax to be imposed on food with a heavy environmental impact by 2025, and issued a report with a series of suggestions for reorienting the food industry towards climate action. "We can't reach our goals without addressing our food system," said Kristin Bash, who leads the Faculty of Public Health's food group and is a coauthor of the report.

Why it's interesting

The concept of healthy eating is expanding to encompass foods that nourish the planet alongside the consumer. "The message is clear," Marco Springmann, a researcher at the University of Oxford who specializes in the health, environmental, and economic dimensions of global food systems, told the *Guardian*. "Without drastic reduction in the production and consumption of meat and dairy, there is little chance of avoiding dangerous levels of climate change."

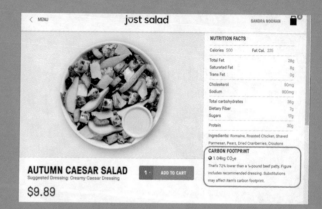

43

Antimicrobial packaging

Packaging companies and brands are responding to consumers' heightened focus on cleanliness with solutions that foster a sense of hygiene security.

In October 2020, San Francisco strategic agency Designsake Studio unveiled Matter, an antimicrobial protective coating that can be used on materials including paper, card, glass, metal and textiles. Matter was created using advanced silver technology, as the metal disrupts a virus's reproduction. It has been certified in the United States by the Food and Drug Administration and Environmental Protection Agency as an antimicrobial technology that provides protection against 99.9% of microbes. Danielle McWaters, founder and CEO of the studio, says that the packaging proves that "you don't have to sacrifice aesthetics for safety or recyclability. We hope Matter can bring joy back to the unboxing experience and create the next evolution of safe and sustainable packaging solutions."

Catering to the large number of consumers who are now cooking at home more often, Rubbermaid launched

"
The antiviral coatings market is forecast to grow at a CAGR of 13.3% between 2020 and 2027, to a value of $1.3 billion
"

EasyFindLids in October 2020. The range of food storage containers features SilverShield antimicrobial technology to inhibit the growth of odor-causing bacteria. "At a time when consumers are cooking more at home, we are pleased to offer a new storage solution that not only helps reduce clutter but also keeps food storage containers free of odors," says Kris Malkoski, CEO of the Food Business Unit at Newell Brands, Rubbermaid's parent company. Researchers at the Verschuren Centre at Canada's Cape Breton University are working on creating antiviral packaging and coatings that could kill the coronavirus on contact, CBC News reported.

The antiviral coatings market is forecast to grow at a compound annual growth rate of 13.3% between 2020 and 2027, to a value of $1.3 billion, according to a report by Allied Market Research. The company noted that increased demand during the COVID-19 outbreak was driving growth, and that "the current pandemic offered opportunity for new product developments."

Why it's interesting
As consumers are hyperaware of a virus's ability to survive on surfaces, expect antibacterial and antiviral packaging to become more important in purchasing decisions.

44
Plane dining

Elevated onboard eating captures would-be travelers' appetites.

Airplane food—once considered a low point of air travel—has become a draw for grounded patrons looking to recreate the travel experience.

In October 2020, Finnair began selling Taste of Finnair, a ready-made line of its business-class meals, in a grocery store in Finland. The menu, which rotates offerings every two weeks, is a fusion of contemporary Nordic and Japanese cuisines. The launch kicked off with an appetizer of roasted carrot and blue cheese mousse, and two entrees: smoked char and chanterelle risotto, and beef with teriyaki-radish sauce, spring onions and rice.

Earlier in the same month, Singapore Airlines hosted a pop-up restaurant on board two Airbus A380s parked at Changi Airport. Demand was so high that the two planned dinners sold out 30 minutes after reservations opened, which prompted the airline to host two additional meals. Like a flight

itself, tickets were tiered by cabin class. The four dining options—first class, business class, premium economy and economy—ranged from a $474 five-course meal served in a private suite to a more affordable $40 option.

For frequent flyers looking for collectibles alongside their meals, Qantas has put catering carts from its recently retired Boeing 747 fleet up for sale. Qantas loyalists were quick to snap up the carts; *Business Insider* reported that 1,000 carts sold in just two hours. They were stocked with mini bottles of

wine and champagne, snacks, candy, business-class amenity kits, throw blankets and first-class pajamas.

Why it's interesting

Plane food is plain no longer; gone are the days of bland microwaved meals. While these endeavors may have been conceived as a stopgap solution for faltering airline business, they point to a continuing evolution in airline dining. In-flight meals are evolving into gourmet offerings that diners choose to eat—even when they're grounded.

45

Ghost kitchens

A new model for the restaurant industry optimizes
operations and prioritizes off-premises dining.

The growing popularity of delivery-first dining, which
proliferated during lockdowns, is opening the door to a new
restaurant concept: the ghost kitchen. Rather than renting and
staffing full cooking and dining spaces, ghost kitchens allow
restaurants to rent workspace in shared kitchens where
cooking is done expressly for delivery and takeout.

Euromonitor estimates that ghost kitchens could be a $1 trillion
business by 2030—and a wave of big players in the food and
drink space is kickstarting the market. In November 2020,
Chipotle introduced its take on the ghost kitchen with the
launch of Chipotle Digital Kitchen. The digital-only prototype
café operates solely for pick-up and delivery, with no dine-in
options.

Midwestern grocery chain Kroger announced a partnership with
ClusterTruck, a delivery-only restaurant startup, in October
2020. Through the partnership, Kroger will provide ClusterTruck
with on-premises ghost kitchens to produce a variety of freshly
prepared on-demand meals, with no service or delivery fees.
Kroger vice president Dan De La Rosa says the partnership is
"an innovation that streamlines ordering, preparation and
delivery."

DoorDash announced its Reopen for Delivery program on October 26, 2020, helping restaurants forced to close as a result of the pandemic to reopen as virtual eateries, operating out of ghost kitchens.

Investors are getting in on the game, too. In July 2020, ghost kitchen company Zuul—which counts popular salad chain Sweetgreen among its clients—raised $9 million to expand in New York City after opening its first Manhattan location in September 2019. The *Wall Street Journal* reported in October 2020 that Travis Kalanick, founder and former CEO of Uber, has invested $130 million in real estate for his ghost kitchen startup CloudKitchens. The same month, SoftBank's Vision Fund invested $120 million in Nextbite, which CEO Alex Canter describes as "a portfolio of delivery-only restaurant brands that exist only on Uber Eats, DoorDash and Postmates."

NYC startup Kitch, launched in January 2020, hopes to create the Airbnb of ghost kitchens. Calling itself a "kitchen matchmaker," the startup connects local eateries with hotel operators, restaurateurs, and other food businesses renting out their kitchens during off-peak times.

Why it's interesting

Prioritizing restaurant space for cooking, rather than dining, follows the path set by the delivery boom, which saw global foodservice delivery sales more than double from 2014 to 2019, according to Euromonitor. "In the same way that, in the last five years, third-party delivery has helped to define the restaurant industry, the next stage of that evolution over the next five years is going to be ghost kitchens and other forms of distributed production," Euromonitor's global head of beverages and foodservice research Michael Schaefer tells Wunderman Thompson Intelligence.

45

WHAT'S GOOD?

EVERYTHING.

(Come on...)

I like the Lo Mein.
Ravioli.
Carnitas.
Veggie burger.
Steak frites.

Sounds good.

ZUUL

46

Breakfast upgraded

More time at home means that breakfast is transforming from a rushed necessity to a ritual that people are increasingly investing in.

In a British study looking at the 12 weeks to June 14, 2020, a Kantar survey showed that consumers ate eggs for breakfast on 68% more occasions than in the same period the previous year, with bacon consumption up 21% and pastries up 25%, as reported in the *Grocer*. And in an October 2020 article for *Business Wire*, US supermarket chain Wholefoods called out an "epic breakfast every day, not just for weekends," as one of its top 10 anticipated food trends for 2021.

"For many people, working from home has meant having the time to slow down and savor breakfast—rather than scoffing a croissant on the commute," says Shokofeh Hejazi, senior editor at British consultancy The Food People. "What's more, 'breakfast' is no longer confined to first thing in the morning. We are seeing traditional breakfast items, like filled croissants or breakfast burritos, being enjoyed throughout the day." Hejazi notes the influence of global cuisine on Western breakfasts, with the popularity of dishes such as Japanese

egg sandos, Malaysian kaya toast, and Mexican breakfast tacos on the rise, alongside "toast 2.0—plain white toast swapped out for homemade sourdough, artisan butter and seasonal jam."

Bianca Bridges, author of *Breakfast London: Where Real Londoners Eat*, says that, alongside the impact of global lockdowns, "breakfast in general is a meal that has been growing in popularity, due to people prioritizing socializing to start their day instead of end with it, as well as a love of breakfast food items." She explains that an increased number of restaurants and cafés releasing breakfast and brunch-themed cookbooks has also led more people to create more elaborate breakfasts at home. "Lockdown has provided people with the time to do this," she says.

Illustrating the breakfast boom in London, Bridges points to innovative bakeries offering new takes on pastries, such as rosemary and sea salt twists at Popham's bakery in London, and salted caramel apple or poached pear and praline custard Danishes from east London bakery Jolene.

Why it's interesting

With people spending more time at home and COVID-19 restrictions leading many to socialize earlier in the day, breakfast is enjoying a renewed appreciation. "Breakfast is becoming more and more of an event," says Bridges. "After restrictions ease, people will be craving experiences. I expect we'll see a rise in notable and experiential dining—whether it's brunch events, dramatic breakfast platters for the table to share, or restaurants creating other-worldly environments, transporting their guests for the duration of their meal."

"
Breakfast is becoming more and more of an event
"

Bianca Bridges, author of Breakfast London:
Where Real Londoners Eat

47

Asia goes plant-based

Food brands are creating plant-based and
cultured-meat alternatives to target health-
conscious Asian consumers.

In mid-2020, Los Angeles-based Beyond Meat, which
produces plant-based meat alternatives, launched its Beyond
Burgers in China's Freshippo supermarkets (also known as
Hema). Asian startups are also introducing plant-based or
lab-cultivated food products as ingredients in alternative
versions of comfort food—such as bao buns, siu mai
dumplings or hot pots—that can fit easily into local cooking
styles.

In recent years, with Asia's rising per capita income, meat
consumption has gone up, but so has demand for meat
alternatives. Across Asia Pacific, the market for meat
substitutes was $15.3 billion in 2019, up 4.75% from the
previous year, according to Euromonitor International.

Singapore-based startup Karana sources organic jackfruit
from smallholder farms in Sri Lanka to create its meat-like
alternative to pork. Karana raised $1.7 million in seed funding
from investors including Tyson Foods and Big Idea Ventures,

with a focus on increasing commercial production and developing a line of ready-to-cook products.

Beijing-based startup Zhenmeat has launched a range of plant-based products tailored to Chinese cuisine such as hot pot and dim sum. Made from plant proteins including pea, soy and brown rice, and fungus-based proteins sourced from mushrooms, the product range includes sausages, steaks, mooncakes and meatballs.

In Singapore, Shiok Meats is researching lab-cultivated seafood, in part to solve the problem of giant shrimp farms, which destroy mangrove forests and can breed disease. By July 2020, it had raised $7.6 million from investors such as US accelerator Y Combinator and expects its products to be available within a few years.

Young people in particular say they are rethinking what they put in their bodies, for the benefit of their own health and that of the planet. In a 2019 Wunderman Thompson Intelligence survey of teens and young adults in nine Asian markets, 56% of respondents say they are trying to eat less meat. COVID-19 has provided a further catalyst for health-conscious, meat-free eating.

Why it's interesting

The end result could be more choices for all. Elaine Siu, managing director of the Good Food Institute's APAC chapter, sees a future where the meat aisle will include a choice of plant-based alternatives, as well as new foods that blend animal and plant origins, making "our food choices more customizable and diverse."

48

Dining redesigned

Cutlery and tableware are being reimagined to reflect evolving dining etiquettes.

Designers are turning their attention to the table in an effort to elevate the distanced dining experience. Design studio March Gut introduced a new serving format in October 2020. The Alma Tray, created for the Biohotel Schwanen in Bizau, Austria, makes serving at a distance easier. Measuring 1.2 meters long—just over Austria's one-meter physical distance requirement—the sleek tray means waitstaff don't need to lean across diners to serve and remove dishes.

Studio Boir is rethinking tabletop design with its New Normal collection. Unveiled in October 2020, the range of high-design tableware accommodates new ways of sharing and serving food, with sculptural pieces including divided serving platters and elongated spoons.

"Our conceptual tableware retains that important social and cultural dimension of dining—sharing," studio founder Ivan Zidar explained. "Boir's tableware bridges the gap between intimacy and distance."

Christophe Gernigon Studio is also working to preserve an element of intimacy while dining out. In May 2020, the French designer revealed the Plex'eat concept. Translucent lampshade-like hoods cover each individual diner and their place setting, or an entire table for two, so diners don't feel isolated when eating out. Gernigon describes the plexiglass hoods as "elegant alternatives that guarantee the rules of social distancing."

Why it's interesting

In "The Future 100: 2.0.20" we charted how restaurants were redesigning their spaces to protect diners and adhere to social distancing measures without diminishing the dining experience. Now, designers are focusing on the details of dining, innovating how it looks to serve and share food. These latest projects point to a more sophisticated and nuanced future of physically distanced dining.

48

49

Intimate dining

**High-end restaurants and culinary start-ups
are positioning private dining as the latest luxury
when eating out.**

In June 2020, the United Kingdom saw the launch of Apt, an intimate dining experience for diners and those in their social bubbles. When the pandemic left the hospitality industry in decline, some of London's top high-profile chefs grouped together to create a new way of bringing gourmets and food together again. As regulations permit, guests can make a booking for a group of up to 10 people and select a chef from Apt's roster, who will create a bespoke menu for the occasion. Events take place in an apartment in east London's Town Hall Hotel, or at the client's home.

Michelin-starred chef Pichaya Utharntharm, also known as Chef Pam, offers a private dining service in Bangkok; The Table by Chef Pam is located in her own home. Parties of four to 16 people can book an exclusive meal experience of up to 12 courses.

> **2020 dining points the way to a future of culinary experiences where privacy and personalization are paramount**

Ecuadorian-American chef Jose Garces' seafood restaurant The Olde Bar is shaking up the restaurant scene in Philadelphia. In October 2020, the restaurant revealed interior renovations that allow guests to enjoy their meal sitting in one of 14 library-themed dining nooks, which lend the feel of a private dining experience.

Bord för En ("table for one") in Sweden catered to those seeking a unique and truly isolated private dining experience. The pop-up restaurant launched in May 2020 and was designed to let single diners enjoy a different kind of meal out.

Situated in the middle of a Swedish summer meadow, 200 miles from Stockholm, it offered entirely no-contact service. Guests dined alone at a single chair and table, helping themselves to a three-course gourmet meal that arrived in a traditional picnic basket delivered via a cable connected to the kitchen.

Why it's interesting

These dining experiences are reviving the excitement of eating out that was lost throughout 2020. They point the way to a future of culinary experiences where privacy and personalization are paramount.

50

Three hot food ingredients

Three hot new ingredients to watch in
the food category.

The Sichuan peppercorn

Having defined the cuisine of an entire Chinese province, the
Sichuan peppercorn is now setting mouths afire across the
world. In recent years, the swift expansion outside China of
hot-pot restaurant chains such as Haidilao and Yang Guo Fu,
serving up simmering soups of peppery meat and vegetables,
has helped spread the peppercorn's numbing charms to the
United Kingdom, Japan, Australia and Southeast Asia.

The Sichuan peppercorn is also making inroads as a
condiment. In 2019, the US-based chef and food writer Jing
Gao ran a successful Kickstarter campaign to launch Sichuan
Chili Crisp, billed as the "first and only 100% all-natural chili
sauce," for export to the United States. The sauce's
ingredients include Sichuan pepper and fermented black
beans, and it has since topped everything from fried eggs to
dumplings to, memorably, vanilla ice cream from the
Wanderlust Creamery in Los Angeles.

Home-grown herbs for teas

Home gardeners are cultivating herbs with calming and immunity-boosting properties for steeping into teas, to use as natural remedies. In New Zealand there's been a growing interest in rongoā, traditional Māori medicinal practices that feature herb teas. Examples include kawakawa, whose heart-shaped leaves steep into a digestive tonic, and manuka, which has anti-bacterial properties.

In May 2020, during New Zealand's national lockdown, Auckland-based *New Zealand Gardener* magazine ran an article recommending herbs for "emotional resilience." They included lavender, passionflower, ashwagandha and chamomile for relieving stress and anxiety, and lemon balm to combat insomnia. The magazine's retail sales held steady during the pandemic, according to Roy Morgan, New Zealand's largest independent market research company, making it a rare bright spot in publishing at a time when several major lifestyle publications in the country closed down.

"You see a surge of interest in gardening following every global recession, like clockwork," Jo McCarroll, editor of *NZ Gardener*, tells Wunderman Thompson Intelligence. "You saw it after the 80s financial crisis, after the 90s dot-com bubble. People think: 'I need to have something in my life that's more real and more manageable.' You're seeing that now."

Koji

Koji, the Aspergillus oryzae mold, has long been prized in Japan for its qualities as a fermentation agent used to make sake, mirin and soy sauce, among other products. Koji is so highly prized for its umami flavor that it is celebrated annually on October 12, Japan's National Fungus Day. Now it is showing up as a prime ingredient in plant-based meat alternatives on western grocery shelves.

For Thanksgiving 2020, Prime Roots, a Californian provider of plant-based meat alternatives, introduced a koji-based "turkey" roast with a meaty taste and texture. The faux turkey's other ingredients include rice, pea protein, pea fiber and vinegar. The koji "turkey" came after the 2020 launch of Prime Roots' meat-free frozen meals at Whole Foods, including koji-based "bacon" mac and cheese and Hawaiian Shoyu "Chicken."

Renowned chefs around the world have spoken highly of the Japanese fungus, including David Chang of Momofuku in New York and René Redzepi of Noma in Copenhagen.

Beauty

51

60

51
Unbound beauty

A new wellness movement is setting the palette for unconventional beauty.

Prolonged at-home comforts may have given a moment to makeup-free beauty and reduced skincare rituals, but as time moves on people are surfacing from their duvets and dusting off cosmetics to reinvent who they will be as 2021 beckons— and they're going all out.

Music artist Halsey's beauty brand About-Face, launched in January 2021, aims to celebrate "the many facets and forms of expression that live in each person."

Byredo makeup debuted in October 2020, exciting beauty enthusiasts with its non-conformist styles, versatile palette and unique packaging. This is the fragrance brand's first cosmetics collection, created in collaboration with avant-garde makeup artist Isamaya Ffrench. "We wanted to create a universal product that could be worn in many ways. I do not want to tell people how to wear cosmetics, but to inspire them," explained Ffrench.

Left: About Face by Halsey
Right: Byredo Makeup. Photography by Daniel Sannwald.
Image courtesy of Byredo

Dazed Beauty Club.
Photography by Till Janz, styling by Georgia Pendlebury, hair by Jose
Quijano, makeup by Georgina Graham

"

Wellbeing has never looked so imaginative, personalized and refreshing

"

Haus Laboratories captures founder Lady Gaga's eccentric looks with its eye-catching collections, meshing matte and gloss with glitters and bold liners. The brand dropped a collection of four-way shadow palettes in November, selecting queer artist ChrisSoFly22 and beauty influencer Biddy to explore intriguing looks. Beauty content is also getting more experimental. *Dazed Digital*, known for covering fringe subcultures, launched Dazed Beauty Club in June 2020, providing exclusive access to a "topsy-turvy world of alternative beauty."

What is provoking this amped-up experimentation? Experts are connecting it to wellness. "Wearing makeup can be a form of self-care," Dr Patricia Celan, a psychiatrist at Dalhousie University, Canada, said in a July 2020 *Dazed Beauty* article. For some, lockdown applied a renewed lens to makeup. In an April 2020 article, *Vogue*'s senior fashion writer Janelle Okwodu described her newfound beauty experience: "The makeup was a confidence boost, but why stop at feeling good when you can go for great?" And so began her journey of "high-drama beauty" and "outlandish transformations."

Why it's interesting
Wellbeing has never looked so imaginative, personalized and refreshing. A year of restraint has unleashed a burst of creativity, as experimental beauty takes over the home and social media, inspiring beauty brands to add versatility to their offerings.

52

Foraged ingredients

Skincare label or locavore dinner menu? New beauty brands packed with foraged and wild-harvested ingredients make it hard to tell the difference.

Alpyn Beauty, which launched at Sephora in February 2020, features ingredients such as mountain-grown huckleberry and chokecherry in its masks and moisturizers. When founder Kendra Kolb Butler moved to Wyoming after a 20-year stint in New York City working for skincare brands including Clarins and Dr Dennis Gross, she was inspired by the resilience of the mountain wildlife. "I was sitting in my backyard one day, which backed up to the Grand Teton National Park, and I was looking at these flowers and they were all Jurassic Park-sized," Butler told the *Financial Times*. "I thought, 'How have these plants found a way to flourish in a climate that makes my skin feel like it's going to fall off my face?'"

The observation is an astute one. Citing research by Urban Ecosystems, the *Financial Times* added that plants which are wild-grown, rather than farmed, have had to adapt to their environment, making them more resilient and nutrient-dense—and therefore also making them more potent and effective as skincare ingredients.

Launched in 2020, North Wales-based Wild Beauty forages ingredients such as nettle leaf and herb robert from founder Lord Newborough's personal estate. "For a number of years, we supplied wild herbs picked by Richard, our forager, to chefs," Lord Newborough told the *Financial Times*. "I had been intrigued through many conversations with him about the beneficial properties these plants and herbs could have for the skin."

Furtuna Skin makes its skincare products using ingredients foraged from a private, organic-certified estate in Sicily that hasn't been cultivated in over 400 years. The volcanic soil, which is fed by mineral-rich waters, enriches plants for a nutrient-dense product. The brand saw 10% growth month over month in 2020, *WWD* reported, and plans to launch an eye cream in March 2021.

Foraging at scale takes patience, though, as production is on nature's schedule. "Before the flower petals are ready to fall, we gather them. Before the seeds are ready to die, we take them; it's an accordion as the seasons change and as different parts of plants are ready to be foraged," Furtuna Skin cofounder Kim Walls told *Allure*.

Why it's interesting
Appetite for foraged and wild-harvested ingredients is expanding beyond the culinary industry. Beauty brands are bottling these hardy and powerful plants to deliver potent results for skincare enthusiasts—while reminding consumers that nature knows best. "These plants have withstood the test of time," said Walls.

53

Science-backed brands

Demand for science-backed beauty products
is on the rise.

Findings from Pew Research Center show that 89% of
Americans have confidence in medical scientists to act in the
best interest of the public, and beauty companies are
increasingly enlisting medical professionals and spotlighting
the scientific credentials of their products.

In July 2020, skincare line Atolla, whose founders include two
former MIT students, closed a $2.5 million round of seed
funding. The science-led company experienced an uptick in
customers during the coronavirus pandemic, *WWD* reported,
citing Atolla cofounder Ranella Hirsch, who shared that the
brand had "5x'ed monthly revenue" in the first half of 2020.

In May 2020, skincare industry darling Augustinus Bader—
named for the stem cell and biomedical scientist behind the
product formulas—released a hand cream created with
proprietary molecules to help counteract dryness caused by

over washing. The brand's patented TFC8 technology is made of amino acids, vitamins, and "synthesized versions of molecules found naturally in skin."

This follows a wave of "skintellectualism" in the beauty industry, which has seen skincare devotees turning to experts in scientific fields—including Fraser Stoddart, who was awarded a Nobel Prize in chemistry and went on to develop a range of anti-aging products—to deliver technical, precise products.

"Consumers want proven performance benefits, and certainly post-pandemic, we will be seeing an increase in clinical, science-backed brands that can evidence claims," Jenni Middleton, director of beauty at trend forecaster WGSN, told *Vogue*. "Consumers have gotten used to hearing from, and trusting the opinions of, medical experts during this crisis."

Why it's interesting

A heightened focus on health is changing consumers' priorities, and they are now looking for scientific credentials when buying beauty products. Expect to see a continued emphasis on science-backed products.

54

Three hot beauty ingredients

Three hot new ingredients to watch
in the beauty category.

Grapes

The grape seeds, skins and leaves that are discarded after winemaking contain some of the most powerful antioxidants in the world—and they're being harnessed for skincare products, thanks to a growing class of vintner-inspired ranges. In October 2020, sustainable skincare brand Circumference launched its first moisturizer, made from grape leaves. The company partnered with family-owned vineyard and winery Bedell Cellars which provides grape leaves that are usually thrown out during the winemaking process.

Cult favorite Vintner's Daughter—started by April Gargiulo, the daughter of vineyard owners in California—was ahead of the curve when it released its second product, its Active Treatment Essence, in 2019, after launching its now-famous grapeseed-based face oil in 2014. When making her products, Gargiulo turns to "the fine winemaking principles of craftsmanship and quality," she told the *Financial Times*.

Bakuchiol

This all-natural, vegan alternative to retinol is making its way onto beauty shelves. With antioxidant, anti-inflammatory and antibacterial properties, bakuchiol is an increasingly popular option for those with sensitive skin. Dr Zenovia, a hormonal skincare line whose range includes a bakuchiol hydrating cleanser, launched at Sephora in October 2020. Beauty brand PSA, available from ASOS and other outlets, launched in November and includes a bakuchiol and rosehip facial oil.

Anchusa azurea

This bright violet wild flower has been thrust into the spotlight thanks to Furtuna Skin. The purple powerhouse is rich in vitamins C and E and fatty acids, and is loaded with antioxidants, making it a potent pick. "Its potential for skin healing is off the charts," Furtuna cofounder Kim Walls told *WSJ* magazine. And, because it's wild-harvested (see trend #52, Foraged ingredients, page 118), it's supercharged with nutrients from the mineral-rich soil in which it grows.

55

Intersectional beauty

Women-led brands are increasingly demonstrating that the beauty industry must and can do better in terms of diversity, inclusivity and intersectional feminism.

Dialogue around the importance of these has infiltrated multiple sectors, from tech to fashion and now beauty. Independent brands are leading the way when it comes to championing intersectional beauty. Geenie, a "culture-first" beauty marketplace founded by Chana Ginelle Ewing, focuses its curation on underrepresented business owners from diverse backgrounds, and on inclusive offerings.

"I consider myself a cultural entrepreneur, and my mission is to think about what an intersectional world looks like, and how to create space for that," Ewing tells Wunderman Thompson Intelligence. Brands that Geenie holds include LGBTQ+ advocate We Are Fluide and indigenous-owned Prados Beauty. "I don't think intersectional beauty is a trend," says Ewing. "The desire for authenticity, which has been used by the marketing industry for a long time, is actually now going to be true."

Toronto-based Yard & Parish is a Black-owned and female-founded online collective promoting independent lifestyle brands for women of color. Founded in 2019, the site stocks beauty, fashion and homeware, and dubs itself "the destination for eco-luxe Black-owned brands."

Demanding transparency and fed up with Black underrepresentation in the workplace, Uoma Beauty founder Sharon Chuter launched the #PullUpOrShutUp campaign on June 3, 2020. It challenged beauty brands to "pull up" and reveal within 72 hours the percentages of Black employees in their organizations. Within 24 hours a number of brands turned in their results, with many admitting they had to do better. This campaign now captures a larger movement fighting for economic opportunities for Black people around the world.

Retailers Nordstrom and Sephora have announced they are dedicating more shelf space to inclusive beauty. *Teen Vogue* has introduced a monthly column dedicated to Black-owned beauty brands, called "Black is Beautiful." Those featured include Shontay Lundy, founder of Black Girl Sunscreen, and Trinity Mouzon Wofford of Golde.

Why it's interesting

Politicized consumers and the intersectional feminism movement are highlighting underrepresentation and calling beauty brands out publicly. It is imperative for brands, retailers and publishers to address intersectionality to remain relevant. "I think that consumer activism will continue to accelerate," says Ewing, "and that people will continue to leverage their economic power to put pressure on industries and companies."

56

Haute haircare

For a growing number of consumers, a workaday shampoo will no longer do.

Customers are increasingly opting for prestige haircare products featuring nuanced formulas that target the health of the scalp and locks with skincare-inspired ingredients.

The prestige haircare market is on the up. According to research from NPD Group, prestige haircare grew by 13% during the first quarter of 2020, making it one of the fastest growing categories in the beauty sector, *WWD* noted. While NPD Group figures showed an overall 10% decline in the market in the tough second quarter of 2020, sales of hair masks and treatments specifically rose 30%, *Happi* reported.

Several prestige skincare brands are driving interest by diving into this category. Cult skincare favorite Drunk Elephant launched its haircare line in spring 2020. It includes products such as TLC Happi Scalp Scrub, formulated with plant oils and a blend of alpha hydroxy acids to break down and dissolve dead skin cells and product build-up on the scalp, which the brand says keeps the scalp nourished and balanced. Also in spring 2020, Dr Barbara Sturm launched her

brand's Scalp Serum, with hyaluronic acid and purslane to improve scalp health and, in turn, the hair's condition. Even cannabidiol (CBD), which has filtered into the beauty market in recent years, is finding a place in prestige haircare. In March 2020 R&Co launched Super Garden, its CBD shampoo and conditioner, with the brand saying that the hemp-derived CBD soothes and calms irritation on the scalp.

"Over the years people started spending lots of money on skincare," Howard McLaren, R&Co cofounder, told *Glossy*, yet, he pointed out, they were still washing their hair with the equivalent of dish soap. "Millennials have become more transparent with brands about what they want and have dug deeper into the ingredients in their haircare and skincare. It has simply been a progress of education," he said.

Why it's interesting

Care for the hair is becoming as important as skincare. Now that consumers have experienced some of the beneficial effects of prestige haircare ingredients, this category could be poised to grow further post COVID-19. Grand View Research reports that the luxury haircare market was valued at $19.95 billion in 2019 and is forecast to grow at a compound annual growth rate of 5.9% between 2020 and 2027.

BEAUTY

ck is a testing facility
open to everyone.

ices provided by Gabisa Medical, PLLC

schedule an appointment.

ENTER ⟶

WUNDERMAN
THOMPSON   XpresCheck

57

Healthcare as selfcare

Beauty services and selfcare rituals are evolving to
incorporate elements of healthcare for elevated
personal protection.

The nebulous concept of selfcare, which has typically skewed
towards wellness and beauty, is now expanding to include
physical health components.

Spas are extending their offerings beyond pampering to add
COVID-19 testing to their list of services. At the end of May
2020, airport spa chain XpresSpa—which has a treatment
menu that includes pre-flight massages and manicures—
announced the launch of new brand XpresCheck, offering
rapid nasal swab COVID-19 testing and blood antibody
testing at airports. After piloting at JFK Airport in New York
City, XpresCheck has rolled out across the United States,
including the Phoenix Sky Harbor International Airport
location, which opened in November 2020.

Alongside rest and relaxation, Sha Wellness Clinic in Spain is
offering peace of mind with free COVID-19 antibody testing
for guests. At the end of May 2020, Lanserhof at the Arts
Club, a luxury spa-meets-gym in London, began offering
COVID-19 antibody tests.

> **"**
> Selfcare is being redefined. Expect to
> see more crossover between beauty, wellness
> and medical categories
> **"**

High-end beauty brands are adding aromatherapy-inspired hand sanitizers to their product portfolios in an effort to ritualize the act of sanitization. After first releasing its hand sanitizer in May 2020, indie beauty brand Curie launched at Nordstrom the following November with sanitizer scents such as grapefruit cassis, white tea and orange neroli. Upscale bath and body brand Noble Isle, whose products are stocked at luxury department stores Selfridges and Fortnum & Mason, released it first two hand sanitizers in August 2020. One is enriched with wild samphire and sea oak, and smells of thyme, lemon and juniper, and the other is fragranced with rhubarb, juniper berry and rosemary. In April 2020, luxury perfume house DS & Durga launched a hand sanitizer based on its popular scent Big Sur after Rain, with notes of young green shoots, wood and eucalyptus.

Why it's interesting

Selfcare is being redefined. Expect to see more crossover between the beauty, wellness and medical categories as sanitization and protection from COVID-19 are increasingly considered key aspects of selfcare practices.

58

Skinfluencers

A new generation of influencers are seeking to refresh the skincare experience.

Interest in skincare products is soaring, partially driven by the recommendations and tutorials of fresh-faced "skinfluencers" on TikTok and YouTube. "Gen Z is turning to TikTok skinfluencers for product advice because they value authentic voices," Liz Flora, a senior beauty and wellness reporter at *Glossy*, tells Wunderman Thompson Intelligence. "Skinfluencers such as Hyram Yarbro are equally known for recommending their favorite products and sharing blunt opinions on what they don't like. This honesty gives them authority in a highly pay-to-play influencer landscape, especially as gen Z has a strong radar for sponcon [sponsored content]."

With its short, snappy video format, irreverent creative aesthetic and large gen Z audience, TikTok is the perfect vehicle for skinfluencers such as Yarbro, whose Skincare by

▶ 3.8M

▷ 91.5K

▷ 239.5K

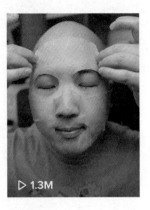

▷ 1.3M

▷ 130.6K

Hyram TikTok account grew from 100,000 followers at the onset of the pandemic to over 6 million in September 2020. A profile of the 24-year-old in the *New York Times* that month carried the headline "The Content Creator Who Can Make Or Break A Skincare Brand." Yarbro holds big-name brands to uncompromising standards in his product reviews, and he's not afraid to slay sacred cows.

Yarbro isn't alone in his approach. Katya-Niomi Henry (@katyaniomi) is a rising 17-year-old skinfluencer based in Ontario, Canada, with 140,000 followers on TikTok. Henry helps her fans avoid paying too much for miracle serums, instead unpacking the ingredient list of popular brands available at retailers such as Costco and Walmart. Former beauty sales rep Young-Seok Yuh has amassed more than a million followers on TikTok for his frank, humor-filled

take on skincare education and product effectiveness, telling his readers, "I have no filter."

It's paying off for the skincare companies that lean in and even collaborate with young customers who are removing the veil from the beauty industry. Traackr reported that skincare brand CeraVe enjoyed a significant bump in sales following a 67% rise in influencer mentions in 2020, according to the *Guardian*.

Why it's interesting

Whether they're heritage companies or up-and-coming new entrants, cosmetics brands are tasked with wooing savvier, more discerning shoppers in the gen Z cohort who are turning to short videos for more than just entertainment—they want no-nonsense education.

59

Brazen brows

With many countries now recommending or requiring face masks to be worn, makeup artists and beauty influencers are focusing on the eyes as the face's focal point, with brows specifically in the spotlight.

According to research from the NPD Group, sales of prestige eyebrow products in the United States rose by 8% during May and June 2020, fueled by "widespread mask usage," the firm said.

Promoting its Hydro Silk Touch-Up razor in October 2020, Schick tapped actress Madison Bailey to appear in an Instagram campaign highlighting how to express oneself via the eyes when wearing a mask. "Many women now are looking for eye and eyebrow products to help accentuate their face above their mask," Melissa Rossi, brand manager at Hydro Silk, told *Adweek*. "Brows are really the new lips."

This trend has also played out on the runways. During the spring/summer 2021 collections, famed makeup artist Pat McGrath created brows at Miu Miu that appeared to have lines shaved into them, while Peter Philips created defined, '90s-esque brows at Acne Studios. Artist Inge Grognard was

behind several statement brows of the season; she daubed orange pigment over eyes and brows at Dries Van Noten, and did brushed-out, ultra-natural brows at Blumarine.

Celebrities and influencers are experimenting with brows, too. Actor, director and producer Michaela Coel sported pink brows that matched her cropped hair when she gave a talk for the *GQ* Heroes series in London. Tanya Compas, the London-based youth worker and LGBT rights activist, wears her brows in tones that span pink, green and silver. As Jared Bailey, global brow expert for Benefit Cosmetics, told the *Guardian* in May 2020, "filling in your brows is the quickest and easiest way to instantly make you look more polished and put together. Brow products are now replacing lipsticks in that way."

Why it's interesting
Brows are the new lips. Statement brows are being championed by makeup artists and influencers whose looks for the season ahead are shaped by a focus on the eyes.

WUNDERMAN
THOMPSON

Left: Tanya Compas. Image courtesy of Instagram
Right: Backstage at Miu Miu SS21. Image courtesy of Instagram via Pat McGrath

60

Waste-free beauty

One person's trash is another person's ... face wash?

It's no surprise that the beauty industry is taking action for the environment. Data reported by Zero Waste Week in 2018—and still referenced today—revealed that more than 120 billion units of cosmetics packaging are produced globally each year, most of which are not recyclable. Niche beauty brands have arisen since then that adopt a more sustainable approach to their products and packaging, and now we are seeing a greater push to rethink the industry, with bigger brands getting involved too.

Creating noise in the United Kingdom is UpCircle Beauty, a leading voice in sustainable beauty. The company repurposes waste and uses it as key ingredients in products. UpCircle's body scrub, one of its most famous items, uses coffee grounds from London cafés which are combined with other ingredients to form an exfoliator. In September 2020 the brand released a body cream that reuses discarded date seeds, crushed into a powder, which help reduce inflammation and keep skin smooth.

In Australia, The Body Shop is also making the most of wasted food products. In October 2020, the company introduced a new range made from lumpy lemons and wonky cucumbers deemed too "ugly" to be sold in supermarkets. Stores in the United Kingdom introduced a similar range in 2019, made from unwanted carrots, and in October 2019 took the step to axe face wipes to reduce the impact on the environment.

Beauty Kitchen is on a mission to create a more circular model for purchasing beauty and personal care products.

In October 2020, the brand partnered with Unilever to launch three Return, Refill, Repeat stations at an Asda supermarket in Leeds, England. Unilever products including Radox shower gel, Simple liquid handwash and Alberto Balsam shampoo can be purchased in reusable aluminum or stainless steel bottles and refilled. Beauty Kitchen says that it will be introducing more refill stations in 2021.

Why it's interesting
The waste-free movement is extending beyond packaging into product formulations as sustainability remains an important issue for beauty consumers.

Left: Unilever and Beauty Kitchen
Right: The Body Shop

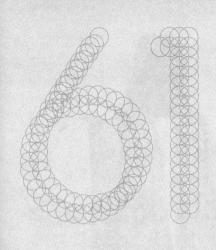

Retail

Escapist retail

Virtual wardrobes and fantastical backdrops
are engaging shoppers' imaginations—and dissolving
retail boundaries.

Digital fashion and virtual spaces are getting dreamy,
transporting shoppers to utopic destinations for otherworldly
escapes. "It's a rebellion against minimal, clean Airbnb-chic
and a return to craftsmanship with an escapist and silly
edge," Kate Machtiger, founder of Extra Terrestrial Studio,
tells Wunderman Thompson Intelligence.

In March 2020, Shanghai-based digital platform Xcommons
partnered with retailer ICY to showcase a virtual runway
show. The immersive 3D showcase for emerging designers
transported viewers to a parallel universe of cavernous pink
rooms and winding sage-green paths.

Virtual fashion house The Fabricant produces one-of-a-kind
designs that only exist digitally. Using 3D modeling software,
it meticulously creates outfits for customers' avatars to wear
in digital environments such as social media or gaming. The
brand presents its creations against dream-like settings such
as pink sand deserts and intergalactic terrains, which reflect
its level of visionary craftsmanship. The company has seen a
spike in interest during the pandemic. "I've never dressed so
many people in my life," cofounder Amber Jae Slooten told
Dezeen in October 2020.

"
These utopian and fictional spaces feed into people's imaginations and appetite for a change of scenery, be it completely possible or not
"

Charlotte Taylor, digital designer

As well as being used by fashion houses to present their collections, fantasy digital renderings are also seeing a rise in popularity in interior design—pointing to a future format for all-encompassing digital stores.

Digital designer Charlotte Taylor collaborates with a roster of 3D artists to realize her soft, utopian virtual spaces, including villas featuring minimalist furniture and homeware objects. Reisinger Studio created a whimsical, open air structure bathed in lilac, with a metallic pillow-like creation and modern acrylic chaise, as part of its Terrace North project. For House by the Cliff, multidisciplinary designer Stefano Giacomello envisioned a structural living room outfitted with tubular furniture and built into a jagged rockface. Loftgarten creative director Paul Milinski designed a series of otherworldly virtual spaces in his Dreamscape series, including Work Party, a light, airy room complete with sunken salmon-pink couch and a cage filled with oversized balls.

These spaces "are designed to transport you along pathways that illustrate inspiration for a potential future and offer a chance to wonder and escape," Milinski told *Designboom*.

Why it's interesting

"The desire for escapism is at an all-time high," Taylor told *Dezeen*. "These utopian and fictional spaces feed into people's imaginations and appetite for a change of scenery, be it completely impossible or not." This desire has further evolved the rise of immersive spaces and experiential stores in bricks-and-mortar retail over the past couple of years, translating them for digital application. Whether IRL or URL, a store is no longer just a vessel for retail but also an experience in its own right, offering fantasy, imagination and escape.

+WUNDERMAN THOMPSON   Left: Borders. Image courtesy of Loftgarten and Paul Milinski
Right: Work Party. Image courtesy of Loftgarten and Paul Milinski

62
Disrupting the dealership

The automotive industry has seen a wave of disruption as dealerships pivot to meet the evolving needs of consumers.

With car dealerships around the world seeing declining footfall throughout 2020, innovative companies are upending the buying process.

In October 2020, Volkswagen Australia introduced its Volkswagen Smallest Dealership to help more customers purchase and customize vehicles online. After seeing online sales increase throughout the year, the company created a unique AR experience, which it launched with a 28cm-high miniature reproduction of a dealership. The model complemented the main virtual showroom, which allows the customer to see what a vehicle would look like in a variety of settings, open and close the doors, interact with the interiors, and even buy online—all from their phone.

Ford is bringing the dealership to buyers' driveways. In the United States, in August 2020 the company launched the Driveway Dealership AR experience for its 2021 F-150 truck. Users can explore the interior and exterior of the vehicle, and see how it would look parked in front of their homes.

Part of the benefit of going to a dealership is the ability to ask questions on the spot. Kia is now offering this service digitally with its Live Stream Showroom, launched in July 2020 for the Middle Eastern and African markets. Personalized virtual viewings and on-demand demonstrations are being rolled out across Qatar, Saudi Arabia, Pakistan, Kuwait, Bahrain and South Africa.

Looking to eschew the idea of a traditional dealership altogether, Lynk & Co's first venue opening, The Amsterdam Club, is more members' club than car showroom—and proposes a new model for car ownership. Lynk & Co was formed through a partnership between Geely and Volvo, and its first connected car is the 01 compact SUV hybrid or

plug-in hybrid, which will hit the market in 2021. Members of the club can choose either full ownership or shared renting schemes, offering a more sustainable approach to driving. The rental process is simple for both sides, with handover processed via an app or the in-car console.

Why it's interesting

As with many industries, the car buying category has seen the shift towards interactive and engaging digital experiences accelerate as a result of the pandemic. With consumers expecting more seamless purchasing processes and flexible renting models, car dealerships are overhauling the traditional buying experience.

Dark stores

A new format is emerging for bricks-and-mortar retail–stores with no shoppers.

Throughout 2020, retailers saw their sales migrate online. In May 2020, internet sales made up 32.8% of all UK retail sales, compared to 19% in February the same year, the British Office for National Statistics reported. In the United States, ecommerce sales rose by 31.9% in the second quarter of 2020, compared to the first quarter, to a value of $211.5 billion, and rose by 44.5% compared to the same period a year ago, according to November 2020 estimates from the Census Bureau.

In response, retailers are adopting the dark store format, which caters to online order fulfillment. In September 2020, Whole Foods Market opened a store in New York City that is closed to the public. The company's first online-only store is designed expressly for order fulfillment and pick-up. Gone are the make-your-own salad bars, coffee stations and eye-catching displays. In their place are longer aisles, bigger freezers, and refrigerated coolers for fresh produce.

The Amazon-owned grocer subsequently turned its San Francisco store into a semi-dark location that is closed to the public in the afternoon. Other grocery chains such as Kroger and Giant Eagle are also experimenting with pick-up only formats, while Macy's converted two of its department stores into dark stores for the 2020 Christmas holiday season, to help meet ecommerce demand.

Walmart is repurposing four of its stores in the United States as ecommerce "laboratories," to test various digital solutions. In November 2020, the retailer announced that it would transform 42 of its regional distribution centers, which normally supply its stores, into pop-up ecommerce distribution centers, to fulfil online orders for the holidays.

George Wallace, chief executive of retail consultancy MHE Retail, says that retailers are "right to explore some of these solutions. If you can reallocate some of your store space as a mini-warehouse for click and collect or to facilitate returns, that can allow you to lever up your online business."

He cautions, however, that many legacy retailers will find these solutions offer only a "temporary fix" to the problem of a surfeit of physical stores due to dwindling in-person traffic. "Twenty years ago, it was about more, more, more stores. That's left a terrible legacy for those companies today," says Wallace. "COVID-19 has accelerated their problems, but those problems were already there. Stores should be fewer, a bit more special, and smaller—that's not really going to change."

Why it's interesting

Inventory and fulfillment are being thrust into the spotlight as retailers pivot to accommodate the ecommerce boom, transforming physical stores to foster a more symbiotic relationship with their ecommerce offer.

"
Twenty years ago it was about more, more, more stores. That's left a terrible legacy for those companies today
"

George Wallace, chief executive, MHE Retail

64
Retail reset

How will the pandemic shape the evolution of retail experiences?

Despite the hope that 2021 will bring looser COVID-19 restrictions and a return to social life, consumers and retailers will continue to be mindful of minimizing touch and close contact with others. For stores looking to entice customers to shop in person rather than online, a demand for IRL experiences that place hygiene high on the agenda has dovetailed with the ongoing trend for creating physical spaces with impact.

"Online avenues can only provide so much," says Kate Machtiger, founder of Extra Terrestrial, a studio that designs and creates "'deep space'—surreal places that build connection through exploration and play." She explains that the experience of interacting with product in person is irreplaceable for many people. "As remote work continues, 'third spaces' that filled the time between work and home will become 'second spaces'—places for escape from the blurred boundaries and monotony of work/home."

Project Earth by Selfridges. Image courtesy of Selfridges

Launched in September 2020, the new MAC Innovation Lab cosmetics concept store incorporates myriad touch-free elements. Plans for the store, which opened at New York's Queens Center, had already been made before the pandemic hit. Its physical-meets-digital ethos offers stations where consumers can virtually try on products or looks created by local makeup artists, while those looking for the perfect foundation can use an infrared touchscreen to shade-match their skin tone.

In response to the pandemic, Selfridges in London announced a five-year sustainability initiative called Project Earth in August 2020. This will encompass working with sustainable materials, prioritizing circularity in consumption—for example, repairing, reselling and renting goods—and putting longevity at the core of its business. "Out of the global pandemic has come an understanding of how fragile and complex our systems are, but also how our planet and people can benefit if we act collectively with a shared purpose," says Alannah Weston, Selfridges group chairman.

Machtiger notes that when it comes to future store design, "even if we can't physically touch the walls of a store, we can create spaces with gravity and substance that generate strong feelings—whether they excite us or calm us." This new retail experience will make greater use of sight, sound and smell, she explains. Materials will be used to convey tactility; sound will create opportunities both for escape and to be present; while smell can be used as a strong reminder of place. "I think relying on crowds to create a dynamic experience was a crutch and I'm excited to see brands focus on the individual moment rather than on creating hype. Whether through escape pods or immersive visual moments, the best experiences will have power alone."

Why it's interesting
While COVID-19 dealt a hard blow to physical retail, it has also brought into sharp relief the power of an IRL retail experience. Whether through more individualized experiences, digital elements, or inspiring, unique design, retailers will strive to make physical retail experiences truly stand out, while keeping customers safe.

65

Live commerce

Retail-tainment moves online with engaging, tailored shopping experiences for digital-first consumers.

Combining the ease of ecommerce with the theater of infomercials, live commerce features a host or influencer live video streaming as they demonstrate products available for purchase and interact with their audience in real time. The format has been popular in Asian markets for several years and is now experiencing a global boom.

The market leader is China, where the 2020 Singles' Day shopping event featured 30 livestreaming channels on the Taobao Live platform, with each one generating more than $15.3 million in gross merchandise value. In May 2020, during the five-day national Labor Day holiday, sales via live streaming platforms increased by 400%. Chinese influencers and brands are selling everything from doorbells to clothing to makeup via the new format.

Live commerce has already hit the mainstream in China, and it is starting to gain momentum in the West. In June 2020, the Canadian ecommerce video streaming platform Livescale announced the launch of a partnership with Shopify, the ecommerce platform of choice for many small businesses, in North America. Livescale had seen a fivefold increase in business requests since March 2020, as reported by *Glossy* in July 2020, with many big-name beauty brands turning to the platform. Urban Decay's US site, NYX Professional Makeup, Kiehl's, It Cosmetics, and cult skincare brand Shani Darden all hosted their first livestreamed shopping events through Livescale in 2020.

"For industries like makeup and color, livestreaming is just going to grow and grow," Crisanta German, senior director of marketing at Shani Darden, told *Glossy*. "Watching someone do a makeup tutorial live and being able to interact with them and ask questions is something that you can't do on a static YouTube video."

Social media sites are also looking to expand their retail offerings by integrating livestreamed shopping. Facebook launched Facebook Shop and Instagram Shop in May 2020, adding live shopping capabilities over the summer in the United States.

Why it's interesting

Live commerce is competing with bricks-and-mortar retail, and its rise in popularity shows that customers are still eager to engage with the combination of entertainment and shopping that in-store experiences offer. Access to brand ambassadors and influencers provides a new level of brand engagement that consumers crave—and can't find in a physical store.

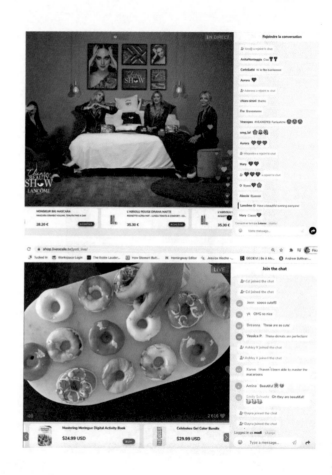

Owning the delivery ecosystem

From food to vaccines, delivery services have graduated from nice-to-have to essential, and companies are expecting continued growth.

The rapid rise of ecommerce in the past year has spotlighted an understated but essential part of the retail chain—delivery. According to a study by the World Economic Forum, rising demand in ecommerce will lead to 36% more delivery vehicles in the world's top 100 cities by 2030, with last-mile delivery expected to grow by 78%.

The Consumer Electronics Show (CES) 2021 became a launchpad for new delivery initiatives. Verizon-owned Skyward and UPS Flight Forward announced connected drone delivery, and Cenntro Automotive Group unveiled the CityPorter electric vehicle, designed for last-mile urban deliveries. General Motors went all out with the launch of its new electric delivery business unit, BrightDrop. The brand aims to make commercial delivery services sustainable with its all-new electric vehicles. FedEx Express has already test-driven BrightDrop's delivery system and is slated to be its first customer when the vehicles officially launch later this year.

In General Motors' announcement at CES, Richard Smith, executive president at FedEx Express, said that the pandemic has greatly accelerated ecommerce and door-to-door delivery. Smith predicted that these sectors will continue to grow, with US residential deliveries expected to reach 100 million packages a day by 2023 (a projection that was originally set for 2026.)

Other players in the electric vehicle marketplace are also fueling investment in the delivery space. Amazon showed off its first electric delivery van, built by Californian startup Rivian, in October 2020. The vans are scheduled to begin commercial deliveries in mid 2021. UK-based Arrival received an order for 10,000 electric vehicles from UPS in January 2020 and hopes to use an $85 million investment from Hyundai to ramp up production. In December 2020, US company Canoo unveiled plans for a "fully electric multipurpose delivery vehicle," with commercial release expected in 2023.

Why it's interesting
As commercial delivery booms, competition heats up with companies planning for a delivery ecosystem future that is sustainable, efficient and safe.

Anti-Amazon retail

Growing backlash to Amazon's monopoly of online shopping carts is driving small businesses to seek alternative solutions.

The shift to ecommerce has accelerated by five years thanks to the pandemic, according to IBM. One of the prime beneficiaries of this shift has been Amazon, whose sales increased by 40% in the second quarter of 2020 compared to 2019. At the same time, small businesses with limited online presence have suffered greatly as footfall to bricks-and-mortar stores has dropped.

There has been a growing consumer backlash to Amazon's dominance in the ecommerce arena, with hashtags such as #boycottamazon trending on Instagram and Twitter. Seizing an opportunity to lure disenchanted consumers away from Amazon, small and medium-sized enterprises (SMEs) with limited online presence are looking to new ecommerce partners to sell their products to new customers.

Shopify, the Canadian-based international ecommerce platform, saw new users increase by 71% in the second

ShopHERE is an amazing way to get your business online for free especially if you don't have a lot of time.

Start selling online today.

Canada   DMS shopHERE
            powered by Google

quarter of 2020 compared to the first. Shopify provides retailers of all sizes with the infrastructure to create their own online store, handling transactions, gift-card options, and deliveries if required. In exchange, it takes a monthly fee and a percentage of each transaction. Shopify, which has partnered with Visa, offers free trials to startups, entrepreneurs and SMES, and offers expert advice for online selling to small business owners.

Seeing the devastation of local retailers, Toronto launched DMS ShopHERE in May 2020. The program helps artists and small businesses develop their online presence in collaboration with various partners, including Shopify, Mastercard, Facebook, Google and the Toronto Association of Business Improvement Areas.

Indian ecommerce site Flipkart launched a program this year to help local kiranas (small shops) fulfill online orders. As of September 2020, Flipkart had onboarded over 50,000 grocery and general stores in 850 cities across India.

Why it's interesting

Online retail is diversifying to better accommodate small businesses. Although ecommerce giants such as Amazon are undoubtedly benefiting from the shift to online retail, SMEs and the companies supporting them are innovating in the face of change and reaping the benefits of going digital. As small businesses integrate into the ecommerce world, consumers will have more options if they wish to go beyond the big retailers and buy local.

> "
> Online retail is diversifying to better accommodate small businesses
> "

68

Influencers become the store

Influencers are moving into live commerce, selling as they go—and taking a cut.

TyLynn Nguyen, a lingerie designer based in Los Angeles, had over 136,000 social media followers at the beginning of January 2021. When one of them likes a trench coat or a pair of jeans the influencer is wearing on her Instagram feed, they can click on the garment and make a purchase.

"Influencers are like the new catalogue," Nguyen told *Vogue* in October 2020. "When you have that database of inspiration, it is so much easier than walking into a store with a whole bunch of stuff on the shelves, and you don't know how to style it."

Live commerce—where influencers sell products in a live stream, taking a cut of sales—is taking off in the United States, and the trend is only going to get bigger. Amazon Live launched in July 2020, and Instagram and Facebook introduced live commerce platforms the following August.

In China, where top influencers can earn millions each year from livestream product sales, the definition of the influencer is already undergoing a democratizing transition. A handful of Chinese mega-influencers have huge fanbases and drive massive sales in mere minutes. Brands have to compete to partner with them by offering them the best deals, which can lead to a discounting spiral and brand devaluation.

As a result, some brands are shifting to nurturing peer-to-peer selling networks, particularly with generation Z and millennials, who compete to earn points on sales that can go towards their own purchases. KFC Pocket Stores on China's WeChat, for example, turn thousands of users' social accounts into franchised stores for KFC, with customized menus and décor—essentially making every user an influencer.

Why it's interesting

Boundaries are blurring between influencers and retailers—between inspiration and point of purchase. The definition of who's an influencer is also blurring, with extreme examples of mega-influencers at one end of the spectrum and individual social media users at the other. But it all speaks to a broader shift. As fashion news writer Emily Farra observed in *Vogue*: "We want to hear from people, not corporations."

The beauty-aisle bleed

Category lines are being redrawn as back-aisle
products make their way onto the beauty counter.

Sephora and Blume believe that period care products belong
on beauty shelves. In September 2020, Sephora began
stocking period products for the first time, adding generation
Z beauty and period care brand Blume's menstrual pads and
tampons to its website, available to Canadian shoppers.

Beauty counters are also making space for hand sanitizers.
Touchland, a European hand sanitizer brand, sold out of
20,000 units in less than 24 hours when it launched at Ulta in
summer 2020, and French hand sanitizer brand Merci Handy
launched at Nordstrom and Ulta in November.

Likewise, beauty brands are adding elevated takes on the
sterilizing product to their portfolios. Eco-friendly personal
care brand By Humankind sold out of its new moisturizing
hand sanitizer 24 hours after launching in April 2020 and
vegan skincare brand Herbivore Botanicals released a hand
sanitizer the following month.

Home goods, too, are being stocked in the beauty department. Beauty textile brand Resorè launched in October 2020 with a medically graded antibacterial beauty towel that kills acne-causing bacteria.

Slip's silk pillowcases, which are marketed as a skincare product, launched at Ulta in 2020. "We have always thought of Slip as a beauty product, and it was our goal to be in the beauty department—not the bedding," said Slip's founder Fiona Stewart. Ulta also sells Kitsch's "hydrating, anti-aging" pillowcases—sales of which grew 240% in 2020, according to the brand's founder and CEO Cassandra Thurswell.

Why it's interesting

As the beauty industry continues to expand, increasingly overlapping with the health and wellness categories, the beauty aisle is expanding with it. Expect to see continued crossover as retailers jump aisles to offer antimicrobial beauty, period skincare and beauty textiles.

70

Clicks and mortar

People still want physical stores, but with digital bells and whistles.

In July 2020, Burberry opened its first "social retail store" in Shenzhen, China's vibrant technology hub. It did so in partnership with Tencent, which owns WeChat, the social media and messaging app with more than a billion users.

A WeChat mini-program allows shoppers to book appointments, reserve fitting rooms and book tables at the café (and unlock special menu items), all the while accruing social currency. Shoppers also get a Bambi-like avatar that evolves as they use it. In the store, each item has a QR code which offers product information when scanned.

The store "marks a shift in how we engage with our customers," Burberry chief executive Marco Gobbetti told the BBC. "When it comes to innovating around social and retail, China was the obvious place to go as home to some of the most digitally savvy luxury customers." Burberry plans to roll out the concept to other stores across China.

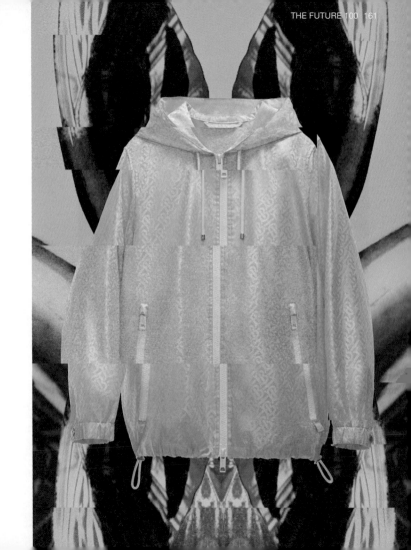

MAC Cosmetics was a pioneer in this field when it opened a "new retail" store in Shanghai in 2019, created by Wunderman Thompson. The MAC store also uses a WeChat mini-program that connects a consumer's physical experiences with their social media. A virtual makeup mirror allows customers to try MAC lipstick colors, an infrared touchscreen matches foundation shades with the customer's skin tone, and there are influencer-created eyeshadow palettes to choose from. The store's second floor hosts influencers' events.

Why it's interesting

The debate over online versus physical in retail is over. Stores of the future will blend both and more, from social media to augmented reality features that go beyond—way beyond—sharing a selfie in the fitting room.

71

Work

80

71

Micropreneurs

Budding entrepreneurs are creatively kick-starting new businesses—and the economy.

A startup boom is in the making, fueled by the pandemic and financial recession.

Krisha Kotak felt the time was ripe to set up her own sustainable fashion brand, Tūla & Tye, in the thick of the pandemic, after being made redundant from her full-time job in travel PR. Kotak, who is based in the United Kingdom, spotted a demand for loungewear, as the uptick in work from home went hand-in-hand with comfort attire. "I've had many business ideas over the years, but never had enough hours in the day alongside a full-time job to act upon any of them," Kotak tells Wunderman Thompson Intelligence. "I think the key is that so many of us were suddenly given the gift of time and the opportunity to slow down and assess what we value."

Kotak is not alone in new entrepreneurial pursuits. On September 12, 2020, Madison Schneider opened the doors of her Kansas bakery. She told the *Wall Street Journal* that launching Lela's Bakery and Coffeehouse during the pandemic "just felt like the right thing to do." In Florida, brothers Nic and Greg Bryon created Pasta Packs, a local meal-kit delivery service, after Nic Bryon lost his job as a

chef. In Rio de Janeiro, Valcineia Machado transformed her green 1969 Volkswagen Beetle into a flower shop after her previous business collapsed during the pandemic, Reuters reported.

With staggering unemployment numbers around the world, many are turning to entrepreneurship as their next career move. In America, for the week ending October 3, 2020, new business applications were up 40% compared to the same period in 2019, according to the US Census Bureau. Experts predict this uptick will continue.

Why it's interesting

Side hustles and embryonic ideas have transformed into full-fledged businesses during lockdown. "It's incredible how many kitchens have turned into tie-dye factories, candle-making labs, art studios, cake shops and so much more," Kotak observes. The key to economic recovery may be in these small businesses blooming.

Pasta Packs by Nic and Greg Byron. Image courtesy of Pasta Packs.

72

At-home empires

The home is now flexing to encompass entire worlds, from the living room to the office and everything in between.

As the work-from-home model, historically a rare luxury in more traditional companies, becomes the norm for many, home design is adapting for flexible functionality.

"What was our home has to become an office or a schoolroom," Ivy Ross, vice president of hardware design at Google, told *Fast Company*. "So how do we build in the most flexibility into our environments so they can accommodate different modes of being?"

Some designers are proposing creative convertible solutions to answer this question. In July 2020, London-based design and architecture firm Jak Studio developed a sofa concept that can be reassembled into a work pod—ideal for small spaces that need to function for productivity as well as relaxation.

"Where, in the past, homes have been designed to have more open, communal spaces, individuals are now struggling to create working areas to boost productivity," the studio told *Dezeen*. "What has become apparent is that homes and furniture need to adapt, providing flexibility and daily changes of use so that we can embrace a new era of working from home."

Other designers are creating more permanent solutions. Boano Prišmontas launched its prefabricated home office in September 2020, which the London studio says can be put together in a day and is "easier to assemble than Ikea furniture." Norwegian firm Livit's Studypod, released in July 2020, is a standalone unit that can be installed in

backyards or garages. The pod comes with a detachable desk, so it can serve as a yoga studio or lounge area, for example, when it's not being used as an office.

This echoes Google's approach. Speaking to *Fast Company*, Ross explained that the brand is not just looking at furniture but also at how a wide range of items can be multiused: "Can you do with less things that do more?"

Why it's interesting

Living spaces are quickly evolving to encapsulate everything from the boardroom to the bedroom, marking an important shift in home design and space functionality.

73

Workcations

Introducing the workcation—a new kind of travel that blends work and play.

The swift normalization of flexible remote working is affording employees a newfound freedom to work from anywhere—and popular holiday destinations are hoping to attract this freshly minted class of wanderlust workers with novel long-term visas and extended-stay offerings.

Dubai is promoting itself as a semi-permanent destination for foreign workers looking for some sand and sun. The Emirati city announced a new remote work visa program in October 2020 which allows visitors to live in the city for up to one year.

"The global pandemic has changed how we live and work. As multinationals and leading startups across the world accelerate their rates of digital adoption, the need to be physically present to fulfill professional responsibilities has been redefined," says Helal Saeed Almarri, director general of Dubai's Department of Tourism and Commerce Marketing.

Dubai joins a growing list of destinations offering similar programs. Barbados was one of the first countries, with the introduction of its 12-month Welcome Stamp in July 2020,

and Georgia announced its Remotely from Georgia initiative in the same month. Estonia and Croatia's digital nomad visas both became available in August 2020, as did Bermuda's Residency Certificate Policy. Iceland launched its long-term work visa in November 2020.

Resorts, too, are offering longer-stay options to attract worn-out workers. The Four Seasons Resort Nevis in the Caribbean unveiled a new package in November 2020 with extended workcation and schoolcation programs, letting parents work in peace from their room or suite while their children attend virtual schooling followed by after-school activities—including sports, swimming lessons, and even marine biology classes.

At the Inns of Aurora in New York's Finger Lakes region, the average length of stay at the resort has increased 112% since it reopened in May 2020, while the number of extended-stay guests at the Vakkaru Maldives has jumped 30% since it started to welcome visitors again in August 2020.

Why it's interesting
As work continues to transition to remote formats, employees are no longer tied to a particular place. Tourist destinations and avid travelers alike are taking advantage of this newly liberated workstyle, advancing digital nomadism—originally charted in "The Future 100: 2018"—from a niche to mainstream practice. As the lines between home, office and getaway continue to blur, brands and businesses have a unique opportunity to redefine how the new luxury vacation looks, catering for both work and relaxation.

"
As the lines between home, office and getaway continue to blur, brands and businesses have a unique opportunity to redefine how the new luxury vacation looks
"

74

Employee activists

Employees are holding their employers accountable, demanding they honor company values.

No longer are people simply using spending power to hold companies to account. Now, they are also bringing the expectation for brands to uphold values into the workplace. Emboldened by waning tolerance of inequality and the waxing momentum for protests on social media, employees in many businesses are raising their voices and demanding more socially conscious and equitable conduct.

In January 2021, Donald Trump's Facebook account was suspended "indefinitely." In June 2020, the platform suffered a massive backlash from employees after executives refused to remove Trump's provocative posts relating to Black Lives Matter protests. Employees felt the posts condoned racially charged violence, while the company deemed them informative and therefore not against Facebook policy. As staff members were working from home, hundreds channeled their anger into a virtual protest, calling on CEO Mark Zuckerberg to take action, as CNBC reported. They set up automated messages saying that they were out of office and refused to work for the day.

In August 2020, Pinterest employees also staged a virtual walkout while working from home. The protest erupted after three high-profile women at the company accused the company of racial and gender discrimination, as the *Verge* reported. In response, on August 13, employees took collective action, replacing their Slack profile images with a photo of the three women, sharing a petition link demanding an end to all forms of discrimination on multiple corporate Slack channels, and then signing off for the afternoon.

Similarly, former employees of the US apparel company Everlane called for a boycott of its products in June 2020, in the wake of allegations of racial discrimination in the workplace, *Buzzfeed* reported. Taking action on Instagram via an account called the Ex-Wives Club, they shared their experiences using the hashtag #BoycottEverlane. Other posts on the page criticize the apologetic statements the company has made, deeming them inauthentic and lacking action. One post even redirects followers to alternative ethical brands and retailers.

Why it's interesting

In a survey carried out for the December 2020 Wunderman Thompson "Generation Z: Building a Better Normal" report, 74% of young people say they refuse to work for a company that goes against their values. With this cohort already entering the workforce, brands and businesses could face grave consequences if they fail to establish and uphold clear values.

75

The chief health officer joins the C-suite

The pandemic has forced a diverse range of businesses to create new chief health officer positions.

When COVID-19 hit, businesses from cinemas to theme parks to malls to restaurants were forced to make swift business decisions, with little public health experience in the C-suite to guide them. That is swiftly changing.

In June 2020, Tyson Foods announced it had created a chief medical officer position and planned to hire nearly 200 nurses and other personnel as part of its COVID-19 monitoring efforts. A month later, Royal Caribbean Group announced its first global health and chief medical officer, to oversee health protocols aimed at protecting its guests, crews and others. Luxury ecommerce brand Farfetch began recruiting for a head of wellbeing at the end of 2020.

Before this, such high-profile roles tended to exist only in organizations such as hospitals, insurance companies and pharmaceutical companies. When Morgan Stanley hired its first chief medical officer in 2018, it was considered an

Viking cruises has hired retired vice admiral Raquel C Bono MD as its chief
health officer

> **"**
> # Will chief health officer be the new leadership position de rigueur?
> **"**

unusual move, aimed at controlling the investment bank's staff healthcare costs.

Due to COVID-19, these types of roles are being considered by a wider range of businesses, and would transcend areas covered by human resources—such as health insurance—as well as by health and safety officers, who tend to work at a local and regional level.

In a June 2020 virtual forum by the Harvard School of Public Health, Richard Edelman, chief executive of the PR firm Edelman, called on companies to hire chief public health officers, who would, he said, have the "rock star status" of chief technology officers.

The role is even more important as businesses reopen around the world. In November 2020, cruise operator Viking hired Raquel C Bono, who led Washington State's medical and healthcare response to COVID-19, and has a distinguished military career, as chief health officer. She is developing protocols as its ships head out again. Viking said it is installing polymerase chain reaction (PCR) testing labs on board its ocean liners and developing shoreside labs for its river ships.

Why it's interesting

For businesses, the pandemic has rammed home the fact that public health and financial considerations cannot exist in silos. Will chief health officer be the new leadership position de rigueur?

76

Virtual-first HQs

Virtual-first offices point to a future of decentralized work.

Around the world, working from home is quickly becoming the norm. In Europe, some countries are even introducing legislation to protect home workers' rights. In September 2020, Germany proposed a law that would make working from home a legal right where possible and regulate the number of hours worked. This follows similar regulations which have been passed in Spain and are being considered in Ireland.

"We cannot stop the changes in the world of work, nor do we want to," German employment minister Hubertus Heil told the *Financial Times*. "The question is how we can turn technological progress, new business models and higher productivity into progress not only for a few, but for many."

Tech companies are leading the charge with inventive, digitally driven solutions—turning temporary mandates into permanent models and paving the way for a flexible and virtual future of work.

Top: WeTransfer. Designed by Luke Vink

Most notable is Dropbox, which is dramatically rethinking its working structure. On October 13, 2020, the tech company announced that it would henceforth be a "virtual-first" company, converting all of its global campuses into Dropbox Studios—spaces for collaboration and community-building, not just solo working. This is a drastic pivot for a company which in 2017 signed the biggest lease in San Francisco's history. Much of its four-building headquarters complex, spanning 730,000 square feet, will now be available to rent.

Other companies are taking a creative approach, programing virtual replicas of offices where employees can gather to socialize and work. WeTransfer opened a virtual office in May 2020, a digital version of its Dutch headquarters where employees can create avatars to roam around, attend meetings, and join happy hours.

In April 2020, Sine Wave Entertainment launched Breakroom, a virtual-world product for remote workforces, which provides 3D offices to companies including Virgin Group and Torque Esports. Italian energy company Enel has been working with Spatial Systems over the past year to assemble workers as avatars in virtual meeting rooms, using a combination of augmented and virtual reality technology.

Why it's interesting

"The tech companies are leading the way on this. I think big offices are finished," predicted Kara Swisher, host of *New York Magazine*'s Pivot podcast. In their place comes the rise of the virtual-first office. As employees disperse and workstreams go digital, workplaces are blurring virtual and physical worlds—opening the door to a new formula for collaboration and a future of distributed work.

77

Gen Z careers

The pandemic has wreaked havoc on gen Z's ambitions as economies falter, family finances shrink, and job listings reflect a stark new reality.

Young people are rethinking their motivations and drivers—their passions, interests, freedom, and need to make money—in terms of how these match with job security and service to society. Early signs indicate that they have an interest in working in the civil service, health or science sectors, ecommerce or other digital services, and logistics. Amazon alone hired 427,300 people globally between January and October 2020, the *New York Times* reported.

In the United States, research carried out exclusively for Wunderman Thompson Intelligence by Civis Analytics in June 2020 found that 39% of those currently enrolled at a college or trade school say the pandemic has affected their choice of a future career, while 28% say it has changed their major or course of study.

Asked to consider the impact of COVID-19 on the economy, 31% say they are now more likely to consider science,

> **31% of US gen Zers are more likely to consider STEM subjects as a result of COVID-19**

technology, engineering and math (STEM) subjects; only 21% say they are more likely to consider social sciences and 18% liberal arts. A few (13%) say they are more likely to consider vocational or trade school to rethink ambitions and motivations.

The quest to match unemployed young people with the needs of society has led to calls for new national programs for youth service. Scott Galloway, a marketing professor at New York University, suggests setting up a Corona Corps—a Peace Corps for our times. In an article for the *Washington Post*, he explained that this new organization would soak up the 18-24-year-olds who can't find work, and employ them for a basic wage as contact tracers, giving them valuable skills in epidemiology, social work and operational management.

Why it's interesting

The pandemic is sharply re-adjusting gen Z's expectations of the world in which they will come of age, a world with different demands and opportunities than before, and one where the value of a college degree is increasingly being questioned. It's also blunted the stigma of unemployment, with young Americans taking to TikTok to creatively document their job hunts and to try to grab the attention of employers.

WORK

78

Climate careers

Climate change is making its way onto curriculums, setting the stage for a rising generation of climate professionals.

In September 2020, Italy became the first country to add mandated climate change lessons to public school curriculums. Students in every grade are now required to study climate change and environmental sustainability for 33 hours per year, reports the *New York Times*.

Universities, too, are adapting their course offerings to address climate change. By 2025, all students at Sheffield University in the United Kingdom—regardless of their field of study—will be required to take a sustainability course. The initiative challenges each department at the university to reimagine their curriculums so that students learn to view a range of subjects through a sustainability lens.

Opened in October 2020, the Greenpoint Library and Environmental Education Center in New York City also points to a climate-literate future. The library and education center is

designed to be "a place for patrons to get their hands dirty and understand the less tangible aspects of our fragile earth systems," said Gena Wirth, design principal at landscape architecture firm Scape, which helped create the building, in a *Fast Company* article.

As education shifts, so do graduates' qualifications and specialties. Research from the US Census Bureau shows that environmental science is a rising field of study. The number of natural resources and conservation graduates in the workforce grew at a rate of 4.59% from 2017 to 2018. Over the next decade, this growth is expected to transform the job market. According to the US Bureau of Labor Statistics, the employment of environmental scientists and specialists is projected to grow 8% from 2019 to 2029, much faster than the average for all occupations combined.

Why it's interesting

Gen Z lists climate change as a top global concern—four in 10 gen Zers from around the globe said climate change is one of the most important issues facing the world, according to a survey by Amnesty International. Gen Zers already make up a quarter of the world's workforce and are bringing their ideals on climate action with them to the office—transforming corporate structures in the years to come.

+
WUNDERMAN
THOMPSON   Greenpoint Library and Environmental Education Center.
Images courtesy of Scape and Ty Cole

79

On-demand offices

The travel and hospitality industries are shifting gears to accommodate a new type of visitor: the 9-to-5 worker.

In the absence of their traditional clientele, hotels and restaurants are repurposing their spaces as rentable offices.

From boutique accommodation to chains, hotels are redesigning their rooms as semi-permanent offices and offering new daytime rates geared towards remote workers. In July 2020, the Wythe Hotel in Brooklyn partnered with coworking company Industrious to transform one floor of guest rooms into rentable spaces. Bedroom furniture was replaced with office desks, chairs and lamps in each of the 13 rooms, and the $200 daily rate includes wifi, unlimited digital access to the *New York Times*, and complimentary coffee and pastries. In September 2020, Industrious partnered with Proper Hospitality to bring the on-demand office concept to Proper hotels in Austin, San Francisco and Santa Monica with daily, weekly or monthly booking options.

In October 2020, the Hilton chain launched WorkSpaces by Hilton across North America and the United Kingdom. At its Conrad hotel in Manhattan, day rates start at $300 and include amenities such as room service delivery for breakfast, lunch and cocktails, plus a Zen Box and discounts on treatments from a nearby Clean Market wellness store.

Marriott Bonvoy is also betting on the personal office business. Its Work Anywhere program, which also started in October 2020, allows loyalty members to check in and out between 6am and 6pm, with no overnight stay.

"The long-term trend of how we fill hotels will likely shift," said Peggy Fang Roe, global officer of customer experience at Marriott. "We're seeing increasing leisure travelers, but it's not 365 days and it's not going to fill all of our hotels."

Cafés are also adapting. In July 2020, Starbucks unveiled a new Tokyo store designed expressly for remote workers. Created in partnership with Think Lab, the second floor of the café is effectively a business center, with enclosed solo working areas and a larger space for collaborative meetings. Customers can reserve the solo workspaces in 15-minute increments, using an app to book, pay and unlock the space.

Why it's interesting
The pandemic has fast-tracked growth in the short-term office rental market, giving rise to on-demand workspaces and pointing to a future where the function of places such as restaurants and hotels is much more flexible. "Spaces that can accommodate that more variable use are particularly important," Wythe Hotel owner Peter Lawrence told *Fast Company*. "I don't think this is true just during COVID—I think this is a fundamental shift that's going to be durable, allowing employees to work from anywhere."

Top: Conrad hotel. Image courtesy of Hilton
Bottom: Starbucks

79

80

Preventing shecession

Women are bearing the brunt of the recession, but new initiatives are attempting to establish gender equality in the workplace.

Women are losing out on jobs and businesses at a higher rate than men, according to the US Bureau for Economic Research.

"We should go ahead and call this a 'shecession,'" C Nicole Mason, president and CEO of the Institute for Women's Policy Research, told the *New York Times*, acknowledging that women are disproportionately affected by the 2020 recession. Globally, women's jobs are 1.8 times more prone to be lost than men's, reported a study by McKinsey. In the United States, women accounted for 55% of the 20.5 million job losses in April 2020, according to the Bureau of Labor Statistics.

Companies are finding ways to support women at this time. American Express partnered with IFundWomen of Color for its 100 for 100 program in November 2020, offering 100 Black female entrepreneurs $25,000 and 100 days of free access to business resources. Amazon and UPS have opted to use their platforms to highlight female founders of businesses. In the

United States, the Women's Business Enterprise National Council is promoting the Women Owned initiative, which helps to raise awareness for female-owned businesses.

While opportunities to support women-owned businesses are available through various programs, there is still a lack of attention given to female employees. In the United States, three times more promotions have been given to men than women during the pandemic, according to a survey in August 2020 by software company Qualtrics and online marketplace the Boardlist.

Why it's interesting

The "shecession" could undo a lot of the progress that has been made by women in the workplace. According to Anita Bhatia, deputy executive director of UN Women, the downturn could be to the detriment of the economy. "This is not just a question of right, it's a question of what makes economic sense," she told the BBC in November 2020. "And it makes economic sense that women participate fully in the economy."

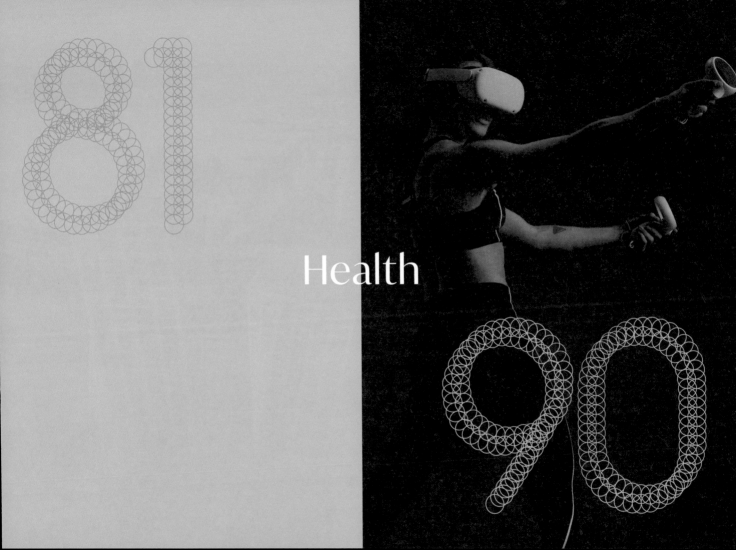

Health

81

Immunity wellness

Wellness offerings are expanding to incorporate immunity strengthening elements for consumers who want to boost their defenses against viruses.

Around the world, "immunity" is becoming a buzzword in the wellness category, with Google searches for the term hitting a five-year high in March 2020—and healthcare brands are adjusting their offerings accordingly.

At the new Six Senses New York, the brand's first North American location, which will open in Manhattan in 2021, wellness offerings will spotlight immunity. The spa will incorporate practices that aficionados have come to expect, such as Ayurvedic treatments and Chinese medicine, and the focus will be on boosting immunity and medical wellness. Services will include diet and lifestyle advice for pre-emptively fighting illnesses and a biohacking program to help guests optimize their fitness. Six Senses pivoted after the pandemic hit and adjusted its portfolio to address a growing desire for treatments that strengthen immunity.

"
The wellness industry is expanding to incorporate immune-strengthening components, which have traditionally been part of the medical realm
"

In October 2020, luxury members' club Spring Place in Manhattan hosted Immunity Morning, an outdoor health session. It was led by Dria Murphy, cofounder of the boutique fitness studio The Ness. All elements of the event—the fitness class, food and drinks served, and products used—were selected for their immunity-boosting properties.

Other companies are also shifting focus. In December 2020, nutrigenomics brand Caligenix launched Immunotype, a supplement based on DNA data research that addresses the human immune system at the level of the genome, marking the company's first foray into the nutritional supplement space. Wellness shots company So Good So You secured $14.5 million in funding in November, which it plans to put toward developing new immunity-focused varieties to meet increased consumer demand. And in October, functional wellness label Remedy Organics launched Berry Immunity, an immune-boosting plant-based protein beverage.

Why it's interesting
The wellness industry is expanding to incorporate immune-strengthening components, which have traditionally been part of the medical realm. Expect to see more wellness products and services incorporating immune system boosters and therapies.

Stay Home
If Sick

Way Forward Signage Co. Photography by Daniel Meigs

82

The iconography of health

The visual language of health is being redesigned to communicate new etiquette.

As health considerations continue to change the way we inhabit and move through public spaces, companies are enlisting designers to help encourage safe behavior. Leading the charge is design company Base, which launched the Way Forward Signage Co in July 2020, following a request from Hastings Architecture for appropriately designed signs. The streamlined notices function as the modern equivalent of traffic signs for indoor spaces, codifying mobility patterns and cueing best-practice behavior.

The objectives were to create a clear, concise and universally recognizable visual language for appropriate behavior during the pandemic and for the messaging not to convey fear. "We made a conscious decision to not only make the visual language and the iconography very simple and universal, but to be optimistic and uplifting," Geoff Cook, a partner at Base, tells Wunderman Thompson Intelligence.

Exit Only

Wipe Area Clean After Use

WAY FORWARD™

Washing Hands Stops the Spread

Mask Required

WAY FORWARD™

Mask Required

WAY FORWARD™

WAY FORWARD™

Max Capacity: 5 Please Social Distance

WAY FORWARD™

Stay Home If Sick

Distance

WAY FORWARD™

Temperature Check

WAY FORWARD™

Max Capacity: 3 Please Social Distance

WAY FORWARD™

Going Down? Use This Stairway

WAY FORWARD™

Max Elevator Capacity:1 Mask Required

hat was Last Thing Touched?

The initiative is jumpstarting the market for consistent corporate design in the era of COVID-19. As offices and public spaces reopen, "the demand for these types of systems will only increase," Cook says.

Beyond architecture, designers are envisioning a hyper-hygienic future. Create Cures, a project initiated by Chinese designers Frank Chou and Chen Min in March 2020, was featured at the Design China Beijing show in September. The project invited designers from all around the world to share solutions for public health problems.

And London-based design studio Bompas & Parr launched a competition in early March 2020 asking designers to encourage handwashing by rethinking sanitizer pumps as well as envisioning "more creative hygiene solutions." The Fountain of Hygiene initiative challenged designers to explore new forms and functions to improve behavioral norms when it comes to the simple act of handwashing.

Why it's interesting

Design thinking is being applied to encourage and enforce healthy behavior. "Design has an important role in helping to solve many of the challenges that we face in daily life," said Tim Marlow, chief executive and director of the Design Museum. As pandemic etiquette becomes cemented in culture, expect to see brands and designers continuing to evolve the visual language of health.

83

Digital nutrition

Social media use and digital content consumption have been linked to depression, anxiety and isolation. But what if digital content could make you feel better, not worse?

"Digital nutrition is the new sixth pillar of human prosperity," Michael Moskowitz, founder and CEO of AeBeZe Labs and a "digital nutritionist," tells Wunderman Thompson Intelligence. He believes that digital content—when administered properly—has the power to boost emotional resilience, combat cognitive drift and maximize human health, potential and happiness. "Content is not story," he explains. "Content is actually chemistry, packaged through the prism of narrative, with tremendous curative potential."

AeBeZe Labs has created a number of tools—including a digital nutrition table of elements, digital nutrition labels and personalized digital nutrition plans—to help people create balanced and nourishing digital diets and build "stronger behavioral and emotional health when consuming media." And, as *Business Insider* reported in February 2020, the company is testing this at scale with "digital pharmaceuticals" developed for the US military.

The company also plans to debut two new products, a neurotransmitter analytics tool and a digital nutrition tracking platform, in January 2021, Moskowitz tells Wunderman Thompson Intelligence.

❝

Digital nutrition is the new sixth pillar of human prosperity

❞

Michael Moskowitz, founder and CEO, AeBeZe Labs

AeBeZe Labs' tools address two key elements alongside digital nutrition: digital hygiene and digital literacy. "People need to know what's in the materials they consume," Moskowitz explains. "They need to understand the risks and rewards of specific digital behavior, and the impact of specific visual or audio assets and experiences. And they need to know when or why to abstain from specific types of digital material to maximize emotional self-reliance."

Why it's interesting
Digital content is being reassessed for its nutritive value. Expect to see more "techceuticals" administering targeted treatments via screens and products that encourage healthy digital diets.

84

Concierge care

Everyday care is being elevated, merging hospitality-grade service and design-led comfort and aesthetics.

Medical providers are shifting their focus to quality time, not waiting time. The Lanby is a new primary care members' club in New York City, slated for launch in autumn 2021, which combines medical care with an experience lifted from the luxury hospitality playbook. Members pay an annual fee of $3,500, which entitles them to unlimited visits to a club facility that is "inspired by your favorite New York hotels and restaurants."

Also included in the fee is 24/7 access to remote care and next-day appointment scheduling via an app. Patients will be assigned a care team comprising a lead physician and a nutrition and wellness advisor, as well as a concierge manager to oversee their personal wellness plan. Beyond medical care, the club will offer regular talks, debates and guest panels alongside a complimentary café.

> **Pioneering healthcare providers are taking service and design cues from upscale hospitality to deliver next-level care experiences**

In London, the "world's first medical gym" celebrated its first anniversary in August 2020. Lanserhof at the Arts Club combines the wellness credentials of the legendary German medical spa with the glamour of one of London's most exclusive private members' clubs. Over six floors, Lanserhof at the Arts Club offers a blend of preventive and regenerative medical services alongside state-of-the-art wellness and training facilities. For an annual fee of £6,500 ($8,645), members can enjoy medical screening and consultation services, a bespoke personal training plan and access to the members' lounge. There is even a butler service for washing and storing workout gear.

The Soke, which opened in London's South Kensington in October 2020, is a new service-led concept dedicated to private mental health and wellness, counseling and coaching services. Founder Maryam Meddin deliberately chose a residential location to set the Soke apart. The calm, stylish space is about much more than pure aesthetics though, being designed to deliver a sense of wellbeing, in contrast to clinical settings which patients often associate with illness, not wellness.

Why it's interesting

Pioneering healthcare providers are taking service and design cues from upscale hospitality to deliver next-level care experiences. There is potential for this service-led approach to go mainstream, as evidenced by the growth of OneMedical Group, which offers concierge care for an annual fee of just $200. Regardless of category, brands must now focus on delivering inspirational customer experiences and service.

84

one

85

Fitness futures

Immersive and enhanced technologies herald a new era of gamified fitness.

Gaming, once a predominantly sedentary activity, is getting an activity boost with new virtual reality (VR) games and systems. In April 2020, Oculus and VR studio Within released a new fitness app called Supernatural. The subscription-based app provides players with personalized workouts and coaching, all within stunning VR landscapes.

The Beat Saber workout, launched in 2019, sees players use controllers as lightsabers to slash color blocks flying at them in a virtual environment. Throughout 2020, new expansion packs were released with updated song tracks, including one called Fitbeat that encourages exercise.

Going beyond the headset, Virtuix will begin shipping its VR treadmill, Virtuix Omni One, in 2021. The system is self-contained and will launch with around 30 games. Players wear a headset, which is provided, and are attached to the

mni one

treadmill with a harness. They will be able to run, jump and kneel on the platform, making this one of the most active and immersive systems yet.

Why it's interesting

The immersive nature of these new games and apps can help people forget that they are working out rather than just having fun. With interactive exercise games, regular push-ups and sit-ups may be consigned to the analog age.

86

Data wellbeing

Managing personal data is draining. New selfcare solutions hope to help ease the emotional strain.

People may not think of privacy breaches as a factor in emotional wellbeing, but consumer experience proves that it is. Pew Research Center findings indicate that Americans feel concerned, confused and vulnerable about data privacy, and research from Wunderman Thompson Data reveals that, after being notified of a security issue with their personal information or data, 55% of Americans report feeling disoriented, 48% violated and 37% frightened.

These visceral reactions are driving a rise in data anxiety. "Privacy is one of those issues that's constantly humming in the back of people's minds—which, over time, can be just as, if not more, damaging to their psyche as major spikes in anxiety," Joe Toscano, founder and chief vision officer of the Better Ethics and Consumer Outcomes Network (Beacon), tells Wunderman Thompson Intelligence.

With data security weighing on people's emotional wellbeing, companies and organizations are designing products and platforms to facilitate digital selfcare and pave a healthier path forward through the data landscape.

In July 2020, Facebook partnered with the Central Board of Secondary Education in India to launch a certified curriculum on digital safety and online wellbeing. Earlier in the year, Mozilla and Tactical Tech presented the Data Detox Kit, which suggests techniques to enhance digital wellbeing, such as how to find clarity among confusing designs, carry out app cleanses, "lock your digital door" and protect virtual valuables. With soothing illustrations of natural landscapes, the Data Detox Kit's vernacular aligns data privacy with modern lifestyle platforms, and positions digital security as a pillar of holistic wellbeing.

Why it's interesting

When confronted with a data security issue, people don't think—they feel. "The impact of privacy issues isn't clearly defined but is, instead, learned through pain and fear," Toscano says. As the data privacy debate matures, expect to see more digital sanctuaries, data cleanses and privacy products offering peace of mind.

+WUNDERMAN
THOMPSON Tactical Tech

87

Virus-proof fabrics

Clothing is on a path to being truly functional. It's becoming the armor we wear to combat disease, optimize our health, maximize our capabilities, and even guard us against the impacts of climate change.

The Full Metal Jacket is a disease-resistant garment launched by British tech-driven fashion startup Vollebak, which is dedicated to imagining the clothing of the future. The jacket debuted in May 2020 and is made of 65% copper—a material that naturally provides antimicrobial properties to kill off bacteria and viruses. The jacket is intended as proof of the value of metal in garments, illustrating its potential as a building block for future clothing innovation.

Swiss textile company HeiQ partnered with Pakistan-based Artistic Denim Mills in June 2020 to launch "the world's first antiviral jeans." The jeans are treated with HeiQ's Viroblock technology, a process that coats fabric with an invisible antiviral film that is effective against viruses within 30 minutes. The technology guarantees at least 30 wash cycles at 60°C

> **"**
>
> ## What you wear is going to enhance your strength. It will become a medicine-delivery system
>
> **"**

Steve Tidball, cofounder, Vollebak

and was certified effective against SARS-COV2—the virus causing COVID-19—following laboratory testing in May 2020. Diesel also launched a pair of antiviral jeans in July 2020, in collaboration with Swedish chemical company Polygiene.

During 2020 we became hyperaware of our vulnerability. As we head into an unpredictable future where the extremes of climate change and the potential for future pandemics could make our environment increasingly challenging, clothing designers are on a mission to make people invincible.

Why it's interesting

Designers are evolving the very fabric of fashion to include materials that are smart, intuitive and protective. "Clothing and technology are going to merge," explained Vollebak cofounder Steve Tidball in an interview with the *Guardian*. "What you wear is going to enhance your strength. It will become a medicine-delivery system."

88

Hyperpurification

Purification standards are getting an upgrade—and are increasingly informing living and public spaces.

Hotels are upping their sanitation practices to reassure guests. Marriott's "Commitment to Clean" campaign, launched in April 2020, included the formation of the Marriott Global Cleanliness Council, which redrafted the chain's best practices with contributions from experts in food microbiology, public health and epidemiology. The hotel group also implemented a new cleaning protocol, which includes the use of UV and leaf-blower-like devices that spray sanitizer. "Suddenly, safety became sexy. Clean was cool," Scott McCoy, Marriott's vice president of operations and guest experience for the Americas, told *Conde Nast Traveler* in September 2020.

Hilton partnered with the British manufacturer of Lysol to revamp cleaning protocols, and consulted with the Mayo Clinic to improve staff training. Four Seasons established a COVID-19 advisory board in May 2020, recruiting specialists from Johns Hopkins Medicine International to update its sanitation practices.

Samsung's AirDresser wardrobe made its stateside debut in July 2020. It was initially released in Europe in 2018 as an at-home dry cleaner but is now being promoted as a hygienic wardrobe. Samsung claims that the device eliminates 99.9% of bacteria in all types of clothing and fabrics.

Italian designer Carlo Ratti believes that clothing disinfectants will continue to play an important role even when COVID-19 restrictions ease and social life resumes. His eponymous design studio, Carlo Ratti Associati, unveiled its Pura-Case decontaminating wardrobe design in April 2020 and began developing a prototype the following July, with plans to launch a Kickstarter campaign. The device will use ozone to sanitize fabric in an hour-long purification process.

Why it's interesting
Cleanliness credentials are becoming a key selling point as decontamination remains a key issue. Purification protocols will likely remain a leading factor in consumer decisions in the months and years ahead.

Left: Pura-Case
Right: Samsung AirDresser

Grief therapy

To address a deluge of cultural traumas, wellness practices are incorporating grief management as a component of overall healthcare.

The pangs of loss have hit especially hard during the pandemic, as restrictions have limited physical interaction and social engagement. Whether it's the loss of a job or a loved one, or the indirect losses people experience from the media's coverage of social injustice and inequalities, addressing intense sadness is a weight many are not equipped to carry on their own, let alone in confined quarters. In response, forward-thinking wellness practitioners are taking a fresh approach to grief management.

In July 2020, inclusive wellness studio HealHaus held a Breathwork for Grief workshop, explaining that "we are deep in a time of collective trauma and also collective grief." Yoga teacher and intuitive healer Michelle Johnson incorporated grief work into her online June 2020 retreat, Healing in Community: A Space for Collective Grief and Liberation. The retreat was intended "to offer a place to honor grief" and examine how "unprocessed grief leads to more suffering," she explains.

Online wellness platforms including Goop and Well & Good have invited grief therapists to write about navigating uncertainty and loss. Therapist Claire Bidwell Smith told Goop that the way grief is expressed is changing. "The suffering is everywhere, so I think we won't have the same urge to put on our armor to face the world, because the whole world is hurting," she said. "And that is another way that we will see one another through this."

Why it's interesting

Practitioners focused on wellness and healing are providing grief therapy offerings that are culturally aware. Creating safe spaces for expression or promoting mindful physical activity is good business. A new era of grief therapy is here, and it's a wellness boon for all.

Calmtainment

Entertainment platforms are transporting viewers into a world of calm.

Content creators are taking a new approach to entertainment by encouraging audiences to practice meditation, mindfulness and selfcare.

Netflix is presenting an antidote to binge-watching. On January 1, 2021, the streaming giant premiered Headspace Guide to Meditation, a new animated series that offers guided meditations and mindfulness techniques, and teaches viewers about the benefits of daily practice. "There's opportunity to be mindful in any part of our day," Andy Puddicombe, cofounder of meditation app Headspace, told Vulture. "So our hope is by presenting this series in this way, it's more than just meditation; it's, 'How do we be mindful in every area of our life?'"

The show is the latest in a slate of mindful consumption offerings sweeping the entertainment industry. In October 2020, HBO Max and mindfulness app Calm partnered to launch A World of Calm, which the platform describes as "a timely antidote for our modern lives." The 30-minute episodes feature relaxing tales narrated by celebrities, including Mahershala Ali, Idris Elba, Keanu Reeves, Nicole Kidman and Kate Winslet, and are "designed to transform your feelings through enchanting music, scientifically engineered narratives, and astounding footage."

Disney also wants to help audiences find calm. In May 2020, the company launched Zenimation on Disney+. The series takes clips from classic Disney animations, such as Aladdin, Peter Pan, The Little Mermaid and Frozen, and overlays them with calming audio for "for a moment of mindfulness," the brand says. The "animated soundscape experience" includes the noise of ocean waves and soft rushing air to help "unplug, relax and refresh your senses."

HBO is encouraging audiences to build selfcare habits. In November 2020, the network released its His Dark Materials: My Daemon app, ahead of the second season of fantasy show His Dark Materials. Users create a personal daemon—described as an animalistic manifestation of one's soul—via the app's personality test, which determines the animal type and character. The daemon then encourages the user to practice selfcare techniques, such as going for a walk or run, reaching out to a friend, or taking time for themselves.

Why it's interesting
The business of mindfulness has skyrocketed during the pandemic. Calm's valuation hit $2 billion in December 2020 after its latest round of funding, and Headspace raised an additional $100 million in 2020. As the demand for mindfulness resources rises, the entertainment industry is enhancing the practice of selfcare with unique, immersive experiences.

Finance

91

100

91

Unbiased banking

Finance is getting an inclusive upgrade.

A rise in neobanks, which operate exclusively online without bricks-and-mortar branches, is addressing the frequently overlooked needs of minority groups.

American rapper Michael Render (Killer Mike) joined forces with former mayor of Atlanta Andrew Young and US network Bounce TV founder Ryan Glover in October 2020 to launch a banking service called Greenwood. Prioritizing Black and Latino consumers, the digital financing app focuses on entrepreneurs who have typically struggled to secure loans from traditional banks.

Simba, a new bank that serves the needs of non-US citizens who have migrated to the country, launched in the United States in summer 2020. "Built for, with and by immigrants," unlike other banks, Simba does not require applicants to have a social security or tax number; only a valid passport and a

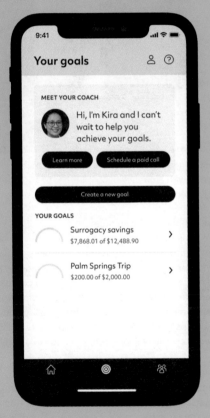

US address are requested to open an account. Simba, which has no sign-up fees and offers low transfer costs abroad, wants to support families to achieve good financial health and even provides funding for financial education programs and community organizations.

Those who identify as LGBTQ+ are getting dedicated new financial offerings too. Daylight launched in November 2020 as part of Visa's Fintech Fast Track Program. It aims to educate and support LGBTQ+ customers throughout every stage of their lives. Financial advisors are trained to address community-specific financial decisions, including transitioning surgeries. The service allows users to display their preferred name on bank cards, without the legal and expensive paperwork that comes with an official name change. Citi has also recognized a need for this, releasing its True Name feature with Mastercard in the same month.

Why it's interesting

Thinking more carefully about the unique needs of different communities is a growing necessity across service industries. Finance is the next sector broadening its offering and becoming more inclusive. Providing more support than their conventional counterparts, these niche alternatives should attract more demand as awareness grows. Going forward, we may see a wave of new banking apps and services that target marginalized communities.

92

Insurtech

Insurtech is the new fintech.

"Insurtech" refers to insurance that employs data, analytics and artificial intelligence to sharpen a market which, traditionally, has been dominated by all-encompassing, broad instruments to pool risk. The result is a raft of new niche products, including those that cover specific activities such as adventures sports, cycling—and possibly driving a Tesla.

Globally, sales of health and life insurance policies increased during the pandemic. At the same time, startups and companies outside of traditional insurance are getting into the game.

Elon Musk said in July 2020 that Tesla will launch "a major insurance company" using data from its electric cars to produce more accurate analysis of risks and ultimately offer cheaper coverage for safer drivers.

A pioneer of bicycle insurance in the United Kingdom, startup Laka focuses on products for cyclists that cover accidents and injury as well as damage to, or loss of, bicycles. Organized as a collective rather than a for-profit company, Laka doesn't charge upfront premiums, but customers share the cost of claims in any one year, with a cap for each member based on the value of the equipment insured. Laka earns a fee for settling claims.

The model echoes the money-for-value ethos of US startup Lemonade, which also takes a flat fee and pays claims, then gives what's left over to a charity of a member's choice. Both Laka and Lemonade make it easy to settle claims. In Hong Kong, the country's first online-only insurance company Bowtie takes the same approach with young, digitally savvy consumers. One ad shows a customer with a leg and two arms in a cast, sitting in a wheelchair, tapping out his claim on a laptop with one toe, with the refrain: "Easy to claim!"

Why it's interesting

Just as fintech is shaking up the previously staid banking sector, insurtech is offering a raft of niche and not-so-niche products, often at lower prices. Leveraging technology, these entrants offer simpler and quicker claims processes.

93

Fin-fluencers

Finance influencers, aka finfluencers, are making finance cool for younger generations.

Gen Zers aren't just turning to influencers for guidance on what skincare products to buy, they're using TikTok and YouTube as a way to learn about personal finance, looking to a rising class of financial influencers.

Their popularity is exploding: finfluencers including Humphrey Yang, Tori Dunlap and Ryan Francis all have follower counts in the hundreds of thousands—Yang has over a million on TikTok. They offer advice on credit, taxes and budgeting, and field questions such as how to invest as a young person and whether it's smarter to buy or lease a car.

The pandemic is increasing this trajectory. Ryan Scribner, a financial YouTuber with 680,000 subscribers as of January 2021, told *WWD* in April 2020 that his viewership increased fourfold for his videos covering coronavirus-related topics. Jamie Fankhauser, a recent business management graduate, started her finance TikTok account in May 2020 and by

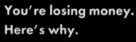

December had over 30,000 followers and nearly 115,000 likes. Her videos cover topics from the stock market and savings to entrepreneurship.

In April 2020, Haley Sacks—the Instagram influencer known as Mrs Dow Jones—announced a new eight-week program to help gen Zers navigate and manage their finances during the pandemic. Weekly themes included jobs, personal finance, healthcare and taxes. "There's so much interest for financial information from people who normally ignore it," she said. "There's so many questions about the future of people's careers, and how they will make money, and how to manage the money they have now."

Why it's interesting

Job losses have skyrocketed. In the United States, unemployment rose to 14.7% in April 2020, the highest rate in the period covered (1948-2020). The recession is hitting young people the hardest: in spring 2020, the unemployment rate for Americans under 25 was 24.4%, compared to 11.3% for workers over 25. Unemployment among people aged 18-29 in the United Kingdom is predicted to reach 17%, the same rate as during the economic crisis of 1984, according to an October 2020 report by the Resolution Foundation think tank. Gen Z audiences are educating themselves to be more financially resilient—and are crowning a new league of finfluencers in the process.

94

Universal income experiments

Governments are reconsidering the concept of universal basic income schemes.

Proposals for some form of universal basic income (UBI) have been thrown out from both the political left and right for decades. Now the societal and economic fallout from COVID-19 has prompted governments to respond to calls for radical state intervention.

In Compton, California, mayor Aja Brown announced the Compton Pledge in October 2020. This experimental two-year plan guarantees a minimum income, undetermined as yet, to selected local residents in the form of monthly cash payments. "People in our community are going through tough times," says Brown, "and I know that guaranteed income could give people a moment to navigate their situation and have some breathing room to go back to school, explore a new career path, spend time with their children, or improve their mental and emotional wellbeing."

Looking past the pandemic, growing social inequality and the potential for artificial intelligence and automation to create mass redundancies is also accelerating action on UBI. Local and national governments in a variety of countries are trialing UBI programs that will likely be scaled up if the promise of early results bears out. According to findings from one Finnish trial that ran in 2017-18, those who participated reported a 37% drop in depression and a 22% increase in confidence about the future.

> "
> In the wake of 2020's economic woes and the spike in unemployment, a new perspective on universal income may point the way to recovery
> "

In Europe, Spain launched a €3 billion program to ensure a monthly national minimum income of €462; payments can be made in full or top up earned income below that level. The plan initially covers 2.5 million citizens who qualify as "vulnerable" under the requirements of the plan—one of the biggest such experiments on record.

South Korean lawmakers have discussed a variety of UBI-type proposals, with one provincial governor advocating extending a pandemic aid plan that saw residents receive a monthly stipend in the form of a "regional" currency, valid for a maximum of three months.

As debates about government-led initiatives continue around the globe, a new US-based app, still in the works, promises an online community approach to guaranteed income. The platform, called Comingle, enlists members to contribute 7% of their weekly earnings to a general fund, which is then distributed among members via a weekly payout.

Why it's interesting

A Pew Research Center survey conducted in August 2020 showed a narrow majority (54%) of Americans oppose a $1,000 monthly UBI for all adult citizens. However, enthusiasm for UBI is strong among certain demographics, including 18-29-year-olds, Democrat voters and people on lower incomes. Similar debates are engaging Canadian politicians and citizens, with the country's parliamentary budget office publishing estimates in summer 2020 for a range of potential minimum income guarantees. In the wake of 2020's economic woes and the spike in unemployment, a new perspective on universal income may point the way to recovery.

95

China fintech

China's online platforms are seeking a share of the growing demand for investment advice.

Chinese ecommerce, messaging and social media platforms are constantly rolling out new services. Now they're moving into investment advice.

Tencent Holdings began offering fund advisory services in August 2020 via its fund distribution platform Teng An Fund and will extend the service to the users of its WeChat messaging service, who number over a billion. This comes after Ant Group—which has one billion users of its Alipay mobile payment app—began offering customized investment advice in a joint venture with US-based Vanguard back in December 2019. Ant is the fintech affiliate of Tencent rival Alibaba and was gearing up for an initial public offering in 2020, until new lending regulations delayed the listing.

The moves are in line with the tech giants' relentless search for ways to monetize their huge user traffic, says Vey-Sern Ling, a senior analyst with Bloomberg Intelligence who covers Asian internet businesses. "The most traditional ways are to get users to play games, show them ads or get them to shop," Ling tells Wunderman Thompson Intelligence. "Traffic redirection, or referrals, are another way to make money off them. I think all the finance-related businesses for these internet companies can be classified into this bucket, whether it's fund advisory, money market funds, wealth management products, brokerage or even online banks."

The tech companies have deep data and analytics capabilities to target fintech users. What's more, the pandemic has boosted digital and social media marketing by fund managers. During China's COVID-19 lockdown, live-streamed investment seminars attracted hundreds of thousands of viewers.

Why it's interesting
China may be playing catch-up in fund management compared to Western markets, but growth will likely be swift and exponential. Ant Group's current regulatory troubles notwithstanding, investing and banking online "will be a structural trend for years to come," says Ling. In future, fintech companies should ultimately face the same regulatory constraints as traditional banks.

Impact investments

Make way for values-based banking.

"Investing in social good is finally becoming profitable," the *New York Times* proclaimed in an August 2020 article, citing research from RBC Capital Markets that showed impact investments—which aim to promote environmental or social good—have outperformed traditional investments during the pandemic. Building on this momentum, investors and financial institutions are making it easier for people to invest in companies with ethical environmental and social policies.

Robo-investor Betterment is helping people invest for climate and social impact. In October 2020, it introduced new portfolios for socially responsible investments (SRIs), allowing its clients to identify and invest in companies with, for example, the lowest carbon footprint, or strong diversity policies as determined by the NAACP.

The same month, JPMorgan announced a new deal with Italian energy company Enel that "highlights finance's green shift," the *Wall Street Journal* reported. The terms of the deal are based on sustainability practices for both companies, with interest rates rising if either side doesn't reach its agreed environmental goals.

In September 2020, the UN Global Compact CFO Taskforce, a coalition of chief financial officers, put together a framework for impact investing at corporate level. It called on other executives to make investment decisions to help achieve the UN's sustainable development goals, which range from ending poverty to taking action on climate change. The group, whose members include senior finance executives from more than 30 companies in a range of industries across the globe, said it is planning to issue guidance, case studies and research on sustainable corporate finance.

In June 2020, investment firm Robasciotti & Philipson made its "racial justice exclusion list" freely available for public use. The list includes all the companies excluded from the firm's portfolios based on unethical practices. Later that month, the Rockefeller Brothers Fund announced that it would begin actively investing in more firms owned by minorities and would publish the diversity of its investment portfolio, starting in 2020. "The lever for change is the capital itself," Stephen B Heintz, president and chief executive of the Rockefeller Brothers Fund, told the *New York Times*.

"Energy and urgency around values-driven investment continue to grow," says Boris Khentov, senior vice president at Betterment. "Investors shouldn't have to guess whether their investments are maximizing the impact they value most, and they shouldn't have to choose between social good and lower costs."

Why it's interesting

Finance is the latest industry to restructure around consumer values. Responding to the growing conscious consumerism movement, banks and financial advisors are shifting their services to make it easy for investors to put their money to good use—and incentivizing companies to operate responsibly.

97

Social media credit

Social media ratings will soon enable credit score boosts.

The business of content creation on platforms such as YouTube, Instagram and Twitch is being taken very seriously by Karat, a startup pioneered by Eric Wei and Will Kim, former Instagram and Goldman Sachs employees respectively. The duo want to reward individuals with credit ratings based on their social media stats and revenue streams.

Challenging the traditional banking model, which is slow to account the credibility of influencers as a stable business, Karat aims to create a new market stream. "The traditional banking system is messed up," cofounder Kim told *Wired*. "It's overlooking these vast swaths of underserved groups. That's where we thought, 'Wait. This is a massive opportunity.'"

The Karat Black Card is the first credit card released by the company and is currently being piloted by a small group of creators. The card, launched in collaboration with payment

company Stripe, does not charge fees or interest for now. The aim is to get the card into as many wallets as possible before scaling up and extending into other financial services such as mortgages.

Why it's interesting

The Instagram influencer market alone reached $5.24 billion in 2019, with over three million posts tagged as "sponsored," according to analytics platform HypeAuditor, which is powered by artificial intelligence. As more content creators, brands and marketers turn to social media as a core business, a new metric system is in the making to help offer financial support where traditional banks are not yet venturing.

98

Crisis savings

Spending and saving habits are shifting in the face of an uncertain financial future.

With rising unemployment rates, a volatile stock market, and a recession with no end in sight, consumers are tightening their belts. More than two-thirds of Americans said the pandemic helped them find new ways to cut back on spending, according to a TD Ameritrade survey at the end of May 2020. Most reported a spike in grocery spending, but had saved money on not eating out, going on trips or buying clothes.

As the TD Ameritrade report showed, most people are being more cautious with their money, tracking spending carefully and sustaining an emergency fund. In a September 2020 survey of more than 2,000 adults conducted by the Harris Poll on behalf of CIT bank, 53% of Americans reported saving more than they typically do between June and September 2020—including 41% of those who identified as unemployed—and 76% planned to continue saving more each month.

Savings rates confirm this. Prior to the pandemic, the savings rate—the portion of monthly income that households are saving—was 7.5%, according to the US Bureau of Economic Analysis. In April 2020, the savings rate reached a record 33.7%, hovering around 20% in the following months, a study from Northwestern Mutual revealed.

Younger consumers, too, are watching their wallets; 70% of gen Zers say that their spending habits have changed as a result of COVID-19, according to October 2020 Wunderman Thompson Data research for Wunderman Thompson Intelligence. Numbers from Wells Fargo show that over 16% of gen Z and 18% of millennials have started saving more for retirement since the pandemic began.

Their attitudes indicate that this is not a fleeting shift. Research by Wunderman Thompson shows that 65% of gen Zers consider themselves savers rather than spenders, 80% agree that spending wisely is more important than earning a lot of money, and 77% make sure to save some money every time they earn or receive it. Financial habits learned during the pandemic are shaping gen Z's identity and will likely inform a lifetime of financial behaviors, perhaps making younger people more financially responsible than older generations.

Why it's interesting
64% of Americans said their spending will be permanently changed because of the pandemic, according to TD Ameritrade's findings. Brands will need to prepare, adjusting their language and approach for the next phase of conservative consumption.

99

Ewallet wars

Looking for alternatives to cash, people around the world are bypassing credit cards and going straight to epayments and ewallets.

The options are numerous. Ewallets are owned by entities ranging from ehailing companies (Singapore's Grab has GrabPay and Indonesia's Gojek has GoPay) to mobile telcos (India's Jio Platforms has JioMoney) to online grocers (India's Flipkart owns PhonePe) to ecommerce marketplaces (Singapore's Shopee has ShopeePay). Malaysia's Touch 'n Go, which started as a smart card for paying highway tolls and parking, now has Touch 'n Go eWallet.

The stakes are high, since partnerships with ewallets are key to directing consumer traffic to vendors and marketplaces through deals and discounts—and are key to retaining custom, too. People tend to be loyal to their ewallet in the same way they are loyal to their bank.

For an idea of how fragmented markets are, look to Indonesia, where market leader ShopeePay has a penetration of 48%, followed by OVO (46%), GoPay (35%), Dana (26%) and

ONLINE PAYMENTS

Buy movie tickets, shop online, book flights and more!

> "People tend to be loyal to their ewallet in the same way they are loyal to their bank"

LinkAja (16%), according to an October 2020 survey by Ipsos. Across Southeast Asia, the use of cash for payments fell from 48% of transactions to 37% in 2020, according to Bain & Co. Ewallet transactions rose from 18% to 25%.

If that's not crowded enough, big Chinese and Western tech companies are swooping in. Facebook and Google both have stakes in India's Jio, while WeChat Pay entered Indonesia in 2020 and Alipay was hoping to formalize its entry into the country in partnership with Bank Mandiri and Bank Rakyat Indonesia at the time of writing. Unlike the early forays of Alipay and WeChat Pay around the world, which were chiefly to cater to Chinese tourists, these latest moves are targeted at local markets.

Why it's interesting

The pandemic has accelerated the move to digital payments, even as governments are encouraging the march to cashless societies. But in some countries, the number of ewallets may be close to saturation point.

100

The new financial advisor

Financial management can be daunting. A new breed
of armchair advisor is changing that.

The economic shockwaves of the COVID-19 pandemic are
being felt around the world—and are leading to a rise in
financial anxiety. At least half of all households in the four
largest US cities report facing serious financial problems—
Chicago (50%), New York (53%), Los Angeles (56%) and
Houston (63%)—according to September 2020 findings from
NPR. Nearly one-third (31%) of US adults say financial anxiety
causes them to feel depressed at least once a month,
according to October 2020 findings from Northwestern
Mutual.

"It's understandable why people are feeling anxious," says
Christian Mitchell, executive vice president and chief
customer officer at Northwestern Mutual. But, he notes, it's
not just the stress that's problematic. Anxiety is also caused
by not knowing how to take control of your finances. "Stress

can be paralyzing, especially if it's coupled with uncertainty
about what action steps can be taken. The key is to gain
control, get perspective, and take action."

In search of guidance, people are turning to their peers for
advice.

Ale Cuadrado began posting finance videos on TikTok in July
2020 to share her frustrations about job hunting during a
pandemic, and was startled by the attention her content
received. One of her clips, about her financial habits living
unemployed in New York City, gained more than 340,000
views. The appeal, she thinks, is in the candidness. Unlike
formal financial education avenues, peer-to-peer learning
affords an honest and approachable entry into the topic. "It's
extremely relatable, especially for the younger generation,"
Cuadrado told i-D. "Most of us are experiencing unemployment
or job insecurity right now, so it is nice to know that we are not
alone."

Dr Bryan T Whitlow, a fellow in pain medicine at the University
of Kentucky, has a similar view. "When you hear it from
someone who's in the same situation," he told the New York
Times, "I think it's more impactful because you know they just
came from where you were."

He is one of a growing group of financial mentees—people
turning to their friends and colleagues for fiscal coaching.

"
In a time of widespread economic anxiety, the financial advisor role is being democratized
"

Dr Ty L Bullard, an anesthesiologist, created a program on personal finance for medical residents at the University of North Carolina, the *New York Times* reported in July 2020. The program encourages residents to start thinking about retirement—and planning for it—early in their careers, with lectures and panels where doctors discuss investing and share some of their financial decisions and mistakes.

Alannah NicPhaidin, a consultant in international trade compliance who lives in Colorado, has become an "accidental advisor" to her friends. She makes it personal, discussing her own budgeting strategies over wine or chocolates before diving into spreadsheets. If you're excited about providing friends with their financial security "and you're able to show how you needed it and what it could do for them in the future, then they get pretty excited too," NicPhaidin told the *New York Times*. "And it doesn't just have to be some boring thing of some old guy telling you, 'You have to budget better.'"

Why it's interesting
In a time of widespread economic anxiety, the financial advisor role is being democratized. People want to feel in control of their finances and are turning to those they trust to guide them—giving rise to a new practice of financial mentorship.

From the experts

What are industry leaders forecasting for 2021? We asked 21 experts across a range of sectors to share their one big prediction for the coming year.

From travel and tech to marketing and beauty, major themes include the expansion of the content multiverse; a continued momentum in consumer activism and higher accountability from brands; technological proliferation and the rise of blended realities; a redoubled appreciation for nature; and the premiumization of at-home dining.

Brands & marketing

"The impact of coronavirus and the events of 2020 have taken their toll on everyone. Health will be a big focus, and as science allows restrictions to be lifted, priority will be given to our mental and physical health. Communities, people and purpose will take precedence in boardroom, as organizations across the world redefine what wellbeing means at home and in the workplace."
Mark Read, CEO, WPP

"The events of 2020 have made consumers more plugged into current events, more willing to be vocal, and more willing to antagonize brands they view as being antithetical to their views or beliefs. In 2021, brands that are caught saying one thing and doing another will face crises that are more ferocious than ever. Brands will need to be able to take a stance— and have a plan for responding to social media users about social, economic, and racial justice issues within minutes."
Nandini Jammi, cofounder, Check My Ads

"People want more accountability. There is a renewed sense of purpose. We have all had time to sit and take stock of what truly matters to us. By the end of 2021, brand accountability will be as important to sales as marketing."
Pooj Morjaria, founder, Did They Help?

"There is going to be a lot of focus on content creators, and there's going to be a very big need for them. That's something I'm seeing now. Innovative marketing agencies are hiring creators—and it doesn't matter if they're in high school. They're going to educate them to be active in different industries because everybody will need a content creator."
Fabian Ouwehand, founder and growth director, Uplab

"I see resilience as the major theme driving brands' choices in imagery next year. While 2020 has been exhausting for everyone in so many ways, our individual and collective determination to move through these challenges has created a widespread consumer focus on nurturing resilience, both locally and globally."
Brenda Milis, principal of creative and consumer insights, Adobe Stock

Tech & innovation

"Even without new releases from Hollywood in January, the content multiverse will continue to expand at a blistering clip. And it's not just speeding up—it's diversifying. In addition to film, scripted TV, reality programming, sports, music, podcasting, gaming, and the rest of the rogue fare, there are new and emerging forms of storytelling and participatory entertainment."
Michael Moskowitz, CEO and founder,
AeBeZe Labs

"Virtual reality is going to be key for taking [remote gatherings] to the next level. When Facebook first came out, they got a ton of traction on the internet and desktops. And then the iPhone came out, and Facebook did a great job of porting over to the mobile phone. I think we're going to have the same transition from phone to headset. The biggest trend that we can ride over the next five years is the emergence of the headset."
Don Stein, CEO and founder, Teooh

"The future won't see the rise of one 'reality' (AR, VR, XR, IRL, URL, etc.) or another, rather than the grand integration of the realities into undefined territory. Coachella will come back, as will the other major festivals, but they will take place alongside virtualized options. Burning Man will double down on the groundbreaking Multiverse it launched this year for those who can't make it to the playa in person. Eventually it will be indistinguishable which reality is in play, as many will be seamlessly integrated together. The future isn't one thing or the other; the future is both, and to what degree."
Justin Bolognino, founder and CEO, Meta

"With the rise of gamification, digital conferences, and streaming services – I anticipate the explosion of interactive digital content platforms to continue in 2021. VR, AR, mixed reality and voice activation have been given a second wind, and I expect to see B2C businesses such as Apple and Amazon to launch mass-market VR and AR sets to reflect the demand."
Nelly Gocheva, Global Head of Content,
Soho House Group

Travel & hospitality

"There will be a small but growing awareness of slow, meaningful travel and experiences, particularly in areas and communities where an influx can disrupt why people went there in the first place. We've seen this with photographers turning off their geolocation, so we don't have hordes of people trampling through ecosystems that are not prepared for large volumes of visitors."
Gareth Chisholm, creative director, Tentrr

"As over-tourism, climate change and COVID converge, they'll become catalysts for deeper reflection on the purpose, value and risks of travel. Meta-travel—travel that teaches you to travel smarter—will come into its own. Expect a greater focus on travel as a therapeutic tool, with travel advisors going beyond the product and a quick sell to share insights in new realms like wellbeing, happiness, flow, creativity, play and transformation."
Philippe Brown, consultant and author of Revisit: The New Art of Luxury Travel

Health

"I predict that we will see in 2021 more integration of the science and the technology world, and tech companies will bring assistive health care goals into their businesses and missions. The traditional physician model is going to change and will incorporate sensors and direct feedback using digital technology so that healthcare extends from the clinic into the home and the workplace."
Sebastain Kunz, medical director at Lanserhof

Finance

"Fintech continues to become more personalized as consumers and businesses seek out products specifically designed for them. Think banking built for freelancers or immigrants or dropshipping entrepreneurs or landlords rather than one generic banking product built for everyone."
Eric Wei, cofounder, Karat

Food & drink

"We may see a continued process where we will eat fewer meals in restaurants, but we will eat more food that is prepared for us by others. And I think that's really the biggest shift that I would point to over the next five years. If the 20th century was all about putting packaged food within, let's say, a 10-minute drive of every consumer, I think the 21st is going to be all about putting prepared food within a click of every consumer."
Michael Schaefer, global head of beverages and foodservice research, Euromonitor

"People are eating more meals at home, but that doesn't mean they don't still want the restaurant/bar/café experience—so we are going to see lots of innovation in respect of at-home solutions for food and drink that is traditionally enjoyed out-of-home."
Shokofeh Hejazi, senior editor, The Food People

"Breakfast is becoming more and more of an event. After restrictions ease, people will be craving experiences. I expect we'll see a rise in notable and experiential dining."
Bianca Bridges, founder, Breakfast London and author of Breakfast London: Where Real Londoners Eat

"We predict a very imminent trend of baking beyond the void. Jelly, with its luxurious texture, glistening surface and comedic wobble, has a role to play. After working with the medium for the last 13 years we are finally predicting a new golden age of jellying."
Sam Bompas, cofounder, Bompas & Parr

Beauty

"We witnessed race take center stage in mass culture in ways we hadn't seen before, but that had been years in the making—with the #BuyBlack movement steadily gaining ground over the last 10 years, the beauty industry was primed for the inclusive conversation. Consumers and employees will continue to drive on the work started in 2020, and use their voices in 2021 to call out (and in) businesses that create untenable atmospheres and perpetuate systemic racism through their practices."
Chana Ginelle Ewing, CEO and founder, Geenie

"Sustainability will remain a large concern and priority for many beauty brands. Sustainability is no longer a niche mission; it's the future of beauty and personal care."
Priscilla Tsai, CEO and founder, Cocokind

Retail

"[I expect to see] the rise of retailers catered to providing convenience. Some will be like Nordstrom's Nordstrom Local concept, focused on allowing customers to pick up and drop off online orders, get alterations, etc."
Jill Manoff, editor-in-chief, Glossy

"The importance of online is increasingly pronounced. For 2021, businesses will break away from 'blanding' (a term we coined) and focus more on how to accurately represent their brands in the digital space in increasingly compelling ways—focusing as much on emotional engagement as sell-throughs."
Geoff Cook, partner, Base Design

About Wunderman Thompson Intelligence
Wunderman Thompson Intelligence is Wunderman Thompson's futurism, research and innovation unit. It charts emerging and future global trends, consumer change, and innovation patterns—translating these into insight for brands. It offers a suite of consultancy services, including bespoke research, presentations, cobranded reports and workshops. It is also active in innovation, partnering with brands to activate future trends within their framework and execute new products and concepts. It is led by Emma Chiu, Global Director of Wunderman Thompson Intelligence.

For more information visit:
intelligence.wundermanthompson.com

About The Future 100
Wunderman Thompson Intelligence's annual forecast presents a snapshot of the year ahead and identifies the most compelling trends to keep on the radar. The report charts 100 trends across 10 sectors, spanning culture, tech and innovation, travel and hospitality, brands and marketing, food and drink, beauty, retail, work, health and finance.

Contact
Emma Chiu
Global Director of Wunderman Thompson Intelligence
emma.chiu@wundermanthompson.com

Editor-in-chief
Emma Chiu

Editor
Emily Safian-Demers

Writers
Chen May Yee, Marie Stafford, Elizabeth Cherian, Sarah Tilley, Maeve Prendergast, Nina Jones, Jessica Rapp

Sub editors
Hester Lacey, Katie Myers

Creative director
Shazia Chaudhry

Cover image
Paul Milinski. Image courtesy of Loftgarten

WUNDERMAN
THOMPSON

書　　名 / 改變未來的100件事—2021年全球百大趨勢
作　　者 / Wunderman Thompson Intelligence
總 編 輯 / Emma Chiu
編　　輯 / Emily Safian-Demers
撰 稿 人 / Chen May Yee, Marie Stafford, Elizabeth Cherian,
Sarah Tilley, Maeve Prendergast, Nina Jones, Jessica Rapp
副 編 輯 / Hester Lacey, Katie Myers

設計總監 / Shazia Chaudhry

協作編輯 / 張玫 Jill, 李慈琳 Ophelia Lee, 張雅帆 Yafan Chang,
劉昀欣 Vik Liu, 江詠延 Yongyan Jiang, 徐慧真 Pin Hsu,
吳芷薰 Emily Wu, 吳靜寧 Zola Wu, 黃靖凱 Kevin Huang,
陳鈺云 Tina Chen, 黃昱嘉 Chia Huang, 王薇涵 Wei Huang,
蔡荃 Sandra Tsai, 高邦旂 Cloud Kao

中文版團隊 / 香港商台灣偉門智威有限公司台灣分公司
翻譯 / 林庭如 Rye Lin

出版者 / 香港商台灣偉門智威有限公司台灣分公司
地址 / 台北市南港區市民大道7段8號13F之五
電話 / (02)3766-1000
傳真 / (02)2788-0260

總經銷 / 時報文化出版企業股份有限公司
地址 / 桃園市龜山區萬壽路2段351號
電話 / (02)2306-6842

書籍編碼 / Z000130
出版日期 / 2021年4月
定價 / 500元

ISBN / 978-986-98992-1-5

+ WUNDERMAN
THOMPSON
A REPORT BY WUNDERMAN THOMPSON INTELLIGENCE

序言

當全世界經歷了 2020 年的挑戰，邁向充滿希望迎接經濟復甦、社會修復之際，審慎樂觀是 2021 年的主要節奏。重大變化正在發生：英國脫離歐盟，拜登和賀錦麗領導美國，許多有效的新冠肺炎(COVID-19)疫苗在全球推出，為後疫情時代帶來一線曙光。

對於品牌來說，事先規劃、了解消費者有哪些行為改變、注入創新創意等，比以往都來得更加重要。《改變未來的 100 件事：2021 年全球百大趨勢》預覽了 100 個趨勢與變化，追蹤今年的發展方向。

科技對文化與經濟的影響正在加速。無論會議、節慶、品牌，紛紛都把遊戲當成「第三空間」，用以接觸現有以及新興觀眾群（第 2 章：遊戲產業新前線），零售業者結合娛樂和電子商務，利用網路直播來創造互動（第 65 章：直播商業模式）；然而在這些機會之中，新的挑戰開始浮現，在討論數位資訊是否環保永續（第 13 章）、深偽技術帶來的影響（第 16 章）時，話題都圍繞在如何創造安全、永續的數位生態系。

因應消費者價值觀影響道德意識抬頭品牌使命走向主流，消費者選擇反映自身價值觀的企業，而這股影響力由於「Did They Help?」這類公司而更加擴大，因為他們會紀錄品牌的行為成效或缺失（第 35 章：道德計分板），企業開始看向更宏大的目標，選擇彼此合作來解決社會與環境問題（第 31 章：品牌共創共生）。

健康議題的重要度上升，擴大延伸到各個企業中，接下來會看到品牌開始發展經營計畫，並將行銷重點放在公共衛生方面，甚至把「衛生長」提拔到管理高層（第 75 章：「衛生長」位居高層）。

這份報告還包含了 21 位產業專家的預測，他們各自發表了一項對 2021 年的重大趨勢預測。

復甦之路由今年開始，各品牌、領導人、社會大眾，都帶領著我們走向充滿希望的旅程，這趟旅程需要我們互相合作、心性堅韌，才能順利修復並邁向更好的未來。

Emma Chiu
偉門智威智庫全球總監
intelligence.wundermanthompson.com

序言

這是我們將「Future 100 改變未來的一百件事」中文版在台灣發行的第四年，很開心得到很多朋友的正面回饋，有人告訴我，這是他們年度策略動腦會議上的必備工具書，也有人跟我分享，他在這本趨勢報告書中發現很多的生意想法，更有朋友謝謝我，可以因著這本書彷彿走了一趟世界之旅，看到全世界正在發生的事。

但不管趨勢如何預測，誰也無法預測在 2020 年竟會有「Covid-19 新冠肺炎」的全球大流行。

因為一場疫情，改變了人們的生活方式。

因為疫情，人們開始保持社交距離。也因為它，民眾對新鮮空氣和開放空間的需求也更加強烈。

因為疫情，大家盡量避免人跟人之間過度接觸，於是我們看到外送服務的大爆發，同時也為全新的概念餐廳打開了大門—幽靈廚房。

因為疫情，實體活動被強迫取消。人們不出門時，待在家總要有事情做來打發時間，因此遊戲產業更加蓬勃發展，甚至未來的會議和企業活動都將奠基在遊戲之上。因此遊戲產業不再單純只為玩樂而存在，《華爾街日報》（Wall Street Journal）甚至預言，過去幾十年來，搜尋引擎、手機、社群網路的地位，往後將由遊戲接手。

在家工作是傳統企業中奢侈難得的運作模式，但現在這種模式已經成為多數人的日常。當關在家，時間久了，總會悶壞，最終還是得往外走，故誕生了「零接觸旅程」（第 14 章）、「與世隔絕的旅行」（第 30 章），反正不需要到公司工作，更有了「工作旅行」（第 73 章）—結合工作與玩樂的全新旅遊型態。

一場疫情，造就回不去的過去與沒想過的未來新常態，人們正找著新方法生活著，然而：社群連結、環境保護、實體與虛擬的結合、重啟懷舊、汽車有機生物概念、飛航減碳化、氣候友善飲食風潮、循環市場、永續與道德、品牌安全、打擊深偽技術、太空探索、星際雲端服務、無顧客商店、社群媒體信用、數位養分、到數位支付轉型，無條件基本收入實驗 .... 等種種變革卻從未因疫情而停下腳步。

因此，我們相信，人們不會被疫情打倒，只是會用更科技、相互理解與彼此關懷的方式生活著。我們更相信，疫情絕對無法將我們隔離，反而讓彼此的心更靠近。

為什麼我們相信？因為這輯的趨勢報告所揭露的點點作為給了線索與信心，讓我們相信明天一定會更好。

鄧博文
台灣偉門智威 董事總經理

01

文化

10

01

戶外體驗再造

當戶外活動成爲大衆生活重心，也順勢帶動了公共空間戶外的創新與投資。

從 2021 年春季開始，在曼哈頓便會有一座漂浮的島型公園位在哈德遜河上。這座公園是由億萬富翁巴瑞・迪勒（Barry Diller）和黛安・馮・佛絲登寶格（Dian von Furstenberg）這對情侶所構想、由赫茲維克工作室（Heatherwick Studio）設計，這兩英畝大的「小島」（Little Island）拓寬了紐約原本狹小的綠地，同時也有草坪、花圃，而水池前的圓形劇場也能夠給藝術家、樂團、表演者提供一個舞台。

哥本哈根的居民則能享受新的水上活動場地。2020 年 4 月，澳洲建築師 Marshall Blecher 和丹麥電影公司霍克斯特工作室（Studio Fokstrot）公開了「哥本哈根島群計畫」（Plans for Copenhagen Islands），這座「Parkipelago」（丹麥語，意指公園）由一串「浮島」共同組成，地點位在該市的港口邊，讓人可以此放鬆、游泳、釣魚，甚至還可以觀賞星星。2018 年的島嶼

模型 CPH-Ø1 和這次的計畫很類似，因為該計畫非常成功，所以有了這次的新計畫。「哥本哈根島群」秉持永續精神，利用鋼材和回收的懸浮物建造而成，繫於海床之上，島上覆有蓊鬱的樹木和綠地，島群下方也有足夠的空間，讓海洋生物得以繁盛生長。

在維也納的閒置綠地上，Precht 設計了一座類似迷宮的「距離公園」（Parc de la Distance），高聳的樹木圍籬隔開了公園裡的不同步道，讓遊客可以在保持社交距離的前提下悠遊綠地。這項設計成功克服了疫情期間因為關閉公園而產生的問題。

在英格蘭，奧雅納工程公司（Arup）為「無牆利物浦計畫」（Liverpool Without Walls）打造讓民眾得以保持社交距離的新戶外座位區。奧雅納和 Meristem Design 以及利物浦市議會合作，目標是打造出調整型的戶外傢俱，並將它們安置到城市的各個角落中。

值得關注的原因：

綠地是形塑未來城市規劃的重要元素，城市裡的戶外據點，對世界各地的城市居民來說，一直都很具吸引力，受到新冠肺炎（COVID-19）的疫情影響，民眾對新鮮空氣和開放空間的需求也更加強烈。城市規劃者要找出永久性的解決方案，藉此打造獲得重金支持的新型文化空間。

01

02

遊戲產業新前線

遊戲產業革命已經來臨。

顧問公司 Activate 的研究指出,大眾遊戲的產值預計在 2024 年前達到美金 1,980 億元,而且這還不包括遊戲用硬體、相關裝置、擴增實境、虛擬實境、廣告的營收。遊戲產業的成長,某部分是因為數位遊戲已漸漸融入至不同類型的活動中,成為其背景元素,不管在演唱會、畢業典禮或是抗議活動中,都能看到數位遊戲的蹤影。

遊戲場景轉型成虛擬文化據點的案例也日漸增多,大眾可以在遊戲裡聚會交流、享受娛樂、談論生意。

遊戲支付公司 Xsolla 認為未來的會議和企業活動都將奠基在遊戲之上。2020 年 10 月,該公司為遊戲產業推出了虛擬的活動平台 Unconventional,用戶可以在平台上創造虛擬角色以參與活動。Xsolla 解釋,遊戲產業的下一步,按理來說就是要邁入活動籌辦的領域,而且這個新平台也想為大眾免除使用 Zoom 而產生的疑慮。該公司的總裁克里斯‧休伊史(Chris Hewish)表示:

「受到疫情影響，實體活動被迫取消，能有效解決不同需求的虛擬活動暨娛樂平台，變得非常關鍵。」

Teooh 公司也親身體驗了這樣的趨勢變革。Teooh 是使用虛擬人物進行交流的虛擬活動平台，從 2020 年 4 月創立後便大受歡迎，執行長唐·斯戴恩（Don Stein）對偉門智威智庫指出，Teooh 在同年 12 月就累積了超過 5 萬名用戶，會議室數量超過 1 萬個，虛擬聚會時長也達到 12,500 小時。

這個平台的用途廣泛，從商務會議到慶生派對應有盡有——Think Global School 是全世界第一所旅居型高中，全校師生每週都會在 Teooh 上集會；2020 年 5 月，Animayo 在 Teooh 上舉辦一場有 800 人參與的電影節；銳步（Reebok）的創辦人喬·福斯特（Joe Foster）則在該平台上舉行個人回憶錄的虛擬新書發表會；Jay-Z 旗下的公司搖滾國度（Roc Nation）在上面推出盛大的發表派對；類似 Alcoholics Anonymous 這類的酒精成癮戒斷會亦曾在 Teooh 上進行聚會。

Epic Games 開發的遊戲《要塞英雄》（Fortnite）也成為新的聚會場地。2020 年 5 月，該遊戲推出非暴力的大逃殺（Party Royale）模式，成為虛擬表演和聚會的新選項，就像 Epic Games 全球夥伴關係總監 Nate Nanzer 說的：「這是個景點。」

這款遊戲現在也成為文化活動的交流平台，2020 年 7 月，遊戲內舉辦了一系列名為「我們合眾國人民」（We the People）的活動，討論美國種族議題。該活動由有線電視新聞網（CNN）的範·瓊斯（Van Jones）主持，嘉賓則是記者伊萊恩·韋爾特羅思（Elaine Welteroth）和傑梅爾·希爾（Jemele Hill），還邀請了麥克·瑞德（Killer Mike）和利爾·貝比（Lil Baby）兩位音樂人參與其中，共同討論媒體、文化、娛樂產業中存在的系統性種族問題。

值得關注的原因：

遊戲產業不再單純只為玩樂而存在，Activate 的共同創辦人暨執行長麥可·沃夫（Michael Wolf）曾表示，遊戲會成為下一個具有主宰地位的科技平台；《華爾街日報》（Wall Street Journal）則報導，過去幾十年來，搜尋引擎、手機、社群網路的地位，往後將由遊戲接手。

文化

03

安心紮根生活

人們逐漸發現這些以大自然為靈感的設計更能帶給大家舒適、安穩的感受。

前所未見的健康危機、社群騷動、政治動亂都讓人煩躁不安，大眾所企盼和追尋的，是穩定人心且讓人感覺踏實、有安全感的元素。

在特別緊繃的日子裡，醫生越來越常為焦躁、憂鬱、高血壓的病人開出新的處方：多接觸大自然。這股風潮現在也蔓延到室內設計領域，設計師用溫暖的大地色系，來打造沉靜、療癒的環境，將自然元素融入到空間中。

Shutterstock 圖庫在 2020 年 11 月公佈了 2021 年的色彩趨勢預測，上榜的有飽滿的金色系、有機棉白色系、深沉的藍綠色系。Shutterstock 圖庫近期的用戶下載數據「顯示出不同的創作思考模式」，該公司的創意總監 Flo Lau 接著說道：「用戶不再選擇代表 2020 年的那種明亮、飽和的顏色。在 2021 年，我們會看到飽滿、自然的配色，代表新的機會，或者用更簡單的方式來看，這樣的色彩選擇，展現的是大眾想到戶外走走的慾望。」

03

Shutterstock's color predictions for 2021 include Tidewater Green.
Image courtesy of About Life and Shutterstock

2020 年 9 月，顏料品牌德利（Dulux）選擇讓人感覺「踏實」的米色調「勇氣大地色」（Brave Ground），當作 2021 年的品牌年度色彩。該品牌解釋道，勇氣大地色屬於自然色系，反應出「我們可以從大自然中獲得的力量。」

PPG 集團也同樣在 2020 年 9 月發布了 2021 年度配色，裡面有三種自然系色調，「讓人心靈平靜、充滿動力，同時也強調同情心和樂觀精神。」這次的配色包含了舒服的中性色、沉靜的藍色、溫暖的土咖啡色；PPG 更進一步解釋，其中一款顏色名為「巨大柏木」（Big Cypress），裡面「帶有薑黃、柿紅的色澤，就像家帶給你的溫暖感受和大大擁抱。」

PPG 集團的高階色彩行銷經理 Dea Schlotter 說道，這種「有機、充滿希望的配色，代表的是我們長期受到過度刺激、過度消費的影響後，開始嚮往簡單及舒適的心態。」

值得關注的原因：

現在室內空間已經成為比以往都還重要的庇護所。而因為大眾渴望穩定，於是開始尋求帶給人溫暖、安全感的色調和空間設計。WGS 的室內設計總監 Gemma Riberti 對媒體《Refinery29》表示，柔軟、可靠、富有彈性的中性色「能打造出療癒、撫慰人心、提供保護的室內空間」。

04

動畫產業復甦

娛樂產業正在推動將動畫變成說故事的
預設模式。

在隔離期間，真人主演的電影被迫停拍，對於成人卡通動畫的需求因此上升，也終於給了動畫師大顯身手的機會，即使未來電影重新開拍，動畫界的文藝復興也會持續進行。

從 CBS 電視台的節目《卡通新聞秀》（Tooning Out the News）到 Hulu 的《外星也難民》（Solar Opposites），首次開播的大人動畫片在 2020 年都有很好的斬獲，就連真人上鏡的節目《黑人當道》（Black-ish）和《踏實新人生》（One Day at a Time），也都加入了動畫特輯。

動畫特輯的其中一個賣點，是大名鼎鼎的來賓。《黑人當道》的動畫片於 2020 年 10 月推出，裡面出現了史黛西・艾布拉姆斯（Stacey Abrams），她是倡議公平投票的團體 Fair Fight Action 的創辦人；而《卡通新聞秀》裡則可以看到艾倫・德肖維茨（Alan Dershowitz）的身影，他是律師、哈佛法學院的教授，也是傑佛瑞・艾普斯汀（Jeffrey Epstein）的辯護律師團成員。

《星際爭霸戰》在 2020 年 8 月推出最新一季動畫《星際爭霸戰：底層甲版》(Star Trek: Lower Decks)，星際迷也暫時可以不用一再重播之前的經典片段了。製作公司以撥接的速度，為星際宇宙增添了一份幽默感，也為《銀河飛龍》(The Next Generation) 和《銀河前哨》(Deep Space 9) 的影迷，加入了一些內行人才懂的笑點。

還有很多部動畫正在製作中：福斯電視 (Fox) 推出 90 年代大片《X 檔案》(The X-Files) 的外傳，希望可以帶動 X 世代具有懷舊情懷的影迷，復興「X 檔案影迷運動」(X-philes)；網飛 (Netflix) 在 2020 年 9 月宣布，他們會以動畫片的形式，重新製作諾曼‧李爾 (Norman Lear) 在 70 年代推出的情境喜劇《好時光》(Good Times)；迪士尼 (Disney) 也把希望放在漫威系列上，推出眾星雲集的動畫影集《假如⋯?》(What If⋯?) 預計 2021 年夏季會在 Disney+ 上映，總集數 10 集。

值得關注的原因：

動畫將是電視產業的未來。全球動畫市場 2020 年的收益大約是美金 2.72 億元，預計在 2026 年以前就會達到美金 4.73 億元，觀眾對大人卡通的偏好一年比一年增高，《辛普森家庭》(The Simpsons) 和《南方四賤客》(South Park) 等經典動畫片表現依然強勁，《青春無密語》(Big Mouth) 和《馬男波傑克》(BoJack Horseman) 等新片也有優秀的表現。除此之外，還有更多的動畫即將上映，就讓我們拭目以待吧！

"
全球動畫市場2020年的收益大約是美金2.72億元，預計在2026年以前就會達到美金4.73億元。
"

05

生態保育野化

日漸興起的綠地復甦運動，目標是希望能修復被
破壞的棲地，讓野生生物和地球從中獲益——
當然還有人類。

自然學家大衛・艾登堡（David Attenborough）在他 2020 年推出
的網飛（Netflix）紀錄片《活在我們的星球》（A Life on Our Planet）
裡大聲疾呼，希望能「野化全世界」。大自然受到人為濫墾後的反撲，
是他希望喚起大眾關注的焦點。

野化，指的是生態系逐漸恢復到大自然能完全掌控該地區、依循自然
模式生生不息的過程。人類在這個重生的過程中，會扮演積極的角色，
幫助大自然恢復原有的生長力，甚至也可能重新引入原生物種。

這種模式能夠幫助生物多樣性，也能對抗氣候變遷的問題。2020 年
10 月，《自然》（Nature）期刊裡有一篇科學研究指出，如果實施野化，
一來能有效對抗溫室氣體的影響，因為植物可以吸收、儲存碳，二來
也能保護野生生物的棲地。

目前最受推崇的野化案例，當屬英格蘭西薩塞克斯郡的聶普堡
（Knepp Castle Estate）。過去，這裡曾被密集地開墾，但從 2001 年
起，當地便啟動了意義重大的野化計畫，希望讓土地回到生生不息
的狀態。現在，幾十年過去了，目前這裡仍有栽種作物，但野生生物
量大幅增加，諸如遊隼和大紫蛺蝶之類的稀有種，也都重新回到
該地生活。

"
我們期許能夠 修復土地、修復自然， 也修復我們自己。
"

Heal主席，楊·斯丹拿得
（Jan Stannard）

Rewilding by Heal: the marmalade hoverfly. Image courtesy of Chris Towler

Top: Trees for Life Dundreggan Rewilding Centre
Bottom: Image courtesy of Trevor Dines and Plantlife

截至目前，許多初期的野化計畫都在私有土地上開展，聶普堡就是其中一個例子。2020 年，英國慈善機構 Heal 成立，希望利用群眾募資的方式，轉化生態貧瘠的土地，包括舊有農地和舊有綠帶。該機構的目標是要讓這些區域成為庇護所，不只讓野生生物得以棲居，也要成為人類的避難地。Heal 的主席楊・斯丹拿得（Jan Stannard）對《衛報》（The Guardian）表示，「我們期許能夠修復土地、修復自然，也修復我們自己。」

卡帕西雅保育基金會（Foundation Conservation Carpathia）則採取了不同的作法，他們買下部分的私有土地，藉以抑制非法伐木，並為羅馬尼亞打造安全的野外環境，甚至還在 2020 年重新引入草食性的美洲野牛。

城市野化計畫也期許能為城市帶來好處：都柏林的三一學院（Trinity College）替換掉精心修剪的草皮，披上長滿野花的植被。野生動物公益機構 Plantlife 希望能將英國道路的路肩打造成野生生態廊道；2020 年，他們在多塞特郡進行了前導試驗，結果非常成功。

值得關注的原因：

各品牌目前有越來越多的管道，能和對抗氣候變遷問題的相關野化機構合作。英國的富豪汽車（Volvo Cars）贊助了杜瑞爾野生生物保育信託（Durrell Wildlife Conservation Trust）的部分修復計畫，其中包括大西洋東南沿岸森林保護區的修復計畫，預計在巴西的熱帶雨林種下 17,000 顆樹。豪華製錶商愛彼錶（Audemars Piguet）資助了位於蘇格蘭高地的公益機構 Trees for Life，成立世界上第一個野化中心，預計於 2022 年開幕。偉門智威數據服務發現，有 58% 的受訪者表示，疫情開始後，他們變得更加重視戶外空間和自然環境。

05

06

實體活動的未來

活動公司和企業都投入了大量心思,想為2021年打造出安全無虞的現場體驗。

2020 年一整年下來,活動規劃公司展現了創意、韌性、科技長才,舉辦了許多創新的虛擬活動;去年多采多姿的活動也為近期的現場演唱會埋下種子,畢竟疫苗推出的時程,目前還未明朗。Virgin Money Unity Arena 自稱是英國第一個專為安全社交距離所設計的音樂空間,他們在 2020 年 8 月辦了第一場演唱會,裡面有 500 座「個人升降台」,而且每座升降台最多只能容納 5 個觀眾,台座之間也保持著六英呎的距離,換算下來,整個場地總共能容納 2,500 人。

世界各地也出現了很多類似的例子,例如芬蘭的 Suvilahti Summer 電影音樂節、荷蘭的開放式劇場。烈火紅唇樂團(The Flaming Lips)也將社交距離提升到新的層次,2020 年 10 月,他們舉辦了一場演唱會,場內所有的觀眾和樂團成員,全都置身在塑膠充氣泡泡中。

音樂節的主辦單位也急著重新開辦室內外大型演唱會,英國的 Glastonbury 音樂節就是其中之一,這場世界最大的音樂節,

文化

目前正如火如荼地籌備中，希望能在 2021 年 6 月如期舉行（活動暫定取消）；因為 2020 年活動取消而無法出席的肯德里克·拉馬爾（Kendrick Lamar）、泰勒絲（Taylor Swift）、保羅·麥卡尼（Paul McCartney），也都重新受邀。創辦人麥可·伊維斯（Michael Eavis）表示，可以安裝大型的檢測設備，來預防新冠肺炎（COVID-19）並保護觀眾。

受疫情影響，即使有虛擬活動，現場演出的活動主辦方還是面臨了收入上的困境。活動產業的命運，取決於他們是否能讓疫情前的觀眾回籠，如果能安全地把這件事做好，可以創造雙倍的效益。現場音樂表演實務雜誌《IQ》的編輯高登·馬頌（Gordon Masson）告訴《衛報》（The Guardian）：「政府可以利用音樂節來測試防疫相關的產品或流程，因為音樂節就像一座臨時的城市一樣。」他也舉例，像是手環這類的科技產品，就可以在演唱會觀眾彼此太過靠近時，發出震動來警告他們。

體驗設計公司 Meta 的創辦人兼執行長 Justin Bolognino 對偉門智威智庫做了簡單的總結：這「不可能」是實體聚會的終結，「要達成目標，一路上會很辛苦，但我們想要繼續舉辦實體活動，一定要繼續！這件事可以刻在我的墓碑上。」他還補充說道，長期下來，我們就可以學會用更安全的方式，來創造擴增實境體驗。

值得關注的原因：

雖然現況迫使未來幾個月內的活動要以完全虛擬的方式舉辦，例如 CES 和 SXSW，但是其他的活動主辦方都開始為演唱會和會議規劃「階段性回歸計畫」，讓所有的參加者都能享有 VIP 級的待遇。

07

粉絲總動員

鐵粉為自己的偶像造神。

以前鐵粉只是接收流行文化,但現在他們也扮演起推廣流行文化的角色,開始在網路上集體創作和偶像相關的內容。

而社群媒體除了讓世界各地的劇迷、影迷、書迷、樂迷,都能和自己喜歡的事物產生連結,更重要的是,它們還讓這些同好互相認識、讓鐵粉自成社群。在美國,Taylor Swift(泰勒絲)有一群叫做 Swifties 的歌迷,碧昂絲(Beyoncé)被一群「蜂巢」(Beyhive)粉絲簇擁,女神卡卡(Lady Gaga)也獲得一群小怪獸(Little Monsters)支持。只要上網發一篇文章,這些粉絲就會開始集體為偶像的歌曲宣傳、為偶像對抗酸民,最近也越來越常看到粉絲社群全力投入社會、政治議題當中。

南韓偶像產業應用了新的科技,和粉絲建立起世界上最獨一無二的互動模式。其中包括播送特別內容的頻道、客製的對話平台,還有受疫情影響而開始舉辦的串流演唱會,演唱會中更加入了擴增實境和虛擬實境技術。他們的粉絲集結在一起,形成了社群,而且除了購買歌曲,粉絲們還會使用不同的裝置,在串流平台上不停輪播偶像的音樂,把偶像推到排行榜最頂端,也會創作並分享和偶像相關的小說、藝術作品、影片合輯。

《華爾街日報》記者，Eun-Young Jeong

> 社群媒體改寫了
> 音樂產業的規則，也提升了粉絲的
> 力量。

男孩團體 BTS 的全球粉絲統稱為 ARMY（「軍隊」之意），他們是善用科技、分享內容、隨時準備好要為偶像動員的最佳狂粉實例。2020 年秋季，在《吉米 A 咖秀》（The Tonight Show Starring Jimmy Fallon）舉行「BTS 週」的時候，ARMY 讓這個節目的社群媒體互動率登上前所未有的高峰，在臉書、推特、Instagram 上的總互動量達到 1,005 萬次，整體漲幅高達 1,300 倍。

「社群媒體改寫了音樂產業的規則，也提升了粉絲的力量。BTS 的粉絲 ARMY，在這方面領先群雄。」記者 Eun-Young Jeong 在 2020 年 11 月出版的《華爾街日報》（The Wall Street Journal）中寫下這段話，當時 BTS 剛拿下該報社頒發的音樂創新獎（Music Innovator）。

韓流粉絲的影響力也不僅限於娛樂領域。2020 年，他們支持美國「黑人的命也是命」（Black Lives Matters）運動，包下他們不打算出席的座位來破壞川普陣營的集會，也為泰國追求民主的抗爭者集資購買安全帽、護目鏡。

值得關注的原因：

鐵粉的特質是全心付出、善用科技，而且他們具有全球視野，因此，他們也從偶像作品的推廣者，變成一股擁有自我意志的強大力量。品牌若能和支持特定議題的粉絲、消費者、群眾站在同一陣線，就能贏得他們的忠心追隨。

08

懷舊媒體復古風

在不太需要用到行動裝置和隨身網路的
疫情期間，消費者開始利用復古娛樂媒體
自我療癒。

樸實的錄音帶常常因為音質不佳而飽受批評，不過我們在《改變
未來的 100 件事：2020 年全球百大趨勢》裡，就在〈類比復興〉
這篇文章中提過這個復古趨勢了，錄音帶的復興運動看似無望，
但這場運動到目前為止仍然持續進行著。據英國官方排行榜公司
（Official Charts Company）指出，與 2019 年相比，英國的錄
音帶銷售量在 2020 上半年翻倍成長，達到 15 年來的新高，流行
歌手「到暑五秒」（5 Seconds of Summer）、女神卡卡（Lady
Gaga）、杜娃・黎波（Dua Lipa）等人的作品更成為錄音帶市場
上的主力，這代表錄音帶這種復古格式，開始擁有新的年輕受眾
了。傳奇韓流偶像 BTS 也對這波潮流有所貢獻，他們最新的兩首
單曲《Dynamite》和《Life Goes On》分別都出了錄音帶和黑膠
兩種版本，而且都在美國的線上商城裡銷售一空。

業界專家有個理論，他們認為回歸的卡帶風潮純粹只屬紀念性
質；但我們發現，與卡帶相容的音樂播放裝置也開始出現在市場
上。香港的 NINM Lab 推出「IT'S OK 藍牙可攜式卡式錄音機」，
是現代版的隨身聽。2020 年夏天，法國新創公司 We Are
Rewind 發布了小型藍芽卡式錄音機的模型，整體造型就像時尚
的家居擺設。

黑膠唱片的復興已經卓然有成，但在 2020 年，我們還是看到更大幅度的成長。美國唱片業協會（Recording Industry Association of America）指出，2020 年黑膠在美國的銷量破了紀錄，是自從 1980 年以來首次超越 CD 銷量的一年。英國的銷量也有所成長，2020 年有望成為 1990 年以後黑膠表現最好的一年，這個數據是來自《衛報》（The Guardian）於同年 11 月的報導。黑膠和錄音帶的樂迷，喜好有些不同，在黑膠領域裡，披頭四（the Beatles）和綠洲合唱團（Oasis）的經典專輯，分別在美國和英國拿下銷量冠軍。

這股懷舊的風潮，也延伸到音樂以外的世界。去年討論度很高的短影音行動串流平台 Quibi 倒閉，但同一年間，舊時代的熱門娛樂「汽車戲院」（drive-in cinema，詳見第 10 章〈免下車體驗升級〉）卻開始復甦。2020 年 9 月，BBC 報導了一系列新開幕的汽車戲院，從俄羅斯到德國、英國，再到南韓，汽車戲院遍地開花；報導中也提到世界最大的汽車戲院「燈塔五號」（The Lighthouse 5）預計在 2023 年於佛羅里達州開幕。

值得關注的原因：

在幾乎所有體驗都仰賴螢幕的時代裡，有些娛樂迷轉而選擇實體的物件，不再一昧追求即時、便利。類比格式的產品讓人覺得踏實，它們也代表生活中所需的儀式感，以及在零接觸的日子裡，大眾所追求的實感體驗。

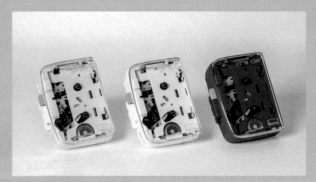

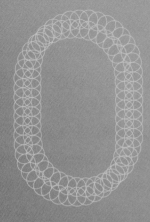

we
are
rewind

電競娛樂進軍黃金時段

電競會是新的好萊塢嗎？

娛樂產業的重心開始轉向電競娛樂，為全新的電競影城打下基礎。

電競比賽創下了許多紀錄，而且不只限於玩家，觀眾也有貢獻。舉例來說，《模擬市民 4》（The Sims 4）在 2020 年第二季開播時，創下了 1,000 萬名不重複觀眾的紀錄，在五、六月期間總共多了 250 萬人；7 月 1 日當天，有超過 16 萬名觀眾，同步收看人氣電競玩家 Ninja 在 YouTube 上玩《要塞英雄》（Fortnite）的直播。

翠貝卡電影節（Tribeca Film Festival）補齊了娛樂和電競產業之間的缺口，他們的顧問群在 2020 年 9 月宣布，他們從 2021 年開始，會在官方演出名單上加入電動遊戲這一項目，也會頒發第一屆的翠貝卡電競遊戲獎（Tribeca Games Award）。翠貝卡娛樂公司和同名電影節的共同創辦人珍・羅森索（Jane Rosenthal）說：「不同的媒體之間原本有一道明顯的分界線，但現在已經變得很模糊了，因為故事變成了遊戲，遊戲也變成了故事。」

娛樂產業的其他大老也同意這樣的說法，2020 年 7 月，索尼（Sony）公告了他們為 Epic Games（創作《要塞英雄》的公司）挹注的巨額投資，金額高達 2.5 億美元，這讓這個遊戲巨匠在整體電玩產業中佔了 1.4%，也預示了更多從電腦螢幕跨越到大銀幕的跨界合作機會。Epic Games 的創辦人暨執行長蒂姆・斯維尼（Tim Sweeney）說道：

「索尼和我們都在創意和科技領域跨界經營，我們對即時產生的 3D 社群體驗也有共識，希望能藉此讓電競、電影、音樂匯流在一起。」為了達成這樣的願景，索尼和 Epic 採取了實際的做法，他們會在 2021 年的美國消費電子用品展（CES）上，舉辦一場「沉浸實境」演唱會，到時候會讓 PlayStation 和 Oculus 的虛擬實境裝置雙雙公開亮相。

有線電視頻道 TBS 在最新的《模擬市民》實境秀裡，發揮了電競娛樂的優勢，他們的新節目《The Sims Spark'd》是由透納體育（Turner Sports）的電競部門 ELeague 負責；對此，《紐約時報》（The New York Times）觀察到，「雖然競爭激烈的電競比賽在世界各地都一直有人在播，但是《Spark'd》已經做好萬全準備，要成為第一個以電競比賽為主的主流實境節目。」這部只有四集的迷你影集於 2020 年 7 月 17 日首播，邀請了 12 位參賽者，要他們在有限的時間內，在這個熱門的模擬遊戲裡創作出最獨特的角色、世界、故事線，有點類似《決戰時裝伸展台》（Project Runway）和《英國烘焙大賽》（The Great British Bake Off）的運作模式。《Spark'd》是《模擬市民》的設計公司 Electronic Arts、華納媒體（WarnerMedia）旗下的透納體育、Buzzfeed 的電競頻道《Multiplayer》共同合作的成果。

值得關注的原因：

過去幾年來，電競的熱門度和影響力都穩定地上升，創造了無遠弗屆的影響：一群新的電競網紅加速誕生，奢侈品零售業也開始注意到他們的影響力，旅遊愛好者和群眾也藉此發洩全身的精力，甚至成為社運活動的交流平台。由於玩家數量大幅成長，大品牌也跟著注入資金，讓電競娛樂提升到黃金時段的層級。

> "
> 不同的媒體之間原本有一道明顯的分界線，但現在已經變得很模糊了，因為故事變成了遊戲，遊戲也變成了故事。
> "

翠貝卡娛樂公司和同名電影節的共同創辦人
珍・羅森索（Jane Rosenthal）

10

免下車體驗升級

從狂歡派對、藝術展演，到美食饗宴，
免下車型態的活動已經有了新的風貌，為大眾提供
各式各樣的現場娛樂選項。

汽車製造商開始將消費者想「待在車上體驗活動」的需求納入考量，日產汽車（Nissan）和旅遊公司 Atlas Obscura 合作，在發表全新車款 Rogue Routes 之前，先行舉辦了一系列的停車場活動，活動自 2020 年 11 月開始，隔年 1 月結束。Rogue Routes 將觀眾載到「隱藏版景點」，讓他們可以在那享受現場音樂演出，聆聽科學家、藝術家、創新人士的演講，還可以欣賞無人機燈光秀以及刺激的特技表演。美國日產汽車的副總暨行銷總監 Allyson Witherspoon 說：「我們希望 Rogue Routes 的宣傳計畫能給家庭更多靈感，讓他們看到這款汽車可以帶來的各種新體驗。Rogue Routes 是以所有他們想得到的需求為出發點而設計出來的車款。」

凌志（Lexus）是另一家翻轉停車場的企業，2020 年 11 月間，這家高檔汽車製造商在洛杉磯舉辦了一場為期三天的「凌志美食劇院」（Culinary Cinema），除了汽車劇院，還包含一客三道菜的餐點。活動票券全部售罄，說明了群眾對這類體驗的興趣。

活動策劃公司也對熱力四射的停車場活動有所期待，德國的Club Index 在 2020 年春天舉辦了「汽車 Disco」（Autodisco）活動，三場汽車派對分別都能容納 250 輛車，活動中也使用具節奏感的汽車喇叭聲取代興奮的人聲尖叫。接著時間來到夏天，英國的「公園酒吧」（Pub in the Park）系列活動改以停車場「花園派對」的形式呈現，裡面有「專為這種特殊時期」設計的現場音樂演出、美食，以及特有的活動氛圍。

藝術展覽也做了適度的調整。Dallas Aurora 藝術雙年展把 10 萬平方英呎的停車場改造成汽車專屬的沉浸式展場「第三區」（Area 3），觀眾可以直接開車進來看展；展期為 2020 年 10 月到 2021 年 1 月。多倫多則有一場 35 分鐘的汽車專屬藝術裝置展「開車來看梵谷」（Gogh by Car），倉庫裡展示了梵谷的作品，並搭配上聲光和投影特效。

除了乘坐汽車，還有其他類似的體驗活動。巴黎的漂浮劇院由冰淇淋品牌哈根達斯（Häagen-Dazs）贊助，2020 年夏季，在拉維萊特（the Villette）的運河盆地上，提供 38 座小船開放給遊客租用。另外，哈根達斯也和 Openaire 合作，在倫敦打造一座漂浮型的劇院，活動為期四週。

值得關注的原因：

觀眾渴望參加實體的團體體驗活動，但也希望可以預防新冠肺炎（COVID-19），於是，汽車順理成章地成為安全的防護網。現在，車廠和活動策劃公司改造了傳統的汽車劇院，融入創新的現場演出，為停車場活動注入全新生命。

+ WUNDERMAN
THOMPSON

Left: Lexus Culinary Cinema. Image courtesy of Lexus
Right: Area 3 at Dallas Aurora art festival

WUNDERMAN
THOMPSON　Gogh by Car

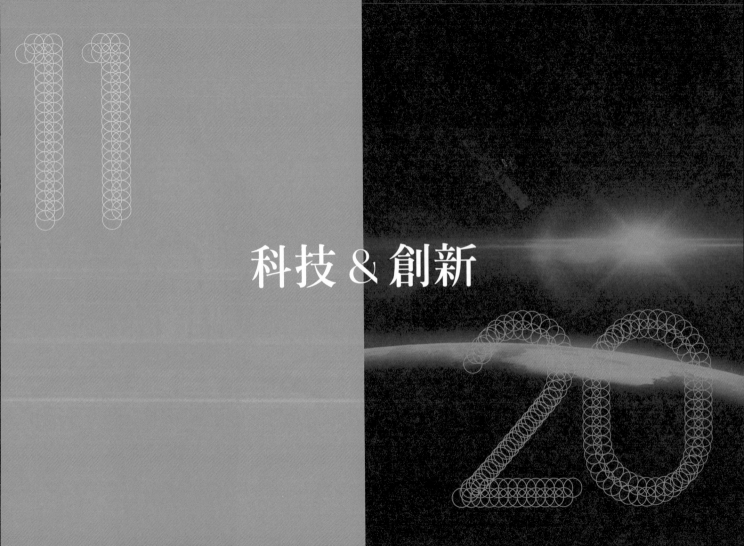

11
科技 & 創新

20

競技運動虛擬化

傳統運動和電子競技已經逐漸整合，和頂尖的職業選手一較高下不再是夢。

2020 年首次停辦的各項體育賽事，激發了體育圈的創意，虛擬運動結合電競的機會越來越多。「很多人突然發現，電競跟傳統運動一樣可以帶來娛樂效果，疫情更加速了兩者的結合。」來自內華達大學拉斯維加斯分校的 Robert Rippee 對偉門智威智庫如此說到。Rippee 是該校國際博弈學院（International Gaming Institute）「餐旅管理暨電競研究室」的主持人。

雖然職業賽車手早就開始用模擬器進行訓練了，但現在有更多品牌投入模擬器市場，為喜好賽車的人提供虛擬賽車體驗。奧斯頓·馬丁（Aston Martin）的目標客群是大手筆的電競玩家，在 2020 年 9 月，他們發布了賽車模擬器 AMR-C01（零售價大約落在 76,300 美元），設計靈感來自奧斯頓馬丁的經典跑車，使用了流線型的設計加上和跑車相同的椅座。對能夠負擔這項產品的人來說，AMR-C01 可帶給買家近乎真實的奧斯頓馬丁極速超跑體驗。

　Aston Martin AMR-C01 racing simulator

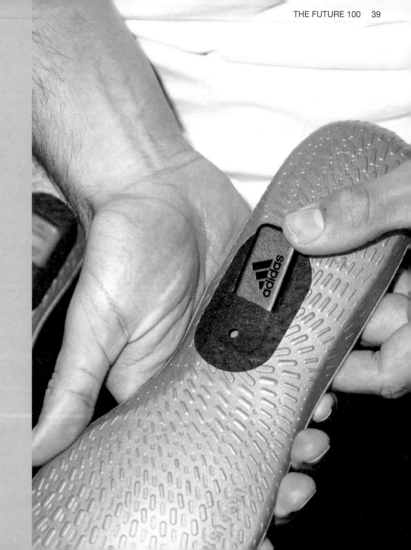

一直以來，業餘玩家都很喜歡在虛擬世界裡，扮演自己最喜歡的運動員來進行挑戰，現在，連職業選手也親身踏入了這個線上國度，運動賽事也因此來到新的高度。Zwift 是單車及跑步的線上訓練平台，他們在 2020 年 7 月舉辦了第一場「虛擬環法自由車賽」（Virtual Tour de France），讓職業車手和業餘玩家一起上場，在同樣的路段一較高下。

2020 年 3 月，愛迪達（Adidas）發表了 GMR 科技鞋墊，讓足球愛好者可以搭配 EA Sports 出產的手機遊戲 FIFA Mobile 來整合、紀錄自己的訓練成果。這款鞋墊可以測量實體比賽中的多項表現，包含得分、攻擊力、距離、速度等，玩家也可以把這些數據匯入遊戲中，換取遊戲虛擬獎勵。

值得關注的原因：

電競和傳統運動之間的界線會越來越模糊，因為以後虛擬體驗和實體活動會更緊密地結合在一起。

+ WUNDERMAN
THOMPSON

Left: Zwift Virtual Tour de France
Right: Adidas GMR smart insole

12

汽車有機生物概念化

汽車設計融入了人類崇尚自然的天性。

賓士（Mercedes-Benz）在智慧車款上做了大膽的嘗試，在 2020
年的美國消費電子用品展（Consumer Electronics Show）上，
他們發布了受阿凡達啟發的概念車款 Vision AVTR，比起汽車，
這家德國車商更希望讓這款車看起來像活生生的生物。賓士的設
計總監戈登·瓦格納（Gordon Wagener）在該活動的系列演講
中提到 Vision AVTR 的設計理念，「我們沒有打算創造一台車，
我們要做的是類似有機生物體的東西。」

這個來自遙遠未來的概念，目的是要「巧妙地和周遭環境融合在
一起，從環境中接收訊息」，裡面涵蓋了很多受自然啟發的特殊
設計。這台車的造型獨特，看起來像爬蟲類動物，例如它青蛙般
的外型、鱗片般的車頂，還有螃蟹般的橫向移動模式。內裝使用
了環保回收材料製成，用色則讓人聯想到大海。另外搭載了直覺
式的操控手勢，包括用手掌驅動的電源和生物辨識系統，讓汽車
開起來就像身體的一部份。

> 在未來的產業生態中，最奢華的產品是結合科技、
> 人本需求、自然元素的結晶。

賓士，Mercedes Benz

現代汽車（Hyundai）也開始擁抱人類喜愛自然的特性，在設計中融入自然相關元素。2020 年 3 月，這家南韓車廠推出電動車款「預言」（Prophecy），車身柔和、圓潤的邊角看起來就像「完美風化的石頭」。這款概念車希望可以「為人類和汽車搭建起情感連結。」

而 Polestar Precept 有著天然、永續的內裝設計，坐墊使用了回收塑膠瓶加工製成，頭枕的材料是回收的軟木塞，腳踏墊則使用了回收漁網重新製作而成。Polestar 是富豪汽車（Volvo）和中國公司吉利（Geely）合作的成果，從 2020 年 9 月起即進入量產階段。另外在 2021 年的消費電子用品展上，凱迪拉克（Cadillac）公布了一款結合生物感應技術的概念車，可以監測乘客的重要生命體徵，繼而調節車內的溫度、濕度、光線、噪音、香氛種類。

值得關注的原因：

過去幾年來，科技產業開始導入更多以人為本、更有機的設計，現在汽車製造業也開始順應這股潮流。能回應人類對自然的追求，以及和生物相關的設計，幾乎成為頂級車款的標配，一如賓士的預測：「在未來的產業生態中，最奢華的產品是結合科技、人本需求、自然元素的結晶。」

13

數據資訊永續經營

人們逐漸意識到數位足跡對環境的影響。

氣候變遷的問題多半聚焦在實體的廢棄物上，但是數位活動也會對環境產生嚴重的影響。彭博社（Bloomberg）的數據顯示，儲存在資料中心的數位資訊不停膨脹，其用電量總共佔了全球的2%，到 2030 年前還會成長到 8%。

不管使用手機還是電腦，我們每發送一封電子郵件、每進行一次 Google 搜尋，都會產生環境成本。在日趨數位化的世界裡，這些數位資訊會像掩埋場堆疊的垃圾一樣日漸增加，對環境造成負擔。根據智庫 The Shift Project 在 2019 年 3 月提出的報告，使用數位科技產生的溫室氣體，佔全球總量的 3.7%，這幾乎相當於航空業的碳排放量（詳見第 25 章〈飛航減碳化〉）。遊戲機也是一大衍生問題，因為製造遊戲設備需要用到礦物成份，丟棄時容易產生安全、環保疑慮。

5G 出現以後，雲端運算和內容串流服務即將再次躍進，準備要改變消費者的工作和娛樂模式。科技巨頭和遊戲平台也為此擔憂，不知道相關的基礎建設是否能應付、是否能在遠端資料中心處理如此巨量的資訊。2020 年英國蘭卡斯特大學（Lancaster University）做的調查預測到，玩家大規模地從遊戲主機跳到串流遊戲平台，會讓遊戲產業在 2030 年前的整體碳排量增加三成。

微軟（Microsoft）和谷歌（Google）也積極地處理相關問題，雙雙宣稱自己的資料中心能達成碳中和。微軟的 Azure 資料中心正在嘗試運用再生能源，他們也引用了 2018 年的內部調查數據：「雲端運算的碳效率比本地運算還高 98%。」

索尼（Sony）在 PS5 裡加入了省電的低耗電模式，新的 Xbox S 系列和 X 系列也都有類似的功能。

值得關注的原因：

數位科技加速實現了遠距工作、線上購物、更大規模的遊戲場景，這也代表品牌在使用數據時造成的環境隱憂會比以往還炙手。可以預期的是，在未來十年內，永續的資料管理方案會是企業對抗氣候變遷的重要發展目標。

"

可以預期的是，
在未來十年內，永續的
資料管理方案會是企業
對抗氣候變遷的
重要發展目標。

"

14

零接觸旅程

航空公司和機場正在致力減少旅途中旅客接觸機會和提高衛生標準。

航空業受到新冠肺炎（COVID-19）重創，因此從登機、行李托運、使用廁所，到機上娛樂，飛航中的所有環節都需要重新審視，藉此提升旅客的信心。

旅經挪威的旅客，可以在 Avinor 公司營運的機場裡，利用旅行科技公司亞瑪迪斯（Amadeus）提供的服務，體驗點到點之間完全零接觸的旅程。這個系統讓人與人之間完全不需要任何接觸，乘客不需使用觸控機台，只要使用手機應用程式即可完成作業。德國漢莎航空（Lufthansa）也在擴大自助櫃檯的服務項目，希望可以寄送簡訊給行李延誤送達的旅客，這樣就可以減少排隊和群聚的時間。漢莎航空同時也為班機誤點、航班取消等狀況，研究相關零接觸準則。

針對整趟旅程中的所有接觸點，航空公司都極盡全力，為旅客提升衛生標準。阿拉斯加航空（Alaska Airlines）導入了安全社交距離登機流程，讓旗下員工可以在六英呎外就能為旅客掃描登機證，所以不管是登機或是印製行李牌，整個過程完全零接觸；除此之外，某些特定航班的乘客還可以事先從阿拉斯加航空的網站或應用程式上預訂餐點，付款則可以利用機上的感應式支付系統

來完成。由於機艙內的設施無法完全零接觸使用（例如機上娛樂和廁所），所以目前設計師努力的方向，是要設計出可以「減少接觸」的模組，範圍涵蓋機艙內的一切設施，就連給皂機、廁所門鎖都不例外。

目前新的旅遊模式裡已經加入了健康防護的環節，但這也讓個人隱私議題變得更加複雜，航空公司和機場如果能找出更好的方式來應用生物特徵辨識資料，就能進一步發展了類似「零接觸安檢」的設備，好比納什維爾國際機場（Nashville International Airport）就有導入這樣的設施，美國運輸安全管理局也開始測試人臉辨識系統。

值得關注的原因：

新的零接觸系統可以保障旅客的安全，也是航空業復甦的關鍵，設計顧問公司 Tangerine 的創意總監麥特·羅德（Matt Round）告訴偉門智威，雖然有隱私問題，但他認為「大家對這些新科技的接受度會越來越高」，就像 911 事件後，旅客也習慣了更嚴格的機場安檢措施。他接著說道，「新冠肺炎（COVID-19）可能也一樣啊，大家會知道這是必要的變化，他們很快就會習慣了。」

體驗混合實境

先別管虛擬實境和擴增實境，混合實境現在正夯。

混合實境（MR）在虛擬世界裡整合了真實世界的物件，藉此創造出新的遊戲環境，因此和擴增實境（AR）或虛擬實境（VR）都不同。虛擬實境的設備太笨重又太貴，擴增實境則需要仰賴行動裝置，基於上述這些限制，加上混合實境能模糊線上世界和真實空間之間的界線，而且變化多端、使用簡便，因此能從中殺出了一條血路，快速躍升成為遊戲界的新星。魔多智庫（Mordor Intelligence）表示，2019 年，混合實境的市場價值落在 3.82 億美元，且隨著軟硬體設備升級，市場還會更快速且大幅地成長。

英雄聯盟世界大賽（League of Legends World Champion-ship）從 2011 年起即在世界各地開打，除了大量的現場觀眾，還有很多人在線收看。然而，2020 年的英雄聯盟錦標賽和去年大部分的活動一樣，因為疫情而有所調整，該遊戲的發行商拳頭遊戲（Riot Games）因此設計了一座高科技混合實境舞台，讓觀眾可以在家享受沈浸式的現場直播體驗。舞台由一組巨大的 LED 螢幕組成，讓遊戲中的虛擬元素可以栩栩如生地呈現在觀眾眼前。

2020 年 10 月，任天堂發表的新款混合實境遊戲《瑪利歐賽車實況：家庭賽車場》（Mario Kart Live: Home Circuit）受到大量的關注。這是他們為 Switch 設計的一款遊戲，玩家可以在家裡的各個角落操控賽車，同時和虛擬世界以及真實世界的物件互動。

混合實境也獲得科技巨頭的關注以及投資，2020 年 7 月，印度公司 Jio Platforms，發表了 Jio Glass 混合實境眼鏡，產品同時獲得谷歌（Google）和臉書（Facebook）的資金支持，臉書在 2020 年 4 月投入了 57 億美元，而同年七月，谷歌也加碼投入了 45 億美元的資金。蘋果公司（Apple）在 2020 年也申請了相關專利，因此很多人預測，蘋果會在近期發表自有的混合實境眼鏡。

值得關注的原因：
由於混合實境能完美結合虛擬世界和真實世界，因此成為提升玩家體驗的最佳解方。數位體驗設計公司 Meta 的創辦人暨執行長 Justin Bolognino 告訴偉門智威智庫：「之後大部分的活動和空間都會配有擴增實境和混合實境這兩層設計」，往後使用延展實境和混合實境「來為空間加入更細微且可以共享的維度」，也會成為大家的日常。

顛覆深偽技術

人工智慧的網路調動日漸擴大，用來打擊深偽技術
製造的影像。

有人利用深偽技術（deepfake）來散布無意或惡意的玩笑，有人
拿來做政治操作和宣傳，但不管用在哪裡，深偽技術都會混淆大
眾視聽，也會動搖社會結構。這些用來散布假消息的工具，是當
今發展高階人工智慧（AI）的反作用力，但 AI 本身也是打擊假消
息的主要武器。

如果惡搞的對象是名人，那就可以利用人工智慧來「學習」他們的
經典動作、手勢，再把這些資料拿來和疑似深偽影像的內容交互
比對，看看哪裡不一致。2020 年 9 月，微軟（Microsoft）發表了
一款影片認證器（Video Authenticator），利用人工智慧來掃描
照片或影片，計算該影像有多高的機率會是深偽影像，這個認證
器可以辨識人類無法察覺到的後製痕跡，例如偵測灰階範圍、圖
片邊界是否模糊等。

其他的認證工具也日漸普遍，微軟的 Azure 已開放創作者在檔案
中嵌入認證和數位函式，可以用來讀取和驗證內容；區塊鏈的時
間戳記也是新興的認證方式。用戶可以利用這些「數位足跡」來
追蹤、驗證內容來源，以及查看檔案修改紀錄。

然而，臉書（Facebook）在 2020 年 6 月舉辦的「深偽偵測挑
戰賽」（Deepfake Detection Challenge）顯示，以人工智慧
來偵測深偽影像的技術，其實還有大幅的進步空間。在這場挑
戰賽中，臉書邀請參賽者測試自己的演算模型，而最後勝出的演算
法只勉強達到 65% 左右的正確率。

南方四賤客（South Park）的作者特雷・帕克（Trey Parker）和
麥特・史東（Matt Stone）也用自己的方式攻擊深偽技術，他們
在自己的 YouTube 頻道「騷動正義」（Sassy Justice）上發表一
系列的嘲諷影片，頻道自 2020 年 10 月推出，利用川普（Donald
Trump）、川普女兒伊凡卡（Ivanka Trump）、川普女婿傑瑞德・庫
許納（Jared Kushner）、演員米高・肯恩（Michael Caine）、臉
書創辦人馬克・祖克柏（Mark Zuckerberg）等人的換臉影像，來
呈現一位當地新聞記者（以川普的臉後製而成的角色）調查某個
專案的故事。大家猜得到這位記者要調查什麼嗎？他要調查的正
是深偽技術。史東告訴《紐約時報》（The New York Times）：
「我們就想惡搞一下深偽技術，因為這樣感覺起來比較不
恐怖。」

值得關注的原因：

由於假消息圍繞著新冠肺炎（COVID-19）和美國 2020 年的總統
大選，因此大眾更加意識到，維護數位環境中的言論可信度是非
常重要的事，但是要對付這些合成影像也帶來新的難題：言論自
由和審查機制之間的界線究竟在哪裡呢？

17

平流層科技吸金

科技業準備開始繞行宇宙，業界龍頭紛紛把目光投向外太空。

2020 年 10 月，美國太空總署（NASA）和諾基亞（Nokia）宣佈了一項合作計畫，要將 4G 網路帶到月球上。他們第一階段的目標是要改善數據傳輸品質，讓太空人可以操控月球探測器、在月球表面上即時導航、以串流方式播放影片，而最終的計畫則是要「驗證人類在月球上棲居的可能性」，諾基亞公司的研究部門貝爾實驗室（Bell Labs）說道。

根據《華爾街日報》（The Wall Street Journal）報導，有分析家預測，與太空相關的雲端服務，其整體累積收益會在十年內達到 150 億美元。微軟（Microsoft）和亞馬遜（Amazon）正準備在這個全新領域一較高下。

微軟和 SpaceX 合作，目標是要推出星際間的雲端服務。這個合作案於 2020 年 10 月公開，希望利用 SpaceX 規劃的低軌道衛星，搭配軌道較高的傳統衛星，來部署全新的雲端運算服務，這個計畫也同時鎖定了公、私部門的太空事業。

亞馬遜網路服務公司（Amazon Web Services）在 2020 年
6 月公開了新的「航太衛星方案」（Aerospace and Satellite
Solutions），由美國太空部隊的前任局長 Clint Crosier 少將
主導。亞馬遜的副總特雷莎·卡爾森（Teresa Carlson）告訴全
國廣播公司商業頻道（CNBC）：「航太衛星工業需要雲端特有的
優勢，也就是敏捷、快速、彈性。在太空競技場上，我們有很多從
事國防和情報業務的客戶都如此表示。」

卡爾森預測：「我們希望之後能在太空中實現 Hulu 或網飛
（Netflix）這類的串流體驗，所以會需要用到和這些程式相同的
技術。」

值得關注的原因：

太空科技產業的投資金額快速增加，企業也在尋找商業契機，希
望能在這個領域中拔得頭籌。

18

雲端遊戲大戰

科技巨頭在雲端遊戲競技場交鋒——
現在正式開打。

遊戲產業的「Netflix」,已經以雲端遊戲的形式出現了,玩家不再需要實體光碟或下載龐大的檔案,只要利用串流服務,就可以直接享受到高畫質的雲端遊戲。

戰場上的主要選手都把目標鎖定在雲端遊戲上,選手名單包含亞馬遜(Amazon)、谷歌(Google)、騰訊(Tencent)、微軟(Microsoft)、索尼(Sony),以及最近參戰的臉書(Facebook)。2020 年 10 月,這家社群媒體公司宣布,要在現有的臉書遊戲平台上加入免費的雲端串流遊戲,一開始雖然只有幾款遊戲,但臉書計畫要擴大遊戲種類,並且提升雲端技術規模,他們遊戲部門(Play)的副總傑森·魯賓(Jason Rubin)說道:「擴張計畫會從2021 年開始,我們打算加入動作和探險遊戲,遊戲裡面會有付費項目,也會有廣告,形式會依遊戲種類和開發者的選擇而有所不同。」

2020 年 9 月，亞馬遜立誓要「改變遊戲的未來」，他們發表了全新的雲端遊戲服務「Luna」。Luna 和其他已經稍有規模的競爭者不同，因為不管是谷歌的 Stadia、微軟的 xCloud 或是索尼的 PlayStation Now，都需要有特定的硬體設備才能使用，但 Luna 的玩家只要使用現有裝置就可以享受它們提供的遊戲串流服務。

中國科技巨人騰訊也透過企業合作迅速提升自家的雲端遊戲技術。2020 年 3 月，路透社報導了騰訊和電信公司華為的合作案，他們共同成立的創新實驗室目的在於打造雲端遊戲平台；騰訊雲遊戲（Tencent Games）推出的「Start」雲端遊戲服務也曾和美國科技公司輝達（Nvidia）合作過。

這些公司的競爭模式和機上盒的競爭情形相當類似，他們知道內容為王的道理，所以致力推出更多的遊戲來達成目標：谷歌的 Stadia 於 2019 年 11 月推出，當時只有 22 款遊戲，但在 2020 年底前，上面已經有超過一百款遊戲了。微軟的遊戲庫 Xbox Game Pass Ultimate 於 2020 年 9 月 14 日上架，推出了 150 款的串流遊戲。

值得關注的原因：

遊戲業出現的這波擾動，和娛樂業的產業演進史相當類似—影視娛樂從原本的公播頻道，演變成後來的機上盒。這樣的轉變吸引了科技巨頭的注意，他們紛紛砸下重金，投入雲端串流遊戲，因為隨選隨玩模式會成為遊戲產業的未來。

矽谷形象重塑

新生代的新創企業努力賦予科技全新的形象，希望科技能成爲一股正面的力量

群眾對科技巨頭的幻想開始破滅，也開始對他們抱持懷疑的態度。《紐約時報》（The New York Times）在 2020 年 10 月的報導指出，美國司法部對谷歌（Google）提告，指控該公司「非法獨佔網路搜尋和搜尋廣告市場」，這可能會導致美國「面臨新一波的信任危機」；在此之前，臉書和亞馬遜也曾受到聯邦政府及州政府的調查，該報社接著提到，「這類調查主要是擔心大公司變得太過強大，因而對國家產生負面影響。」

在這樣的氛圍下，年輕企業開始擁抱利他主義，嘗試用更有道德、更具包容力的精神來打造品牌及產品。Gen Z Mafia 自稱是「年輕工程師的社群」，裡面的應用程式和遊戲工程師都會遵守彼此共同信奉的價值觀，他們的作品包括 MegaBlock、Vibes.fyi 等，前者可以讓用戶一鍵「封鎖劣質推文（tweets）、推文作者，還有所有對那則推文按讚的人」，而 Vibes.fyi 的用戶則可以上線分享「當天值得開心的事情」，並且能讓用戶「感受到人與人之間的連結」。

2020 年 6 月，科技巨頭的年輕員工之間瘋傳著「目 - 口 - 目（eye-mouth-eye）」這樣的表情符號。雖然看起來像一家新創公司，但其實這是專為黑人和跨性別族群設計的勸募平台，希望能為這些族群實現司法正義，也兼顧他們的心理健康。雖然平台的做法受到部分人士的批評，但這群工程師在網站上寫道：「我們是一群隨性、成員組成多元的年輕科技人，我們不安於科技業的現況，相信自己有能力推動整個產業改變，讓科技業多加反思自身的行動。」他們也提到「業界多數人還是熱衷於研發排外的社群軟體，常常忽視全世界上各個邊緣族群真正的需求，把他們排除在我們的發展過程之外。作為一個產業，我們可以做得更好。」

在氣候科技的領域，在 2020 年底以 32 億美元賣掉資訊公司 Segment.io 的彼得・萊因哈特（Peter Reinhardt），創立了新公司 Charm Industrial，把生質廢料（來自植物或動物的廢料）轉換成生質油料，這款油料可以注入深層地底中，達成負碳排放，也可以轉化成能作為燃料或化工材料的綠色氫氣（詳見第 25 章〈飛航減碳化〉）。

矽谷對氣候科技的關注還有另一個篇章，《石英財經網》（Quartz）提到新創加速器 Y Combinator 曾公開徵求投身除碳技術的新創企業，讓除碳成為 2020 年末的一波新潮流。

值得關注的原因：

政府和人民已經不像以往一樣可以無限包容科技巨頭恣意擴張的舉動，Accountable Tech 在 2020 年 7 月公開的一則研究顯示，有 85% 的美國人認為科技巨頭的權力過大。不過，年輕一代的工程師仍然深信科技可以改變未來，所以他們也開始尋求更富正義的方式來為科技賦予新的想像。

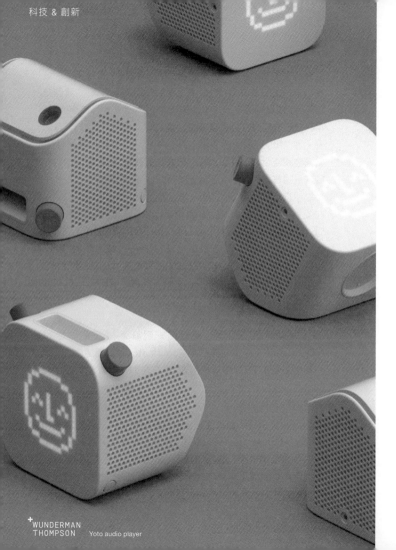

20
守護α世代

現在網路身份無所不在，這對Z世代之後的α世代
來說又代表什麼呢？

日常生活中的各個層面都開始出現在網路上了，電腦資訊「冰冷、只是一連串 0 和 1 的排列組合」，這樣的形象已經漸漸淡化，由新的風貌取而代之：電腦資訊已經成為匯集個人化數位身份的場域了。

有些父母想要為小孩管理「網路形象」，所以對這些家長來說，上述現象再真實不過了。美國育有 18 歲以下孩童的父母當中，有 53% 的家長（57% 的媽媽、48% 的爸爸）表示，他們「非常擔心」小孩照片的隱私和安全問題，有 58% 的母親希望兒童使用的裝置可以加入更安全、更具隱私的選項。上述數據引用自偉門智威數據庫。

科技巨頭還在研究能讓父母安心的做法，讓他們可以不必擔心小孩的數位足跡。根據商業雜誌《Fast Company》於 2020 年 9 月的報導顯示，亞馬遜（Amazon）在旗下所有對兒童友善的智慧裝置上都「建立了一座有圍籬的安全花園」。同年 2 月，臉書的兒

童版通訊軟體 Messenger Kids 也稍微改良了家長監控功能，讓家長可以在應用程式中輕鬆地管理小孩的隱私權設定，該公司也更新了隱私權條款，在裡面加入了對兒童友善的詞彙和插圖。

還有些公司主打的就是隱私優先的服務，2020 年 11 月，Rego Payments 推出全新數位錢包 Mazoola，這款應用程式遵守《兒童網路隱私保護法》（Children's Online Privacy Protection Act，簡稱 COPPA），也會教導小朋友財務觀念，讓小朋友可以從父母認可的商家購買商品，並以點對點（peer-to-peer）的方式支付，保護孩童身份。

倫敦公司 Yoto 和設計工作室 Pentagram 合作，推出「讓兒童自行操控」的音樂播放器 Yoto Player，上面捨棄了相機、麥克風、廣告，使用觸控式智慧卡片來取代，也有多款有聲書、播客節目和音樂可以收聽，並使用近距離無線通訊技術來開啟。

值得關注的原因：

和網路隱私有關的疑慮從出生的那一刻起就已經存在了，據資安公司 AVG 表示，美國有 92% 的兒童在兩歲前就有「網路身份」了，因為他們的父母喜歡「曬小孩」（千禧世代的父母喜歡在社群媒體上分享小孩的照片）。現在家長已經開始注意到兒童的隱私問題了，所以品牌也開始思考兒童網路隱私會為他們帶來的影響。

WUNDERMAN
THOMPSON　Yoto audio player

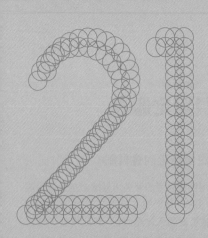

21

旅遊 & 觀光

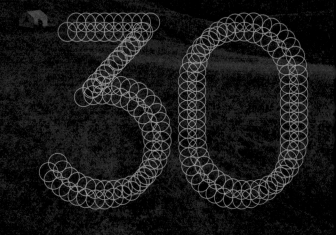

30

21

會員限定服務

奢華旅遊服務走向會員制。

2020 年 7 月，深受好萊塢明星歡迎的著名洛杉磯飯店馬爾蒙莊園（Chateau Marmont）宣布，他們會在接下來的 12 個月內轉型為會員限定的飯店。會員要購入物產股份，藉此換取入住飯店、享受專屬用餐區、個人管家服務的機會，該飯店也為會員提供存放私人物品與延長住宿時間的服務。緊接在馬爾蒙莊園酒店之後，飯店老闆安德烈‧巴拉茲（André Balazs）也計畫將會員模式拓展至其位於米蘭、巴黎、東京、倫敦、紐約的其他飯店。

從 2020 年 8 月開始營運的奢華旅行俱樂部 Manifest 也為會員提供了「出走之旅」—精心策劃、團員少、搭乘私人飛機的奢華旅行。

其他高級旅遊俱樂部則因新冠肺炎（COVID-19）爆發，迎來前所未見的需求熱潮。奢華旅行俱樂部 Inspirato club 主要業務是為客戶代訂旅館與私人豪宅，會費從每月 600 美元起跳，該俱樂部的共同創辦人布倫特‧韓德勒（Brent Handler）向《紐約時報》（New York Times）表示，他們在 2020 年 7 月見證了「近九成的住房率，是歷年來最高紀錄」。

另一個會員制俱樂部是渡假飯店 Exclusive Resorts，執行長詹姆斯・亨德森（James Henderson）在 2020 年 8 月時向《紐約時報》（New York Times）表示：「我們見證了自 2013 年以來需求最高的一年。我們在 8 月時簽下了 10 年前就已經在潛在會員名單上的客戶，他們之所以在這個時候決定入會，是因為此時此刻，他們需要我們為其提供的安全與信任。」

值得關注的原因：

專屬渡假勝地和私人交通對奢華旅遊業並非新鮮事，但這些升級方案代表著會員制越來越熱門，而他們的目標客群則是尋求私人精英旅遊方案的客戶。

22

家族旅行三代同行

經歷數個月封城分離，許多人紛紛決定要展開家族旅行。

家家戶戶都因新冠肺炎（COVID-19）而縮小社交圈，再加上部分旅遊限制放寬，祖孫共聚一堂的家族旅行，成為現下許多家庭認為可行且風險較低的渡假選項，智遊網（Expedia）資深公關經理克莉絲蒂‧哈德森（Christie Hudson）向《今日美國》（USA Today）如此表示。有鑑於此，受多人團體歡迎的私人渡假別墅，業績也比其他類型的住宿業者恢復得更快。

「有些人只與自己的小家庭成員或一等親互動，但包含我在內的其他人，則是將社交圈延伸至祖父母輩。」哈德森表示，「後來我們延伸據點到戶外，一起踏上家族旅程。」

MMGY Myriad 和《旅遊市場報告》（Travel Market Report）在2020 年 8 月 24 日至 9 月 8 日之間，針對 440 間北美旅遊顧問公司進行調查，結果顯示，旅遊業有四成的客戶對國內旅遊有興趣，只有兩成的人在詢問國外旅遊。另外，每 10 位客戶中就有大約 4 位對多代家族旅遊展示高度的興趣；同時也有大概四成的人對小家庭旅遊有興趣。

> **祖孫共聚一堂的家族旅行，成為現下許多家庭認為可行且風險較低的渡假選項。**

美國華盛頓特區的法律圖書館館員阿蕾娜‧蘿威（Arlene Rowe）向《旅遊者雜誌》（Condé Nast Traveler）表示，她與丈夫本來夢想著要帶剛出生的小孩一起踏上他們第一次的國外家庭旅遊，但因為疫情的關係，他們被迫更改計畫，最後他們選擇和雙方父母及其他家族成員一起到維吉尼亞州的安娜湖租民宿渡假。在家族成員紛紛接受了病毒檢驗與自主隔離後，一家人終於能團聚，共同慶祝其中兩對夫妻的結婚紀念日，祖父母也終於能在相隔多月後再次抱抱小孫子。

蘿威說道：「真的就是在花時間陪伴彼此，因為以目前來說，相處時間難能可貴。我們等於是把一整年的節日擠在同一個假期裡一次慶祝了。」

值得關注的原因：

在亞洲，近年興起一股祖孫同遊的旅行趨勢，他們通常是把以往在故鄉團圓的農曆新年聚會改成家族旅遊的形式。而現在因為國際旅遊仍然受限，加上家庭相處時光成為第一考量，亞洲以外的旅遊品牌也可利用這個機會跨足多代家庭的團體旅遊業務。

23
旅宿服務重新設計

由於顧客開始尋求安全、符合社交距離的住宿環境，但又同時想維持人際連結，因此許多旅館開始重新思索，有哪些方案可以提供給顧客。

繭居型獨立空間、戶外空間寬敞的場地、幅員遼闊但又友善的公眾區域，都成為新冠肺炎（COVID-19）時代中，旅宿業的設計特色。

整合建築、設計、空間規劃的顧問公司金斯勒（Gensler），於2020年9月在其網站文章中寫到：「從過往經驗來看，城市、建築、疫情之間的共生關係一直都很複雜，疾病會改變我們的城市型態，也會推動都市發展。」該公司也提到，「新冠肺炎加速了我們對轉型的需求，旅宿服務業也是此次疫情下受到最大衝擊的行業之一。」

金斯勒公司點出了其中一項變化，那就是有些空間需要成為多功能空間，好比客房和公共區域。「客房要打造成多功能室，讓人可以在同一個空間內，進行許多種不同的活動，好比說工作、休憩、

Birch hotel. Image courtesy of Adam Firman

> "
> 客房要打造成多功能室，讓人可以在同一個空間內，進行許多種不同的活動。
> "

金斯勒（Gensler）

用餐、運動，或者與親朋好友聚會。公共空間也需要轉型，才能同時降低風險又能匯聚群眾。」

倫敦建築事務所 Tate Harmer Architects 的合夥人杰瑞・泰特（Jerry Tate），在 2020 年 6 月出刊的旅遊設計雜誌《沉睡者》（Sleeper）中指出，他們的旅宿建築規劃工作常以「自給自足的住宿空間」為特點。他以 Tate Harmer Architects 在英國南唐斯國家公園（South Downs National Park）內設計的「高地公園」（Upland Park）計畫為例，此計畫以伙食自理的生態旅館取代「大而不當的飯店」。泰特表示：「以主流趨勢來說，顧客現在想要的，不只是在房間泡泡茶而已，他們希望能在裡面進行更多活動。如果能在空間內打造更多可以滿足住客需求的設施，住客就能自行選擇是否要進入旅館其他人潮較多的區域。」

新冠肺炎的爆發更鞏固了「旅館成為出走選項」的概念。2020年7月，美妝品牌馥蕾詩（Fresh）的創辦人蘿特柏葛（Alina Roytberg）和葛來茲曼（Lev Glazman）於紐約哈德遜推出創客旅館 The Maker Hotel。蘿特柏葛在隔月出刊的《Glossy》雜誌中提到，這家飯店的設計理念是要「打造出可以遠離喧囂的地方，但又不是與世隔絕的那種出走」，而且「現在看來，這件事又更重要了。」

贏得《星期日泰晤士報》（Sunday Times）2020 年度最佳飯店獎的樺木飯店（Birch），位於倫敦外圍的赫特福德郡，座落在 55 英畝大的綠地上；這棟建築物原為豪華大宅，帶有慵懶奢華的美感。在設計飯店時，他們選擇以「重新聯繫」為主軸，不在房間內裝設電話和電視；他們也希望善用周遭環境的優勢，計畫在 2021 年開放戶外泳池，並且將馬廄整修成頂級餐廳。《星期日泰晤士報》將此飯店評為「焦慮壓抑時代下的一縷春風。」

值得關注的原因：

顧客希望能同時保有自由，又能防範新冠病毒，因此在未來幾年內，這都可能會對飯店設計產生連帶的影響。為了回應如 Airbnb 等出租平台的競爭，旅宿業總是希望能營造出「離開家但又像回到家」的感受；隨著能夠自給自足的住宿選項日趨熱門，這樣的趨勢也加速了旅宿業對上述目標的追求。

24
旅遊補助獎勵

國家渴望重振旅遊業，因此付費吸引旅客前往渡假。

義大利政府希望以國內旅遊刺激國家經濟，因此於 2020 年 6 月推出「假期津貼」，計畫撥出 24 億歐元補助國內旅行。這項計畫最高補貼低收入家庭 500 歐元，讓他們能留在國內旅行，而不是選擇出國。西西里島則希望以「看見西西里」（See Sicily）觀光票券吸引遊客，此票券可在島內的旅館與景點兌換使用，而且活動也預計延長至 2021 年 12 月。日本政府也在 2020 年 7 月推出「來去旅遊」（Go To Travel）推廣計畫，提供國民在交通、住宿、觀光景點、零售商店及餐廳等方面的多項優惠，折扣高達 50%。

馬爾地夫移民署、觀光局、機場，以及馬爾地夫國營行銷與公關公司（Maldives Marketing & Public Relations Corporation）共同設立了會員計畫，用來獎勵經常前往當地旅行的旅遊常客。他們在 2020 年 12 月推出里程積分計畫「Maldives Border Miles」，將會員分成三個等級，旅客可依據拜訪次數和時間長短賺取不同的積分，並藉此獲得獨家優惠、服務與獎勵。

各國景點也紛紛推出傳染病保險給付做為旅行誘因，在 2020 年 8 月初期，加納利群島的觀光部與產業暨商務部聯合了法國保險業者安盛（Axa），免費為旅客提供傳染病險，將新冠病毒的感染納入保障之中。航空業則是利用免費的新冠肺炎（COVID-19）保險，鼓勵旅人再度踏上飛航旅程：阿聯酋航空（Emirates）在 2020 年 7 月 23 日成為首間給付新冠肺炎開支與隔離費用的航空公司，其他航空業者也迅速跟進，例如加拿大航空（Air Canada）和西捷航空（WestJet）都推出了免費的 COVID-19 旅遊險，西捷航空也將提供此服務延長至 2021 年 8 月 31 日。在 2021 年 3 月 31 日前，維珍航空（Virgin Atlantic）也會贈送所有乘客一份免費的 COVID-19 全球保險。

值得關注的原因：

從國家級會員積分計畫、旅遊補貼，再到傳染病保險給付，旅遊業以全新企劃刺激觀光，鼓勵國內外旅客再次踏上旅程。

25

飛航減碳化

氫能源飛機的夢想是否能成眞？

《大氣環境》(Atmospheric Environment) 期刊於 2021 年 1 月發表了一篇文章，完整地分析了全球大氣狀況，據其調查顯示，飛航佔了全球碳排放總量的 3% 以上。即使 2020 年被迫中斷，飛航引發的長期效應仍無減緩跡象，國際航空運輸協會 (IATA, International Air Transport Authority) 目前預估，航空旅遊到 2024 年就會回復到疫情前的水準了。

為推動減碳飛航，碳足跡極低、甚至可以達到零碳排放的氫燃料，成為替代石化燃料的新選項。歐盟的「乾淨天空」(Clean Sky) 計畫在 2020 年 6 月的報告中指出，透過氫能源與技術，可以讓飛航對全球暖化的衝擊減少 50% 至 90%。

2020 年 9 月，英美研究零碳排飛航的創新企業 ZeroAvia，以改造過的 M 級 Piper 六人座飛機成功完成了一趟 8 分鐘的飛行，使其成為世界首見的氫燃料電池商用機。該公司也將接著進行一連串的商用預備測試，執行長米弗塔科夫 (Val Miftakhov) 認為，他們能在 2023 年前開始載客飛行。

要能成功利用氫燃料，就得先解決一連串的難題，例如燃料儲存的安全問題，以及所費不貲的燃料運輸、補給設施等，這些層面目前也亟待創新。位於奧斯陸的歐洲再生能源集團 Norsk e-Fuel 日前宣布，他們將打造歐洲第一座以氫氣為基礎的再生飛航燃料廠，且將於 2023 年開始營運。

氫能源是否能在近年內成為商用飛機的實際選項仍有人存疑，但飛機製造業的巨擘空中巴士（Airbus）已承諾投入此一技術，並在 2020 年 9 月宣布「ZEROe」，以三種氫燃料動力概念，他們也相信旗下的商用氫能飛機最早可於 2025 年開始運行。他們的競爭對手波音公司（Boeing）也表達了對氫燃料的強烈興趣。

值得關注的原因：

即使以氫為動力的旅行還未成熟，但來自航空業和能源業的各大巨頭已意識到石化燃料對環境的影響，因而出資投入氫燃料技術。據《全球環境變遷》（Global Environmental Change）期刊估計，光是 2018 年一年下來，航空業的碳排放量對氣候造成的損害即可達到美金 1,000 億元。隨著越來越多公司承諾彌補這些損害，且氫動力相關的研究動能持續增長，未來將出現更多與氫能相關的商機。具有前瞻性的企業應該已經開始思索如何利用減碳商機來獲利了。

26

地下渡假村

飯店設計不著痕跡地融入自然景觀中，讓週遭的美景與靜謐依然如常。

當前日益流行的旅宿設計除了尊重當地環境，也重視住客與大自然之間的連結。意為地面之屋的「Casa na Terra」是一棟內嵌於葡萄牙蒙薩拉斯地區的建築，隸屬精品旅店集團 Silent Living 旗下，這棟建物由建築師愛瑞斯馬塔司（Manuel Aires Mateus）設計而成，內含三間套房，以及一座可以遠眺阿爾奇瓦湖的大露天平台。愛瑞斯馬塔司向設計雜誌《Wallpaper》表示：「由於這棟房子位在不能搭建建物的區域內，所以我們的生態責任就是要讓建物融入景觀，不留痕跡。」

Sharaan 渡假飯店是由法國建築師尚·努維爾（Jean Nouvel）設計的地下概念旅館，預計於 2024 年完工。這棟有著 40 間客房的渡假飯店，設計理念於 2020 年 10 月發表，他們會在不破壞歷史、遺跡、風景的前提下，把飯店蓋在沙烏地阿拉伯的阿盧拉沙漠峭壁之中，就如努維爾所說：「我們的建物不應危害到人文和時間累積而來的恩典。」

而在美國，想要逃離一切的人可以真的住到「與世隔絕」的岩石底下。2020 年末，訂房網站 Hotels.com 推出一項獨特的住宿體驗，讓旅客有機會入住新墨西哥洲地下 50 英呎的質樸人造洞窟，且這個獨特的體驗只能從他們的網站上預訂。該網站之所以推出這樣的體驗，是為了在 2020 年 11 月的美國總統大選期間，讓想要緩解「選舉壓力症候群」的人好好放鬆，享受一個不受現代設備干擾的週末長假。

值得關注的原因：

以保護或保育環境為主軸的旅遊體驗越來越多，建築師於是開始設計可以融入自然的旅館，讓住客有機會欣賞未經破壞的優美自然環境。.

27
旅行泡泡成形

想要出遊的旅人不願離家太遠，
活化在地旅遊商機。

由於旅遊業受到限制，旅人開始將目標轉向在地旅行。已經有不少國家選擇性地開放邊界，允許來自鄰近地區的旅客入境。澳洲和紐西蘭即是首批宣布「冠狀病毒走廊」計畫的國家，不過這條走廊一直到 2020 年 10 月才開放，而且只有單向通行：澳洲開放讓紐西蘭人入境，但紐西蘭並未提供同等機會。

Airbnb 的報告指出，隨著新冠肺炎（COVID-19）持續發燒，在地旅遊的趨勢也隨之上漲。在 Airbnb 上預訂 200 英哩內的民宿訂單比例，從 2020 年 2 月份的三分之一暴漲到 5 月份的五成以上，且在該平台並未投注任何行銷資源的情況下，美國在地民宿的訂房業績也在 5 月 17 日至 6 月 3 日期間，相較於 2019 年的同期有所增長。Airbnb 也提到，在德國、葡萄牙、南韓、紐西蘭，本地訂房數也有相似的成長趨勢。

《紐約時報》（New York Times）於 2020 年 6 月時預測,「在航空業放寬管制、旅客負擔下降之前,渡假模式會和 1970 年代類似。大家可以試著想像一下這個畫面:開在高速公路上的車輛,後座塞著大包小包的行李,小朋友開口問著『我們快到了嗎?』這樣的場景。」

值得關注的原因:

Airbnb 執行長布萊恩 · 切斯基（Brian Chesky）於 2020 年 6 月接受美國全國廣播公司商業頻道（CNBC）採訪時表示,在全球疫情下,旅行模式從「搭飛機變成搭車,從大城市轉向小景點,從旅館回到住家」,而旅人也開始重新探索在地景點,取代路途遙遠的異國之旅。

"
旅人開始重新探索在地景點,取代路途遙遠的異國之旅。
"

28
住宿訂閱經濟

旅店重新打造訂閱收費模式，
吸引了越來越多的數位遊牧客群。

美國奢華旅宿品牌 Inspirato 推出「Inspirato 通行證」，會員每月支付 2,500 美元的固定費用後，就能不限次數地預訂品牌精選別墅或飯店，不需另外收取住宿費、附加稅或其他費用，該品牌同時推出每月 600 美元的「Inspirato 俱樂部會員方案」，選取這個方案的會員可以入住 Inspirato 精選的飯店，並享有會員住宿價。該品牌表示，他們提供的訂閱模式可以「鼓勵大家多多渡假」，創辦人兼執行長布倫特・韓德勒（Brent Handler）也向《彭博商業周刊》（Bloomberg）表示，Inspirato 讓合作的飯店可以在不公開提供折扣、不傷害品牌形象的情況下，提高館內的住宿率，而且他們會「負責向飯店預訂空房、支付費用，所以消費者永遠不會看到房價。」

總部位於巴拿馬的全球住宿平台 Selina，則提供了長期住宿以及享用共同工作空間的旅宿選項。2020 年 10 月，該公司收購了 Remote Year，後者主要的服務內容是安排海外工作和海外旅

遊計畫，據此，旅遊業情報平台 Skift 指出，此次收購計畫可為 Selina 提供「新的契機，讓他們可以邁入旅宿業，投資前景看好的飯店和旅館。」Selina 也在 2020 年 8 月推出通行方案，讓會員可以用較低的費率購買旅遊點數，或是在旅館內長住 1 個月、3 個月，甚至 6 個月，並提供共同工作空間供會員使用。「數位遊牧族群的崛起，會讓旅宿業看到前所未見的最大變動。」Selina 的共同創辦人兼執行長拉斐爾·慕瑟里（Rafael Museri）向 Skift 如此說道。

Oasis 旅遊公司也看準與遠距工作者相關的商機，他們了解遠距工作者對探索景點和久居在某些據點的渴望（而且現在這群人可能已經不用進辦公室上班了），於是在 2020 年 10 月推出「Oasis 護照」，使用者只要支付月費，就可以在三到六個月的期限內旅居全球各地：三個月的拉丁美洲通行護照月費為 1,625 美元起，而歐洲通行證則為每月 2,150 美元起，「如果可以在巴塞隆納、巴黎、布宜諾斯艾利斯之間待個 3 到 6 個月，又何必一整年只待在紐約呢？」該公司如此說道。

值得關注的原因：

2020 年的大事件加速了遠端工作的發展，但也對國際旅遊形成阻礙。訂閱制住宿方案成為飯店與民宿吸引住客的方式，也成為企業轉型的方向，現在他們將目標客群鎖定在遠距工作者身上，而非以往的觀光渡假客。這項趨勢可望在疫情後再度強化，正如接案平台 Upwork 於 2020 年 5 月的調查預測，在新冠肺炎（COVID-19）後，美國約有五分之一的勞動人口將完全轉型為遠距工作者。

"
在新冠肺炎（COVID-19）後，美國約有五分之一的勞動人口將完全轉型為遠距工作者。
"

29

旅程資訊超展開

交通類應用程式提供使用者豐富的資訊，
使旅程盡可能達到安全和永續。

交通類應用程式早就成為智慧型手機不可或缺的一部分，而現在它們不僅為用戶提供方向，更加入了新功能，讓使用者可以為身體健康或地球環境作出更聰明的選擇。

為了讓通勤者享受更健康、更安全的旅程，谷歌地圖（Google Map）於 2020 年 9 月加入新冠肺炎（COVID-19）的案例資訊，透過應用程式內建的層疊功能，將此資料疊加在上層，顯示出七天內各區域的平均確診數。

倫敦交通局也在 2020 年 8 月推出應用程式「Go」，並在裡面加入了與健康相關的資訊，例如提供乘車資訊讓民眾能避開擁擠的火車班次，藉此防止病毒散播，或者為用戶提供步行和騎乘自行車的通勤選項。

2019 年推出的行動版應用程式 Float，可讓居住於美國和新加坡的使用者找到最符合經濟效益、安全，同時又兼顧生態永續的旅行方法。2020 年 10 月，Float 宣布他們將與以健康和安全為重點的「舊金山小黃計程車」（Yellow Cab of San Francisco）合作，提供加州人更安全、方便的交通方式。

值得關注的原因：

有環境意識的消費者越來越重視交通運輸對自身健康和外在環境造成的影響，因此他們也期待應用程式能協助他們，讓他們能踏上更公開透明的旅程。

30
與世隔絕的旅行

2021年關鍵字：偏遠秘境、私人島嶼、杳無人煙。

2021 年的旅遊熱點將不再是人口密集的大城市，而是能徜徉在空曠戶外空間的地方。

「即使有了疫苗，戶外空間還是很吸引人，而且在家關了一整年後，想要外出接觸自然的欲望會更強烈。」Tentrr 的創意總監蓋瑞士‧契澤姆（Gareth Chisholm）向偉門智威智庫如此表示。Tentrr 是營地出租界的 Airbnb，他們與全美私有地主合作，提供獨特又舒適的豪華營地。契澤姆表示，該公司在疫情前成長飛快，目前也已經在營地中導入嚴格的新冠肺炎（COVID-19）預防措施了。

Tentrr 有超過 800 座的豪華營地，例如位在紐約卡茨基爾山的廢棄動物園，露營者能從園區進入綿延數里的登山路徑；在猶他州崎嶇陡峭的斯坦恩內克國家公園（Steinaker State Park）內，他們也提供附有家具的營地，讓旅客可以在鄰近的水庫區從事水上活動。克里斯荷姆表示，大家在尋求的是可以讓人「眼睛一亮」的僻靜景點，像是可以親臨瀑布或者遠眺壯闊美景的地方。「大家在找的不只是渡假勝地，他們也想要好好探險一番。」

預訂營地和採買裝備的需求也急遽增加。2020 年 5 月，在英國政府宣布解除隔離限制後，當地的營地預訂公司 Cool Camping 業績成長了五倍。英國零售商約翰路易斯百貨（John Lewis & Partners）、阿斯達超市（Asda）、Halfords 等，都表示露營裝備的銷售額在 2020 年夏季有所成長。

野外探險的風潮也使得陸路旅行跟著盛行起來，大眾開始往鮮為人知的野營地前進。在美國，與陸路旅行相關的關鍵字在谷歌（Google）上的搜尋量比去年增加了將近兩倍，尤其在夏季達到最高峰，因為冒險家紛紛在夏季躍上吉普車或休旅車，準備體驗陸路就可抵達的全新疆域。

經過深思且更有意識地旅遊也是孤立主義者的旅行要點。克里斯荷姆觀察到，「雖然大家都喜歡遙遠的異域，但有越來越多人意識到搭乘飛機或巨型郵輪對環境產生的衝擊，這些想法會影響較有意識的旅人，他們也會因此考慮在地旅遊或者開車就可到達的景點。」

值得關注的原因：

隨著旅遊業開始回穩，渴望心靈平靜並與人保持距離的旅客，會更加偏好融入自然、冒險、孤獨的旅程。

品牌 & 行銷

31

品牌共創共生

新型領導力是品牌之間放下競爭、彼此合作，共同處理社會和環境議題的能力。

Z 世代看待品牌使命的方式有了新的標準，2020 年 10 月，偉門智威數據服務做的調查顯示，美國有 80% 的 Z 世代覺得品牌有責任改善大眾生活，有 82% 的人更認為品牌之間應該放下歧異、通力合作以達成更重要的目標——而眾品牌也洗耳恭聽。

7 月時，微軟發起降低碳排放的計畫「降至零碳排」（Transform to Net Zero）來因應氣候危機，他們和八家企業合作，包括 Nike、賓士、聯合利華、達能（Danone）等，希望在 2030 年前一起成為負碳排放的企業。2019 年後期，古馳（Gucci）的執行長馬可‧畢薩力（Marco Bizzarri）首度提出「執行長的碳中和挑戰」（CEO Carbon Neutral Challenge），希望其他企業加入他的行列，一起減少溫室氣體的排放量，響應的企業包括二手精品寄售網站 The RealReal、義式咖啡品牌 Lavazza，以及軟體公司 SAP。

在疫情期間，品牌合作能讓各品牌以更迅速的方式研發產品。2020 年 4 月，英國起家的跨國藥妝集團葛蘭素史克藥廠（GSK）和法國藥廠賽諾菲（Sanofi）合作，共同研發新冠肺炎（COVID-19）疫苗。

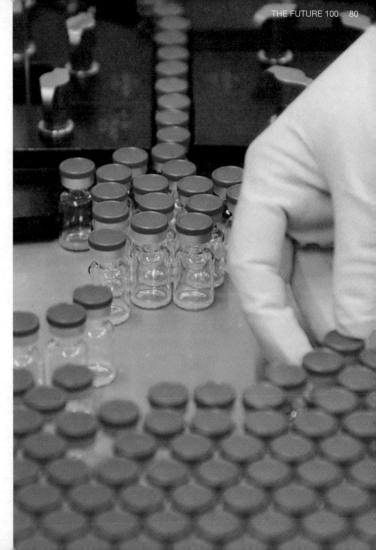

"

美國有80%的Z世代覺得品牌有責任改善大眾生活，有82%的人更認為品牌之間應該放下歧異、通力合作以達成更重要的目標。

"

同樣地，美國藥廠輝瑞（Pfizer）和德國生技公司生物新技術（BioNTech）也協力研發出極為成功的疫苗，並在 2020 年 12 月初取得英國許可，英國也因而成為第一個核准該疫苗的國家。

2020 年 5 月 25 日，喬治·佛洛依德（George Floyd）在美國警方的逮捕下不幸過世，此舉激起全球抗議行動，眾人也對系統性的種族歧視深感憤怒，許多品牌即時回應了這個議題。Nike 在 5 月 29 日貼文：「讓我們一起成為改變的力量」，並附上反歧視的影片，傳達了「就這一次，不要去做」（For once, Don't Do it.）的訊息。隔天，愛迪達（Adidas）轉發了 Nike 的文章，並寫下：「只有並肩才能前進，只有並肩才能改變」，和 Nike 並肩同行。

為了解決「職場上的少數民族」失業問題，有 27 家公司在 2020 年 8 月聯合舉辦了「紐約就業執行長會議」（New York Jobs CEO Council），與會者包含摩根大通集團（JPMorgan Chase）、亞馬遜（Amazon）、IBM 等，該會議的目標是希望在 2030 年前，從低收入的非裔、拉美裔、亞裔族群中，雇用十萬名員工。

值得關注的原因：
在文化層面從「我」到「我們」的精神轉變，現在也延伸到了品牌上，品牌所想要展現的是「團結就能帶來改變」的精神。

32

人際連結的視覺語彙

廣告商和品牌要如何傳遞團結，
又不會顯得不負責任呢？

擁擠的群眾和大型聚會場景，對 2021 年來說依然不甚恰當，既然如此，廣告商和品牌要如何利用畫面傳達社群意象呢？

「在家中拍攝 360 度的生活畫面是主要的做法，因為這種手法既能呈現安全社交距離，也可以呈現各式各樣的生活風格和活動。」奧多比圖庫（Adobe）中負責主管創意與消費者洞見的米莉絲（Brenda Milis）如此告訴偉門智威智庫。米莉絲解釋，疫情期間，品牌緩慢地摸索出拍攝主軸，其中包含連結、互助、健康等等，也在不同場景中拍攝小團體共度時光的畫面，以傳遞這樣的主題，他們拍攝的小團體包含家庭、伴侶、「隔離艙」（quarantine pods）內的成員等等。

Airbnb 要傳達的核心概念是社群，2020 年 6 月，該公司推出一支名為〈靠近一點〉（Go Near）的廣告，希望刺激在地旅遊並推動經濟成長。廣告選用的圖片是度假中的三五好友，以非正式的視角來呈現畫面。

亞馬遜的廣告〈演出還要繼續〉（The Show Must Go On）發布於 2020 年 11 月，裡面描述的是一名年輕舞者，她選擇為家人、朋友、鄰居表演舞蹈，因而成功克服 2020 年的困境。亞馬遜的全球創意副總西蒙·莫里斯（Simon Morris）說道：「今年，我們常常可以看到大眾展現了不屈不撓的精神，也看到群體的力量，我們的電視廣告受此啟發，同時我們也想對此致敬。」

先把 2020 年 Zoom 視訊會議裡由人臉群像所傳達出的團體參與感拋在腦後吧。品牌和廣告商在 2021 年選擇拍攝小型群體之間的親密互動，來表達新的一年專屬的群體參與感。

值得關注的原因：

群體的意義已經和以往不同了，就像米莉絲說的：「我真的很開心可以看到大家越來越常因為彼此理解而組成一個一個的群體，也有越來越多人發現，大家不需要共處一室就能建立群體或支持彼此。」

+
WUNDERMAN
THOMPSON
Left: The Show Must Go On commercial by Amazon
Right: Go Near campaign by Airbnb. Image courtesy of Airbnb

33

TikTok 抖音廣告效應

Z世代的市場潛力正在改變廣告活動和品牌訊息—抖音（TikTok）早已蓄勢待發，要在2021年藉此大舉獲利

Z 世代最喜歡的應用程式「國際版抖音」（TikTok）是驅動短影音廣告成長的主要動力，但同類的社群影音平台 Triller 也加入競爭（這兩家公司目前正在為某項專利打官司），2020 年 10 月，Triller 宣布要和數位廣告平台 Consumable 合作，要在影片之間置入 Consubmable 提供的廣告。

國際版抖音「TikTok」也從中國版抖音身上學到一課。在中國，抖音選擇協助用戶利用內容來獲利，而不是像 Instagram 或臉書（Facebook）一樣，聚焦在大品牌的廣告上。「去年抖音在中國幫助 2,200 萬名創作者賺取超過 70 億美元的收入。」Uplab 的創辦人暨品牌成長總監 Fabian Ouwehand 對偉門智威智庫如此說道。

"
TikTok
除了往更成熟的社群
電商邁進，也成爲
定義時代的創意
生產中心。
"

國際版抖音「TikTok」也追隨了中國版抖音的腳步，在 2020 年 6 月推出內部廣告平台，也就是商業版抖音（TikTok for Business）；同年 10 月，他們整合了 Shopify 的服務，在應用程式中導入了網購服務。

這樣的發展結果對品牌來說相當有利，但抖音還是會把創作者擺在第一順位。Ouwehand 說道：「TikTok 最重要的資產就是他們的創作者，所以他們都會借力使力。你可以看一下上面的各種流行趨勢，再看一下它們為什麼成為潮流，你會發現，這其實都歸功於創作者。」

值得關注的原因：

TikTok 在平台上加入廣告和網購功能，讓品牌除了能往更成熟的社群電商邁進，也能成為定義時代的創意生產中心。除此之外，能有像 Triller 這樣的競爭者緊追在後，倒也不是一件壞事。

34

名牌跨入循環經濟

從古馳（Gucci）到優衣庫（Uniqlo），
時裝品牌一一邁入二手市場。

這樣的趨勢是受到永續思維以及全球經濟蕭條而造成錢包變薄的現象所影響；對精品品牌來說，這樣還能順便抑制仿冒品流通。

The RealReal 是在那斯達克上市的大型精品寄售平台。繼 Stella McCartney 和博柏利（Burberry）之後，古馳也於 2020 年 10 月宣布要與該平台展開合作，雙方合作的線上商店 Gucci x TRR 不僅讓用戶寄售二手精品，也供應由古馳直接出貨的商品。此次的合作案緊接在古馳發表第一個持續發展系列服飾 Gucci Off the Grid 之後，這個系列主打以有機、回收、生質布料製作而成的熱門中性服飾。

> 2019年二手市場的成長速度比整個
> 零售市場還快25倍。

The RealReal 的創辦人暨執行長茱莉·溫萊特（Julie Wainwright）對時尚雜誌《Vogue》說道：「每一秒鐘都有一整輛垃圾車那麼多的布料被送到掩埋場或焚燒掉。時尚產品不能一直成為垃圾，我們要購買好的產品，也要在用不到的時候把它們重新賣掉。直接和品牌合作對我們來說很有意義，我們可以運用他們的影響力來宣導循環時尚的重要，就像我們這次跟古馳的合作一樣。」到了 2024 年，二手服裝市場預計會從目前的 280 億美元，成長到 640 億美元，這個數據來自以舊金山為總部的 ThredUp，他們自稱為「世界最大的線上二手商店」。從 ThredUp 的年報可以看到，2019 年二手市場的成長速度比整個零售市場還快 25倍，總消費人數高達 6,400 萬人。

優衣庫也推出 Re.Uniqlo 計畫，回收自家生產的二手羽絨夾克，並重新製成新的羽絨外套，該計畫在 2019 年於日本啟動，隔年10 月也在新加坡推出，還會接著延伸到 27 個海外市場。優衣庫從 2006 年就開始徵集二手衣物，稍加分類以後，再透過聯合國難民署和其他機構把衣物捐給需要的人；在日本國內，這家快時尚品牌也把無法捐贈的衣物做成燃料或吸音原料使用。

值得關注的原因：

品牌開始意識到，二手市場即將成為循環經濟中的重要齒輪，積極參與循環時尚業務，不僅能幫助品牌打擊仿冒品並從二手販售中獲利，也能提升產品在一級市場的售價。

35

道德計分板

品牌的作為，對於消費者來說，從未如此重要。

根據 IBM 在 2020 年出版的調查報告顯示，有四成消費者的購買行為會受到「使命感」影響，而《富比士》（Forbes）雜誌也在探討使命感是否為 2020 年的主流。

為了回應這股成長中的道德導向消費趨勢，監測品牌行為的網站開始浮現，企業也紛紛將品牌價值提前，即使擁抱那些價值會對品牌營運產生挑戰也在所不辭。2020 年 10 月，迪士尼在旗下串流平台 Disney+ 上架某些老電影時，會在片前加註警語：「本節目內含對某類人士或文化的負面描述」，另外也會加上以下字句：「相對於移除節目，我們選擇承認其中的負面影響，從中學習，也開啟對話，一起創造更兼容並蓄的未來。」這些電影包括《與森林共舞》（The Jungle Book）、《小姐與流氓》（Lady and the Tramp）、《小飛象》（Dumbo）等等。

2020 年出現的線上平台《Did They Help?》記錄了企業和公眾人物的各種「優劣行徑」，並為其評分。訪客可以查詢品牌或人物在面對不同事件時的優劣表現，包括新冠肺炎（COVID-19）和「黑人的命也是命」運動（Black Lives Matter）等。創辦人摩爾加利艾（Pooj Morjaria）對偉門智威智庫表示：「雖然過去品牌可能缺乏道德意識或責任，但他們現在絕對都有這樣的意識了。」

Covid-19

Our full list of companies and their actions regarding Covid-19

Show [　] entries

SORT BY:	Title	Rating	Added
	TELUS	24	05 Oct 2020
	MORRISONS	15	11 Jun 2020
	Walmart	13	27 Mar 2020

LGBTQ Rights

Show [　] entries

SORT BY:	Title	Rating	Added
G	Google	3	27 Aug 2020
	Starbucks	3	28 Jun 2020
	American Express	1	27 Aug 2020
	Walmart	1	28 Jun 2020
	General Mills	1	18 Jun 2020
	Urban Outfitters	-1	27 Aug 2020
	Comcast	-1	27 Aug 2020

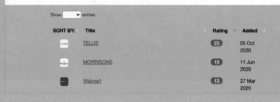

"

雖然過去品牌可能缺乏道德意識或責任，但他們現在絕對都有這樣的意識了。

"

《Did They Help?》線上平台創辦人
摩爾加利艾（Pooj Morjaria）

企業購買的廣告，可能會出現在與其價值觀相反的內容旁邊，這是自動化、程式化的廣告採購可能造成的結果，為了防範這個現象，南丁・潔米（Nandini Jammi）和克萊兒・阿特金（Claire Atkin）在 2020 年成立了品牌安全顧問公司 Check My Ads，創辦人潔米對偉門智威智庫解釋道：「如果你購買廣告的時候，把你的廣告和某種價值觀不同的內容並置在一起，兩者概念不一致，這樣就會產生問題。你等於是你把你的廣告預算，拿來對你的顧客表達你要維護（或者貶抑）的價值觀。」

在價值觀導向的背景下，品牌積極地展現了自身的道德意識，就像精品品牌蔻依（Chloé）的執行長里卡爾多・貝里尼（Riccardo Bellini）在 2020 年 11 月的發言，他說該公司以使命感為核心（例如社會利益是他們關心的面向），他們也建立了少女教育基金，並將社會企業家帶進相關供應鏈中，他對《WWD》表示：「品牌代表的意義、他們的信念、價值觀，都會跟商品和包裝一樣重要。」

值得關注的原因：

面對新冠肺炎、「黑人的命也是命」運動，以及令人擔憂的政治局勢，集體社會責任成為 2020 的首要工作目標，消費者對自身擁護的價值採取強硬立場，他們也希望品牌能展現這樣的精神。因此，不管是品牌本身或者外部獨立平台，都致力以更透明的做法來展現企業的道德意識。

36

靈活經營創造體驗

創新企業開始尋找利用閒置場地或閒置資源的新
方法，打造出富有彈性的複合式體驗。

泰國航空（Thai Airways）改造了飛機椅座和頭等艙菜單，提供
給地面上的旅客享用。2020 年 9 月，該公司的曼谷總部出現了一
家快閃餐廳，餐廳內部使用了閒置的飛機座椅和汰換下來的飛機
內裝，還請空服員來為顧客端上飛機餐。（更多與飛航飲食相關
的內容請見第 44 章〈機上餐飲饗宴〉）

2020 年 4 月時，疫情不僅讓航空業停擺，也影響了休閒娛樂
產業，全球電影院幾乎都被迫關門。立陶宛的維爾紐斯機場
（Vilnius airport）於 是 和 維 爾 紐 斯 國 際 電 影 節（Vilnius
International Film Festival）展開合作，讓機場跑道變身成汽車
劇院，並將它取名為「航空劇場」（Aerocinema）。

中國某家電影院決定轉型成鮮食超市以求生存。據《環球時報》
（Global Times）報導，網路上流傳著一部影片，可以看到位在
北京朝陽區的這家戲院外面大排長龍，好多人等著進去採買。

值得關注的原因：

這些例子不只告訴我們品牌與企業能在困境中為大家帶來歡樂，
也顯示了靈活經營與跨界合作在面對多變時局時有多重要，這些
創意做法讓大家看到全新的體驗模式帶來的效益，企業可以採取
這類彈性的經營方針來營運旗下空間。

37

品牌安全

品牌安全是傳遞品牌價值時的最新考量，
而且上下文的情境至關重要。

品牌安全是什麼呢？廣義來說，就是維護品牌聲譽；具體來說，則是要注意旗下廣告投放的場域。由於機靈的消費族群日益龐大，對於有意吸引這群消費者的品牌來說，品牌安全也變得漸趨重要。

品牌安全顧問公司 Check My Ads 的共同創辦人南丁·潔米（Nandini Jammi）對偉門智威智庫說到，「顧客現在看待廣告的方式和以前不同了。」現在的消費者看的不只是訊息，還會深入探討品牌的道德意識、行為、價值觀，最近還多了一項新的考量，也就是廣告曝光的位置，因為這也代表著品牌的價值。

潔米和另一位共同創辦人克萊兒·阿特金（Claire Atkin）一起在 2020 年 6 月成立了這家品牌安全顧問公司，為的就是要處理他們在不斷變動的消費生態中，親身觀察到的錯誤策略。雖然品牌傳達的訊息可能和他們本身的價值觀一致，但是廣告如果投放到錯誤的位置，就能毀掉一切。

「我們現在身處在廣告環境和廣告本身一樣重要的時代，你下廣告的地方有時候甚至比你的廣告本身還重要，因為廣告環境要不就是強化你的訊息，要不就是削弱這些訊息。」潔米如此表示。

熱門的社交平台也提升了與品牌安全相關的保護措施，讓企業更能掌握自身廣告出現的位置。國際版抖音（TikTok）自 2020 年 10 月開始與品牌安全平台 OpenSlate 合作，確保企業在 TikTok 投放的廣告不會出現在有問題的內容旁邊。OpenSlate 的執行長麥克·亨利（Mike Henry）表示：「內容和脈絡已經比以前更重要了。」

同月，YouTube 將 ZEFR 指定為品牌安全合作夥伴，希望能在 2021 年完成並推出與品牌安全相關的措施。

值得關注的原因：

潔米談到：「品牌開始了解到，若要守護品牌安全，他們就必須獲得群體的認可。」品牌傳達的價值可以傳播得比產品本身還更遠，而品牌價值包羅萬象，從品牌行動、企業對待員工的方式，到廣告出現的場域，全都包含在內。

Check My Ads

Take back control of your ads.

Keep your brand away from fake news, disinformation, and hate speech.

38

溝通活動著重振奮人心

面對一整年的疾病、貧苦、難關,品牌和廣告商試
著要鼓舞群眾,尤其在節慶期間。

2020 年的齋戒月期間,印尼流動電信公司 (Telkomsel) 推出一
支名為〈持續做好事〉(Continue Doing Good) 的廣告,裡面呈
現了該公司用戶利用視訊通話與親友維繫感情的畫面。身為印尼
最大的電信業者,他們也提醒客戶可以把用不到的通話和數據額
度轉讓給需要的人,也可以捐款或者轉播與信仰相關的內容,總
之就是要告訴大家:在家的時候也要持續做好事。

在英國,國際版抖音 (TikTok) 也在 2020 年 5 月推出第一支電視
廣告,被關在家裡的主角群利用這個短影音平台來保持樂觀正向
的生活態度。廣告的主角包括女子樂團混合甜心 (Little Mix)、
饒舌歌手天霸泰尼 (Tinie Tempah)、知名主廚戈登 · 拉姆齊
(Gordon Ramsay),還有代表社會大眾的人群(跟他們的貓),
這支廣告也是抖音大型數位行銷專案〈曖曖內含光〉(A Little
Brighter Inside) 的其中一環,這個專案呈現了多位名人和創作
者在抖音上分享的閉關生活日常。

一樣在英國,百貨公司約翰路易斯 (John Lewis & Partners) 和
連鎖超市維特羅斯 (Waitrose & Partners) 製作了溫馨的聖誕企
劃,他們每年的聖誕廣告都扣人心弦,因此備受期待。他們 2020

"

這裡要傳遞
的訊息是，每個人都
有責任確保全體社會
大眾的安全。

"

年的廣告也特別讓人動容，在〈付出一點愛〉（Give A Little Love）這支廣告中，八位藝術家各自創作了短片，並以日常生活中的小小善行串起整支廣告，讓大家看到美好的小事如何鼓舞身邊的人。約翰路易斯和維特羅斯希望能利用這支聖誕廣告募集到 400 萬歐元（折合台幣約 1 億 3500 萬元）來做公益。

英國連鎖藥妝店博姿（Boots）也以行善為主題，拍攝了一支聖誕廣告。廣告裡出現的肥皂、沐浴球、泡泡，一起哼著歌曲，唱著「現在世界需要的是愛～」，博姿希望透過這支廣告來鼓勵大家捐贈肥皂和其他清潔用品給需要的人。在廣告的最後，博姿也寫到，他們捐贈了 100 萬歐元（約台幣 3380 萬）予關注衛生的慈善機構 Hygiene Bank。

2020 年 11 月，印度防蚊噴霧品牌 Goodknight 為慶祝兒童節，拍攝了一支描繪正常生活的廣告。男孩在餵自己的嬰兒弟弟，還把湯匙想像成飛機；爸爸在點祈福蠟燭的時候，年輕女孩趕忙把爸爸的袖子從燭火旁拉開；女兒提醒爸爸出門前要記得噴防蚊液……裡面對疫情唯一的著墨，只有爸爸臉上戴的口罩。

這支廣告要傳遞的訊息是，每個人都有責任確保全體社會大眾的安全，就連小朋友也不例外。居住在孟買的偉門智威規劃總監帕利（Rishabh Parikh）如此說道。

值得關注的原因：

新冠肺炎（COVID-19）疫苗的成功，讓大家在疫情中看見一線曙光，但目前還是有很多人需要幫助，所以這些廣告讓我們看見，原來在鼓舞他人的同時，自己心裡也能充滿希望。

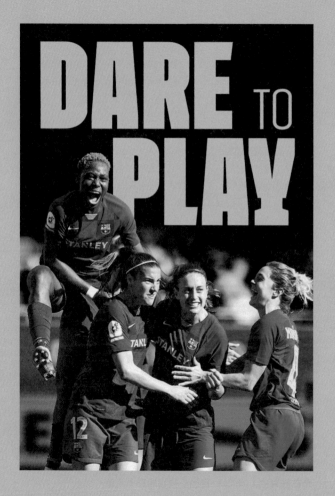

39

粉絲忠實度

運動產業努力打下基礎，
和日漸增加的粉絲更多線上互動。

疫情中斷了大眾現場觀看比賽的機會，卻也讓股東重新看到在網路上和粉絲互動的價值，往後在線上和粉絲互動會成為不可或缺的重要環節，甚至還有機會提升粉絲的忠誠度。

為運動迷打造的全新數位互動模式，在疫情前就已趨於成熟，以區塊鏈為核心的 Chiliz 公司就是一例，他們在 2019 年 11 月推出粉絲互動應用程式 Socios.com，執行長德雷福斯（Alexandre Dreyfus）也提到「現在 99% 的運動迷都不在現場觀賽了」，這樣的娛樂模式「受到社群媒體、全球電視轉播權、運動明星的個人魅力影響」，已成為全球現象。因此 Socios.com 讓運動迷可以在程式中賺取獎勵和積分，藉此和喜歡的隊伍互動，粉絲代幣可以經由收集、購買、贏取等方式累積，粉絲可以使用代幣來投票和參與市調，進而影響隊務發展。代幣就像虛擬的會籍，讓持有人有資格得獎、購買商邊商品，還能享有獨一無二的體驗。

新冠肺炎（COVID-19）的爆發讓這股趨勢來到前所未有的高峰，2020 年 9 月，板球隊伍「孟買印度人隊」（Mumbai Indians）推出不少創新的虛擬功能，讓他們的粉絲社群「Paltan」更加團結，其中包括和三星（Samsung）合作推出的 Paltan Play，讓粉絲能在比賽期間利用小視窗來互相較量、預測比賽結果，預測項目包含跑分和每局進球數等等。

北美西甲（LaLiga North America）採取了獨家做法，善用觀看派對來為西班牙足球狂粉提供 VIP 服務，他們在 LiveLike 平台上一連舉辦了 5 場獨家觀看派對，由森姆・艾托奧（Samuel Eto' o）、迪亞哥・佛蘭（Diego Forlá）等人主持，比賽過程中也有一系列的球員問答直播，也能開啟線上聊天室功能。

除了這些在比賽期間推出的有趣線上活動以外，粉絲也想近距離收看和選手或比賽相關的大小事，所以傳奇足球隊巴賽隆納足球俱樂部（FC Barcelona）也推出了一系列的娛樂媒體，在 2020 年夏季，他們推出獨家串流平台 Barça TV+，讓粉絲飽覽選手大小事，裡面匯集了 1,000 小時以上的賽況直播、經典畫面重播、獨家幕後花絮等等。該隊伍還養了一支自己的後製團隊，專為 Barça TV+ 製作影音內容，包含原創紀錄片、系列影片，甚至還拍攝了以足球為主題的影集。

Barça TV+ 是巴塞隆納足球隊粉絲會員俱樂部 Culers 白金會員的福利之一，是現有會員制的進化版，他們為會員提供完整的線上服務，另外也有各項折扣和抽獎機會。

"
在線上和粉絲互動會成爲不可或缺的重要環節，甚至還有機會提升粉絲的忠誠度。
"

值得關注的原因：

在這個全新的粉絲互動世代裡，跨平台的體驗模式和沈浸式娛樂，讓品牌有了吸引消費者的全新管道，甚至還能提昇粉絲長期的忠誠度。世界摔角娛樂品牌（WWE）總監史蒂芬妮・麥馬漢（Stephanie McMahon）在 2021 年美國消費電子用品展（CES）的座談會中，談到未來的粉絲體驗，「如果要讓科技和運動成功交匯在一起，那就得創造出情感價值，要和觀眾產生情感連結。」

品牌學院

品牌聯名課程是否在未來會成為教育的一環嗎？

教育制度正面臨轉變，品牌也趁機跨入教育領域。聯合國教科文組織統計，2020 年因為封城的關係，導致全球超過 15 億名學生需要在家自學，這對許多教育體系來說是很重大的難關，但同時也為品牌提供跨足教育領域、協助學校師生的機會。

2020 年 11 月，英國匯豐銀行（HSBC）宣布要和非營利的金融教育團體 Young Money 合作，為 3 到 11 歲的幼童推出金融學習平台 Money Heroes，平台上也為家長和老師提供資源，內容涵蓋預算管理、金融犯罪等各類題材。

臉書（Facebook）一直以來也為學校師生提供各類傳統課綱以外的學習題材。2020 年 8 月，該公司推出教學中心 Educator Hub，讓學生能接觸反種族歧視、數位識讀、身心健康等相關課程，也為老師提供資源，推出「線上學習管理」等教師專屬的課程。

為了幫助學童了解環保生活態度，超越肉類公司（Beyond Meat）和社會教育平台 EVERFI 合作，讓美國師生可以免費使用與環保永續議題相關的教育資源。他們為 2020 年開始的新學年推出線上課程，內容包含氣候變遷、生態多樣性等議題，也會在 2021 年陸續加入線上學習活動來加強學習效果。

值得關注的原因：

品牌教育的概念並非前所未見，麥當勞早在 1961 年就創設過漢堡大學（Hamburger University）了，但是現在企業尋求的是更深入、更具影響力的管道，不只是要訓練他們現在和未來的員工，還要教育未來的世代。

食品 & 飲品

41
用餐體驗無與倫比

**顧客在社交距離的新時代，
仍不忘尋求難忘的美食體驗。**

為了服務尋求特殊餐飲的顧客，餐飲經營者開始打造符合安全社交距離的高級用餐環境。

在布達佩斯，米其林星星餐館 Costes 將精緻餐飲提升至全新境界。2020 年 10 月 17 日，Costes 在被稱為「布達佩斯之眼」的摩天輪上供應一套四道菜的晚餐，讓賓客可以一邊享用美食，一邊在四人座包廂內欣賞令人屏息的城市美景。新冠肺炎（COVID-19）期間的旅遊限制讓旅遊人數下滑，卻也讓 Costes 餐廳的負責人葛翰達（Károly Gerendai）有機會實現自己的景觀餐廳夢。路透社（Reuters）的報導指出，售價 155 美元的晚餐套票在數日內就已售罄，且因為活動大受好評，葛翰達還宣佈將於 2021 年的春季再加場舉辦。

巴黎奢華飯店 Les Bains 在創立之初原本是座公共浴場，2020 年 9 月時，他們將 1885 年就已經存在的地下泳池抽乾並重新規劃，改造成私人專屬的用餐空間，這是他們「Les Bains Confidentiels」企劃的一環，用意是要向顧客展現飯店內奇特出

眾的獨特空間,除了泳池餐廳,顧客也可以選擇在飯店的附屬夜店裡預定私人席位,這家夜店可是曾經接待過米克‧傑格(Mick Jagger)、娜歐蜜‧坎貝兒(Naomi Campbell)及凱特‧摩絲(Kate Moss)等名人的夜店。

在小棕櫚島溫泉度假會館(Little Palm Island Resort and Spa)裡,餐廳開放預約的時段是由潮汐來決定的。這座度假會館位於佛州小火炬礁島上,要價 1,000 美元的「沙洲晚餐組合」於 2020 年 9 月推出,會為顧客提供一組五道菜式的雙人晚間套餐,且將私人餐桌設在沙灘旁的淺海中。

值得關注的原因:
外食習慣正在慢慢改變,高級餐廳發揮創意,為顧客提供專屬、獨特、無可比擬的用餐環境,在不犧牲用餐氛圍下,仍能遵守安全社交距離的規範。

41

Les Bains hotel swimming pool, now drained and repurposed

42
氣候友善的飲食風潮

「氣候飲食主義者」賦予健康飲食全新的意義。

全球約有四分之一的碳排放量和食品生產過程有關,因此消費者開始採取行動。民調機構 YouGov 於 2020 年 1 月的調查指出,為了降低飲食對環境造成的衝擊,千禧世代中有五分之一的人口正在改變飲食習慣。為了回應消費者對地球健康的期待,品牌和平台紛紛推出新產品或服務,協助消費者了解飲食習慣對環境造成的影響。

在 2020 年 10 月,潘娜拉麵包(Panera Bread)在菜單中加入碳足跡標籤。這間連鎖咖啡麵包店與世界資源研究所(World Resources Institute)攜手合作,評估該品牌有哪些餐飲合乎低碳標準,並依此鑑別出最符合氣候友善思維的產品。

「了解我們吃的東西對環境的影響,是大家在對抗氣候變遷時都能踏出的一小步」,潘娜拉品牌執行長尼倫・喬達里(Niren Chaudhary)接著指出,「身為食品企業,我們有強大的使命感,要和大家分享這資訊,並鼓勵顧客和我們一起做出改變。」同月,奇波雷墨西哥燒烤(Chipotle)也推出追蹤永續指數的工具 The Real Foodprint,協助顧客分析餐飲的永續指數,包含碳排放量和省水量等主要指標;該餐飲業者也與受千禧世代歡迎的科學網紅比爾・奈(Bill Nye, the Science Guy)合作,透過國際版抖音(TikTok)影片展示 The Real Foodprint 追蹤工具的使用方法。

連鎖沙拉店 Just Salad 認為注重健康的食客會像計算熱量那樣計算碳足跡，他們從 2020 年 9 月開始實施全新的碳足跡標籤計畫，在菜單上標明所有品項的碳排放量。

這些新計畫「推動了一股社會風氣，讓大家除了想要降低熱量攝取、降低開銷、簡化 iPhone 使用程序之外，也開始認真思考如何減碳。」Just Salad 的永續主管桑德拉・諾南（Sandra Noonan）如此表示。

2020 年 11 月，英國健康領域專家共同成立的協會提出呼籲，希望政府於 2025 年前對嚴重衝擊環境的食品加徵「氣候稅」，並發表報告且提出一系列建言，讓食品業者能轉而配合氣候行動。「如果要達成目標，就必須解決食品業的體制問題」，身為這份報告的共同作者，公眾衛生學院（Faculty of Public Health）的食品組負責人克莉絲汀・芭絲（Kristin Bash）如此說道。

值得關注的原因：

健康飲食的概念已經拓展到更大的範疇，要能同時支持地球，又能為消費者補充營養。英國牛津大學（University of Oxford）的馬可・斯賓曼（Marco Springmann）專門研究「全球糧食系統的健康、環境與經濟」，他向《衛報》（The Guardian）表示：「這裡要傳達的訊息十分明確，若不大幅降低肉品和乳製品的產量和食用量，要防止氣候變遷加劇至危險等級，機會可說是微乎其微。」

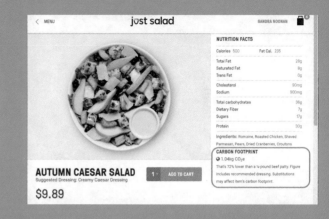

WUNDERMAN
THOMPSON　Top: Just Salad
　　　　　　　Bottom: Chipotle

43
包裝講究抗菌保護

包裝業者和各大品牌為因應消費者對衛生的
高度關切，推出可加強衛生的產品。

2020 年 10 月，舊金山設計公司 Designsake Studio 推出多用
途抗菌防護塗層 Matter，可應用於紙張、卡片、玻璃、金屬、織品
等等多種表面上；產品採用了先進的銀塗層技術，可以中斷病毒
繁殖。Matter 同時也獲美國食品藥物管理局（FDA）和環境保護
局（EPA）認證，證明此種抗菌技術可提供高達 99.9% 的抗微生
物防護。該公司的創辦人暨執行長丹妮愛爾・麥華特（Danielle
McWaters）指出，這款包材證明了「我們不用為了安全或回收的
考量而犧牲美感。我們希望 Matter 可以讓人找回開箱的樂趣，並
創造出安全永續的新一代包裝方式。」

由於現在有大量的消費者開始在家中下廚，Rubbermaid 於是在
2020 年 10 月推出「易找蓋」（EasyFindLids）保鮮盒，這系列的
商品使用 SilverShield 抗菌技術製成，可以抑制會產生異味的細
菌生成。「目前這段時間，消費者比較常在家中烹飪，所以我們很

> **"**
> 在2020年至2027年間，抗病毒塗層市場的
> 年複合成長率預計達到13.3%，
> 總值上看美金13億元。
> **"**

樂意提供可以同時解決囤積問題，又不會讓保鮮盒產生異味的產品。」諾威公司（Newell Brands，Rubbermaid 的母公司）食品企業部門的執行長克里斯・馬柯斯基（Kris Malkoski）如此表示。另外，加拿大廣播公司（CBC News）的報導也指出，加拿大卡普頓大學（Cape Breton University）Verschuren 研究中心的研究員正在開發抗病毒包裝及抗病毒塗層，用來殺死物體表面接觸到的新型冠狀病毒。

依據美國聯合市場研究公司（Allied Market Research）的報告來看，2020 年至 2027 年間，抗病毒塗層市場的年複合成長率預計達到 13.3%，總值上看美金 13 億元。該公司指出，新冠肺炎（COVID-19）爆發期間的相關需求增加，是推動這波成長的主因，且「目前的疫情也提供了研發新產品的契機」。

值得關注的原因：
由於消費者十分了解病毒存活於物體表面的能力，抗菌和抗病毒包裝將成為企業做出採購決策時的重要考量。

44

機上餐飲饗宴

飛機餐再進化，擄獲無法飛行旅客的食慾。

飛機餐以前被視為空中旅行最無趣的環節之一，現在卻成為仿造飛航體驗的重要元素，吸引被禁足在地面上的旅遊愛好者，一同踏上餐飲旅程。

2020 年 10 月，芬蘭航空（Finnair）開始在芬蘭超市內販售起商務艙供應的機上餐點，並取名為「芬蘭航空的滋味」（Taste of Finnair）。餐點品項每隔兩週循環一次，是融合北歐和日式風格的現代料理。開賣日的菜單先以烤紅蘿蔔和藍紋起司慕斯為開胃菜；接著是兩道主菜：煙燻紅點鮭與野菇燉飯，以及照燒蘿蔔醬牛肉佐青蔥配飯。

同月初，新加坡航空（Singapore Airlines）也在停泊於樟宜機場的兩架 A380 空中巴士上，設立了一家快閃餐廳。這項餐飲活動十分熱門，兩台飛機的晚餐席位在預約開放後的 30 分鐘內旋即售罄，促使航空公司再度加開兩場晚餐活動。餐券與機票一樣依艙等分級，共有四種選項：頭等艙、商務艙、豪華經濟艙、經濟艙，範圍從價值美金 474 元的私人包廂加五菜套餐，到美金 40 元的小資選項都有。

除了飛機餐之外,如果飛行常客想要收藏紀念品,可以參考澳洲航空公司(Qantas)出售的機上餐車。這些餐車來自近期退役的波音 747 班機,澳航忠實旅客紛紛上線搶購,據《商業內幕》(Business Insider)透露,澳航的一千輛手推車在兩小時內即販售一空。這次出售的餐車上面還附有小瓶裝的酒類和香檳、糖果零食、商務艙洗漱用品、毛毯、頭等艙的睡衣。

值得關注的原因:

飛機餐不再無聊,平淡無味的微波餐點早已不復存在。雖然這些大膽嘗試可能只是讓搖搖欲墜的航空業延續生計的權宜之計,卻也點出機上餐飲逐漸進化的現況,現在,飛機餐已經進化成美食饗宴,連在地面上的旅客也想一嚐美味。

45

幽靈廚房

餐飲業以新的經營模式，改善運作方式，將主力鎖定在外帶餐飲上

外送優先的餐飲越來越熱門，在隔離期間更是遍地開花，為全新的概念餐廳打開大門——幽靈廚房。幽靈廚房業者不將資金花在廚房與用餐空間的租金和人事費用上，而是租借共用廚房完成料理，以外送或外帶的形式供應給顧客。

全球市調公司歐睿國際（Euromonitor）預估，幽靈廚房的產值可能在 2030 年前上看美金 1 兆元，許多餐飲業的龍頭也紛紛跨足此市場。2020 年 11 月，連鎖餐廳奇波雷墨西哥燒烤（Chipotle）也導入了幽靈廚房的概念，打造了網路限定的餐館原型「奇波雷數位廚房」（Chipotle Digital Kitchen），只提供外帶和外送服務，沒有內用選項。

中西部連鎖超市克羅格（Kroger）則於 2020 年 10 月宣佈，他們將與專營外送服務的新創餐廳 ClusterTruck 合作。透過此一合作案，克羅格超市將為 ClusterTruck 提供場地，讓他們可以在超市內販售現點現做的餐飲，因此顧客也無須支付服務費或外送費。克羅格公司副總裁德拉羅沙（Dan De La Rosa）表示，這次的合作將成為「讓點餐、備料、外送過程變得更精簡的創新之舉」。

2020 年 10 月 26 日，外送服務公司 DoorDash 宣佈了一項「外送重生」（Reopen for Delivery）計畫，協助受疫情影響而倒閉的餐廳在幽靈廚房裡作業，並以虛擬餐廳的形式重新開張。

投資客也加入了這場戰役。幽靈廚房業者 Zuul（熱門連鎖沙拉品牌 Sweetgreen 也在他們的客戶名單上）於 2019 年 9 月在曼哈頓開設第一個據點後，又在 2020 年 7 月募集到 900 萬美元，讓他們能在紐約拓展市場。《華爾街日報》（The Wall Street Journal）在 2020 年 10 月的報導中指出，優步公司（Uber）的創辦人暨前執行長特拉維斯‧卡拉尼克（Travis Kalanick）為他新成立的「雲端廚房」（CloudKitchens）購入價值 1 億 3000 萬美元的房產。同月，軟銀願景基金（SoftBank's Vision Fund）也為 Nextbite 注入 1 億 2000 萬美元的資金，依照 Nextbite 執行長艾力克斯‧坎特（Alex Canter）的說法，他們是「一家打造外送餐飲品牌的公司，他們的商品只出現在優食（Uber Eats）、DoorDash、Postmates 等外送平台上」。

2020 年 1 月份成立的紐約新創公司 Kitch 則希望打造幽靈廚房專屬的 Airbnb 平台，並稱自家產品為「廚房配對工具」，讓當地餐館能和飯店業者、餐廳經理，還有其他能在離峰時間出租廚房的餐飲業者互相配對、合作。

值得關注的原因：

歐睿國際指出，隨著外送產業蓬勃發展，餐廳經營者改將重點擺在「料理空間」而非「用餐空間」上，2014 年到 2019 年間，全球餐飲外送業的營業額也成長了兩倍以上。歐睿國際的飲食服務研究部全球主管麥克‧沙非（Michael Schaefer）向偉門智威智庫表示，「過去五年以來，第三方外送服務為餐飲業的經營模式下了新的定義；按照同樣的邏輯來看，未來五年的餐飲演化方向，將會由幽靈廚房和其他分散式生產型態來定義。」

WHAT'S GOOD?

EVERYTHING.

(Come on...)

I like the Lo Mein.
Ravioli.
Carnitas.
Veggie burger.
Steak frites.

Sounds good.

ZUUL

45

46

早餐大變身

隨著待在家的時間變長，早餐也從囫圇吞棗的例行
公事變成值得好好享受的生活儀式。

據週刊《Grocer》報導，凱度模範市場研究公司（Kantar）在英
國做了一份為期 12 週的調查報告，調查於 2020 年 6 月 14 日截
止。凱度在這份報告中表示，與前年同期相比，消費者在吃早餐
時食用雞蛋的比例提高了 68%、培根食用量也上升 21%、烘焙糕
點也多了 25%。而且在同年 10 月，《美國商業資訊》（Business
Wire）也寫到，美國連鎖超市全食超市（Whole foods market）
在 2021 年的十大食物趨勢預測中，喊出了「不只週末，每天都該
享用豐盛的早餐」的宣言。

英國食品顧問公司 The Food People 的資深編輯希賈茲
（Shokofeh Hejazi）指出，「對許多人而言，在家工作代表有時
間可以慢下來好好吃頓早餐，不用在通勤時倉促吞下可頌麵包。
另外，『早餐』也不再只專屬於『早餐時段』，我們觀察到傳統的
早餐品項，例如夾心可頌或墨西哥早餐捲，在其他時段也有很多
人享用」。希賈茲也提到世界料理對西式早餐產生的影響，像是
日本雞蛋三明治、馬來西亞咖椰吐司、墨西哥早餐塔可開始日益
流行，還有用自製天然酵母酸麵包、手工奶油抹醬、當季果醬取代
白吐司的「吐司升級趨勢」。

"
吃早餐越來越像
在參與盛會。
"

《Breakfast London: Where Real Londoners Eat》
作者，碧安卡．布莉基（Bianca Bridges）

《倫敦早餐：正港倫敦人吃什麼？》（暫譯自 Breakfast London: Where Real Londoners Eat）一書的作者碧安卡．布莉基（Bianca Bridges）指出，受到全球居家隔離的影響，「整體來說，早餐越來越受歡迎，因為大家會想在一日之始就開始進行社交活動，而不是等到一天快結束時才開始，而且大家也很喜歡吃早餐類的食物」。布莉基解釋到，有越來越多餐廳和咖啡廳在出版早餐和早午餐食譜，這也讓更多人開始在家自製精美的早餐，「居家隔離讓大家更有時間來做這件事」。

談到早餐在倫敦的蓬勃發展，布莉基提到創新麵包店也在烘焙糕點上大展新意，如倫敦 Popham 烘焙坊的迷迭香海鹽麻花麵包，以及來自東倫敦 Jolene 烘焙坊的鹽味焦糖蘋果或者燉梨果仁糖卡士達丹麥麵包等。

值得關注的原因：

由於在家的時間變多，再加上新冠肺炎（COVID-19）的疫情限制，導致許多人一早就會開始進行社交活動，早餐也因此重新受到大家的歡迎。布莉基表示，「吃早餐越來越像在參與盛會，等到限制放寬，大家會更渴望參與各種體驗，所以我認為以後會看到不少餐飲體驗活動崛起，可能是早午餐活動、共享超豐盛早餐拼盤，或者可能有餐廳會為顧客打造超凡脫俗的環境，外加接送賓客前來用餐。」

47

植物性飲食風行亞洲

食品大廠針對關注健康的亞洲消費者推出植物肉和人造肉品的各種選擇。

在 2020 年年中，位於洛杉磯的超越肉類公司（Beyond Meat）生產了植物性替代肉品，並在中國超市「盒馬鮮生」推出「超越漢堡」（Beyond Burgers）。亞洲新創公司也引進了植物性替代肉品或實驗室生產的人造肉，讓創新食材可以輕易地融入當地的飲食風格，用來製作刈包、燒賣、火鍋等療癒食物。

近年來，隨著亞洲人均收入逐漸上漲，肉類食用量隨之升高，而肉類替代品的需求也跟著增加。全球市調公司歐睿國際（Euromonitor International）指出，2019 年亞太地區的肉類替代品市場約占了 153 億元，與前年相比增加了 4.75%。

總部位於新加坡的新創食品公司 Karana，則向斯里蘭卡小農收購有機波蘿蜜，用來製造類似豬肉的替代肉品。Karana 向泰森食品（Tyson Foods）和創投基金 Big Idea Ventures 等投資人募得美金 170 萬元的種子資金，目標是大規模生產和開發即食產品。

位於北京的新創公司珍肉（Zhenmeat）食品，則是推出一系列為中式料理（如火鍋或港式點心）量身打造的植物性產品。他們使用來自碗豆、大豆、糙米裡的植物性蛋白成份，以及來自香菇的真菌蛋白，生產的產品包含香腸、牛排、月餅、肉丸等。

新加坡的 Shiok Meats 公司則在研究實驗室生產的人造海鮮，為求解決大型養蝦場破壞紅樹林的問題以及後續滋生的疾病。截至 2020 年 7 月，該公司已從美國創投加速器 Y Combinator 等投資者募得美金 760 萬元，預期在未來幾年內即可開始販售。

年輕族群更表示，他們會為了自己的身體健康與地球的健康，重新思考吃下去的食物。2019 年，偉門智威智庫在 9 個亞洲市場中

針對青少年和年輕人進行調查，結果顯示，有 56% 的受訪者表示自己正試著減少肉類飲食。新冠肺炎（COVID-19）也進一步催化大眾對健康和無肉飲食的關注。

值得關注的原因：

最後大家都能有更多的選擇。優質食品協會（The Good Food Institute）的亞太區董事總經理 Elaine Siu 預測，以後超市的肉類區將包含更多植物性替代品，以及混合動植物來源的新食品，讓「大眾的食物選擇更貼近個人需求也更多元」。

48

用餐新常態

因應用餐社交距離規範的轉變，賦予刀叉與餐具的
設計新的樣貌

許多設計師將注意力轉移到餐桌上，設法提升安全社交距離下
的用餐體驗。March Gut 設計工作室於 2020 年 10 月推出全新
餐服組合「奧瑪托盤」（Alma Tray），是專為奧地利比曹地區的
飯店 Biohotel Schwanen 打造的餐服用具。這款托盤長達 1.2
公尺，正好符合奧地利的 1 公尺安全距離規範，除了可以讓服務
生在保持安全社交距離的情況下更輕鬆地上菜，光滑的表面也讓
服務人員無需將身體前傾靠近用餐者，即可上餐或收拾餐盤。

設計工作室 Studio Boir 則重新構思餐具的風貌，推出了「新常
態」（New Normal）系列餐具，2020 年 10 月公開的這組時尚餐
具中，分隔式大淺盤和加長型湯匙都為大眾提供了共享菜餚與上
餐的全新方式。

Studio Boir 的創辦人伊凡·席達（Ivan Zidar）解釋：「我們的概
念餐具保留了社交與文化層面的用餐習慣，那就是『分享』的精
神，Boir 的餐具傳遞了親密感，同時又能保持社交距離。」

設計師哲尼貢的同名工作室 Christophe Gernigon Studio 也致
力將外出用餐的熟悉感保留在設計中。2020 年 5 月，這位法國
設計師發表了「玻璃飲食」（Plex' eat）概念，運用類似透明燈罩
的頭罩獨立隔開每位用餐者和他們的用餐區，也提供另一款雙人
頭罩同時罩住兩位用餐者，讓用餐者在外食時不會覺得受到隔離。
哲尼貢認為這種以有機玻璃製成的頭罩是能「遵守安全社交距離
的優雅產品」。

值得關注的原因：

在《The Future 100: 2.0.20》一書中，我們觀察到餐廳為維護安
全社交距離所提出的措施，在不犧牲用餐體驗的情況下，重新規
劃空間來保護用餐者；現在，許多設計師則將重點放在用餐細節
上，並在上菜服務和分享食物的方式上有所創新，這些最新的設
計專案點出了未來的用餐方式，除了優雅精緻，同時也能遵守安
全社交距離規範。

48

49

私密用餐體驗

高級餐廳和飲食新創公司紛紛將私人用餐定義為全新的奢華外食方案。

2020 年 6 月，Apt 在英國正式推出，讓用餐者和處於同個社交泡泡內的夥伴一起享受私人的用餐體驗。由於疫情導致餐旅業業績下滑，於是倫敦幾位最知名的廚師開始聚在一起，共同打造出讓饕客可以再次享用美食的全新方式，他們會在許可範圍內接受團體預約，人數最多 10 人，顧客從 Apt 的廚師名單中挑選主廚後，他們所選的主廚會為活動量身打造一份菜單。用餐地點可在倫敦東側的市政廳公寓飯店（Town Hall Hotel），或是在客戶家中享用。

米其林大廚烏薩薩木（Pichaya Utharntharm），或稱潘主廚（Chef Pam），即在曼谷提供私人用餐服務「潘主廚餐桌」（The Table by Chef Pam），地點就位在她自己的家中。為數 4 至 16 人的派對團體可以向她預定專屬菜單，菜式最多可達 12 道。

> 2020年的用餐方式，
> 指出了未來美食料理體驗首重私人化
> 與客製化的趨勢。

美籍厄瓜多主廚荷西·加塞斯（Jose Garces）的海鮮餐廳 The Olde Bar 改寫了費城的餐廳文化。在 2020 年 10 月，該餐廳公開整修後的內部裝潢，讓顧客可以從 14 個以圖書館為主題的用餐角落中選擇其一入座，為用餐者帶來私人用餐體驗。

瑞典餐廳 Bord för En（意為「一人餐桌」）則為尋求單人用餐體驗的人量身打造獨特的餐飲服務，這間快閃餐廳於 2020 年 5 月開張，讓單一用餐者能在戶外享用不同的餐點。餐廳地點位於斯德哥爾摩 200 哩外的瑞典夏季草原中，他們能為顧客提供完全零接觸的服務：賓客可在單人餐桌椅上獨自用餐，並自行端出裝在傳統野餐籃內的三道佳餚，而野餐籃會透過與廚房相連的繩索送到用餐者身旁。

值得關注的原因：

這些用餐體驗讓人重新燃起對外出用餐的興致（這是 2020 年所沒有的），也指出未來美食體驗首重私人化與客製化的趨勢。

50

三大最夯食材

食品產業中最值得期待的三種熱門食材。

四川花椒

四川花椒主導了整個四川省的料理,現在這種火辣風味更延燒到了全世界。近年來,中國連鎖火鍋店海底撈與楊國福麻辣燙迅速擴張到海外,熱辣的花椒湯頭配上肉品和蔬菜,讓這股花椒魔力大幅延伸至英國、日本、澳洲及東南亞。

四川花椒也以調味料的形式出線,在 2019 年,住在美國的主廚暨美食作家高靜(Jing Gao)在募資平台 Kickstarter 上推出「四川辣椒脆」(Sichuan Chili Crisp),產品大獲好評。他們打出這樣的口號:「為出口至美國而製造的第一款(也是唯一一款)100% 純天然辣醬。」此辣醬的成份包含四川花椒和發酵黑豆,可搭配任何食品享用,從炒蛋到水餃,再到讓人印象深刻的香草冰淇淋(由洛杉磯冰淇淋店 Wanderlust Creamery 推出),非常百搭。

自家種的泡茶香草

家庭園藝愛好者開始種植具舒緩功效且能提升免疫力的香草，並泡在茶中作為天然療法使用。紐西蘭近期掀起對「rongoā」的熱愛，這是一種傳統毛利療法，搭配香草茶服用：可以將心型葉片的植物卡瓦卡瓦（kawakawa）浸泡在健胃藥中，或加到具有抗菌功效的麥蘆卡蜂蜜（Manuka honey）裡。

2020 年 5 月，當紐西蘭正值全國封鎖階段，奧克蘭的園藝雜誌《New Zealand Gardener》即在其中一篇文章中推薦有助「復原情緒」的草藥配方，成份包含可以舒緩壓力和焦慮的薰衣草、西番蓮、印度人蔘、洋甘菊，再搭配能減輕失眠症狀的檸檬香蜂草。根據紐西蘭最大獨立市調查公司羅伊・摩根（Roy Morgan）指出，當時很多生活風格刊物都停刊了，但這本雜誌的零售量卻在疫情期間穩定成長，使其成為紐國出版業的罕見亮點。

「每當全球經濟衰退時，大眾對園藝的興趣就會突然上漲，而且屢試不爽。」《New Zealand Gardener》園藝雜誌的編輯麥卡羅（Jo McCarroll）向偉門智威智庫如此表示。他接著說道：「80 年代的金融風暴、90 年代的網際網路泡沫也都是這樣，大家會想：『我的生活裡需要一些更真實、更可掌握的事物』，現在我們也可以看到這個現象。」

麴

米麴這種發酵劑早已受到日本長期推崇,可以拿來作清酒、味醂、醬油和其他產品。米麴因其鮮味而廣受好評,日本甚至會在每年10月12日的國定真菌節慶祝此一食材,而現在它也成為植物肉的主要成份,出現在西方國家的雜貨架上。

2020 年的感恩節時,加州植物肉公司 Prime Roots 推出以米麴製作而成的烤「火雞」,吃起來的味道與口感都像肉一樣,除了米麴以外的其他成分還包含米飯、碗豆蛋白、碗豆纖維、醋。在推出「米麴火雞」之前,Prime Roots 也曾在 2020 年於全食超市(Whole Foods)推出無肉冷凍餐點,包含米麴製成的「培根」起司通心麵及夏威夷醬油「烤雞」。

全球知名主廚也對這種日本菌類讚譽有加,其中包含紐約桃福餐廳(Momofuku)的張碩浩(David Chang)和哥本哈根 Noma 餐廳的雷勒·雷哲度(René Redzepi)。

51

美容

60

51

自由的美

全新的心理健康風潮崛起,為美麗下了新的定義。

在舒適的家中待久了以後,無妝美感和簡易保養風潮開始出現;但隨著日子一天天過去,大家終於要鑽出被窩,撢去化妝品上的灰塵,在 2021 年於前方招手之際,準備走向戶外,也重新開始尋找適合自己的妝容。

音樂人海爾希(Halsey)的美妝品牌 About-Face 於 2021 年 1 月推出,為的是要擁護「每個人身上的不同面貌以及各種表達自我的方式」。

Byredo 在 2020 年 10 月首次推出美妝產品,他們不循規蹈矩的風格、萬用的彩妝盤、獨特的包裝,都讓美妝愛好者大為振奮。這是這家香氛品牌第一次推出彩妝產品,他們和前衛彩妝師馥蘭琪(Isamaya Ffrench)合作。「我們想要做的是萬用的產品,可以用各種方式疊擦,因為我不想告訴別人要怎麼化妝,我想做的是啟發他們。」馥蘭琪如此說道。

Left: About Face by Halsey
Right: Byredo Makeup. Photography by Daniel Sannwald.
Image courtesy of Byredo

美容

"
幸福感從來沒有以如此具有想像力、獨特又創新的方式來呈現。
"

Haus Laboratories 推出了吸睛的彩妝系列、帶有光澤感的霧面和亮面彩妝、大膽的眼線產品⋯⋯精準地呈現出創辦人女神卡卡（Lady Gaga）的怪誕美妝。Haus Laboratories 一系列的四合一眼影盤於 2020 年 11 月上架，請來酷兒藝術家 ChrisSoFly22 和美妝網紅 Biddy 分別示範特色妝容。彩妝本身也越來越有實驗精神，以報導邊緣次文化為主的雜誌《Dazed Digital》，在 2020 年 6 月成立了美妝俱樂部 Dazed Beauty Club，讓成員能夠獨家體驗「亂無章法的另類妝容」。

是什麼造就了這種讓人興奮的實驗風格呢？專家把這種現象歸因於心理健康。加拿大戴爾豪斯大學（Dalhousie University）的精神科醫師策蘭（Patricia Celan）博士對美妝雜誌《Dazed Beauty》說道：「上妝是一種自我關懷（self-care）的方式。」而對某些人來說，隔離政策也讓彩妝有了新的面貌，在 2020 年 4 月號的《Vogue》雜誌中，資深時尚專欄作家歐可娃都（Janelle Okwodu）如此描述她新發現的美妝風潮：「以前化妝是為了增加自信，但如果還可以更好的話，為什麼不去試試呢？」她也因此展開了「高調戲劇美妝」和「新奇改造」旅程。

值得關注的原因：
幸福感從來沒有以如此具有想像力、獨特又創新的方式來呈現。一整年的壓抑讓創意在此刻爆發，實驗型美妝攻占社群媒體與個人媒體資料庫，也啟發美妝品牌推出更萬用的商品。

Dazed Beauty Club.
Photography by Till Janz, styling by Georgia Pendlebury, hair by Jose Quijano, makeup by Georgina Graham

52

野摘原料

這是保養品成分的標籤，還是本地料理的菜單？
全新美妝品牌使用了野外摘採的原料，讓人難以
分辨產品種類。

Alpyn Beauty 於 2020 年 2 月在絲芙蘭（Sephora）上架，他們
在面膜和保濕產品中加入了種植於山區的越橘莓（huckleberry）
和 北 美 野 櫻（chokecherry）。創 辦 人 芭 特 勒（Kendra Kolb
Butler）在紐約住了 20 年，服務於不同的美妝品牌，包括克蘭詩
（Clarins）和 Dr Dennis Gross；後來芭特勒搬到懷俄明州，受
到山區野生生物堅韌的生命力啟發，因而創立了自有品牌 Alpyn
Beauty。「有一天我坐在後院，望向後面的大提頓國家公園
（Grand Teton National Park）。我看了看那些野花，他們的尺
寸都像侏羅紀公園裡走出來的花一樣。於是我就想，在這種氣
候環境下，我的皮膚都快從臉上剝落了，為什麼這些植物能在這
裡長得這麼繁盛？」芭特勒對《金融時報》（Financial Times）如
此說道。

她的觀察非常敏銳。《金融時報》引用了城市生態系統（Urban
Ecosystems）的研究並提筆寫道，相對於人為種植的植物來說，
野生植物必須適應當地的環境，所以都能堅韌不拔又能吸收飽滿
的營養，這也讓它們成為保養品的強效配方。

以北威爾斯為基地的保養品牌 Wild Beauty 於 2020 年上市，他們從創辦人紐伯勒勳爵（Lord Newborough）的莊園中，採集了蓁麻葉和漢菈魚腥草當作原料。紐伯勒勳爵告訴《金融時報》：「多年來，我們的採集專家理查（Richard）一直親手採集各種野生植物，供應給大廚使用。我跟他聊天的時候常常聽他說到這些植物對皮膚有多好。」

Furtuna Skin 從西西里私人農莊採集原料來製作保養品，這座農莊通過有機認證，400 多年來都未有耕種活動。當地的火山土經由飽含礦物成分的水源灌溉，讓植物能從中吸取飽滿的養分。根據雜誌《女裝日報》（WWD）報導，該品牌 2020 年的每月營收都有一成的漲幅，他們也預計於 2021 年 3 月推出眼霜產品。

採集大量原料需要很多的耐心，因為野生植物順應的是自然的規則。Furtuna Skin 的創辦人金·沃爾斯（Kim Walls）告訴《Allure》：「我們在花瓣掉落前就先蒐集花瓣，在種子枯死前就先去採集種子，一切都是依循四季的變化來進行；植物在不同的時節裡會有不同的部分可供採收。」

值得關注的原因：

不只餐飲業愛好鮮採野摘的原物料，美妝產業也開始運用這些極具效力的植物，來為熱衷保養的群眾提供有效的產品；他們同時也讓消費者看見了大自然的智慧。「這些植物都經過了時間的淬煉。」沃爾斯如此說道。

53
科研品牌

獲得科學研究背書的美妝品牌，
其產品需求量正在增加。

研究中心皮尤研究中心（Pew Research Center）的研究發現，89% 的美國人相信醫學研究會以全人類的福祉為優先考量，美妝品牌也開始徵招醫學專家，並主打產品經科學實驗認證的功效。

美妝品牌 Atolla 的創辦人當中包含兩位曾就讀麻省理工學院的學生，2020 年 7 月，他們在種子輪投資中募到 250 萬美元的資金。《女裝日報》（WWD）在報導中引用了創辦人荷許（Ranella Hirsch）的發言，她說這家以科學為導向的公司在疫情期間的消費人數增加，2020 年上半年的每月營收也成長了五倍。

保養品牌奧古斯汀・巴德（Augustinus Bader）以調製品牌保養配方的幹細胞生醫科學家巴德為名，在 2020 年 5 月，他們推出高分子護手霜，幫助擊退過度清潔造成的乾燥現象。該品牌的專利配方 TFC8 以胺基酸、維他命調和而成，並另外加入了以合成技術製成的類天然肌膚分子。

延續美妝產業的「智慧肌膚」風潮，保養愛好者也成了科學領域的專家，研發效果精準的技術產品，其中包括獲得諾貝爾化學獎的佛瑞塞‧史多達爾（Fraser Stoddart），他研發了一系列的抗老產品。

趨勢預測公司沃斯全球時尚網（WGSN）的美妝部門主管密德頓（Jenni Middleton）向《VOGUE》表示：「消費者想要的是功效獲得證實的產品，在疫情後，我們會看更多品牌獲得臨床實驗認證。另外，眼前的危機也讓消費者開始習慣聽取醫學專家的建議，並且更加信任他們。」

值得關注的原因：

對健康的高度重視改變了消費者的習慣，現在消費者追尋的是獲得科學認證的美妝產品，因此接下來可以看到更多強調「科學實驗背書」的產品。

54
三款熱門美妝成分

三款美妝產業值得期待的熱門保養成分。

葡萄

葡萄籽、葡萄皮和葡萄葉都含有某些世界頂尖的抗氧化成分,在葡萄酒商間接催生了越來越多的相關產品後,這些釀酒後用不到的原料,現在也被用來製作美妝保養品。2020 年 10 月,永續肌膚保養品牌 Circumference 推出第一款保濕產品,產品主要使用釀酒時剩下的葡萄葉製成,原料是和家族產業型的葡萄莊園暨酒廠 Bedell Cellars 合作取得。

廣受推崇的 Vintner's Daughter 由加州葡萄莊園主人的女兒佳吉蘿(April Gargiulo)成立,他們在 2014 年推出當前知名的葡萄籽美容油以後,又在 2019 年接著推出第二款產品「活性精華素」(Active Treatment Essence)。佳吉蘿告訴《金融時報》(Financial Times),在製作產品時,他們使用的是「頂級釀酒原則所使用的工藝技術和優良品質」。

補骨脂酚（Bakuchiol）

這款全天然純素成分是視黃醇（Retinol）的替代品，現在也躍上了保養品櫃位。補骨脂酚具有抗氧化、抗發炎、抗菌的特性，因而成為敏感肌族群漸趨熱愛的品項。荷爾蒙肌膚保養品牌 Dr. Zenovia 生產了補骨脂酚保濕潔面乳，並於 2020 年 10 月起在絲芙蘭（Sephora）上架。美妝品牌 PSA 於同年 11 月推出，可以從購物網站 ASOS 或其他平台購買，他們的產品也包含以補骨脂酚與玫瑰果製成的美容油。

牛舌草（Anchusa azurea）

這種亮紫色的野花受到保養品牌 Furtuna Skin 採用，因而成為目光焦點。牛舌草富含維他命 C、E、脂肪酸，因為飽含抗氧化劑所以成為相當有潛力的保養成分。Furtuna Skin 的創辦人金·沃爾斯（Kim Walls）告訴《華爾街日報》（The Wall Street Journal），「牛舌草修復肌膚的功效遠遠被低估了」，而且因為它是野生摘採的植物，所以會從飽含礦物質的土壤中吸取滿滿的營養成分（詳見第 52 章〈野摘原料〉）。

55

多元交織型美妝

在多元文化、平權價值與多元交織型女性主義上，
由女性發起的品牌可以讓大家看到美妝產業必須
要做，而且可以做得更好的面向。

與這個議題相關的討論已經滲透到許多領域當中，從科技領域
到時尚圈，現在再到美妝產業；其中，獨立品牌在多元交織型美
妝領域領先群雄。「以文化為優先考量」的美妝賣場 Geenie 由
夏那·吉內爾·尤因（Chana Ginelle Ewing）創立，該平台合作的
對象多為名氣不足且店主來自多元文化背景的品牌，平台上供應
的產品也會以平權價值為考量。

「我認為自己是文化企業家，我的任務是思考多元交織型的世界
會是什麼樣貌，然後想想該怎麼為這樣的世界提供平台。」伊雯
告訴偉門智威智庫。Greenie 販售的品牌包含支持 LGBTQ+ 團
體的品牌 We Are Fluide，還有原住民品牌 Prados Beauty。伊
雯說道：「我不覺得多元交織型美妝是一種潮流，追求真實是行
銷產業長期以來使用的策略之一，現在也終於成真了。」

位於多倫多的 Yard & Parish 是一個黑人女性所創辦的線上合作社，推廣專為女性有色人種設計的的獨立生活品牌，他們的網站於 2019 年創立，供應美妝、時尚、家居用品，並自稱為「環保奢華的黑人品牌集散地」。

Uoma Beauty 創辦人茱德（Sharon Chuter）對黑人在職場受到的待遇深感不滿，要求企業開誠布公。她在 2020 年 6 月 3 日發起「# 檢查或閉上嘴」（#PullUpOrShutUp）的活動，希望邀請美妝品牌在 72 小時內檢視並公開企業內部的黑人僱員比例。活動開始後的 24 小時內，已經有許多品牌公開內部數據，並承認他們還可以做得更好。這個活動也引發了更大規模的關注，鼓勵大家為世界各地黑人的經濟狀況奮起行動。

諾德斯特龍百貨公司（Nordstrom）和絲芙蘭（Sephora）相繼宣布，他們會在架上為平權品牌保留更多櫃位。《TEEN VOGUE》則開啟了每月專欄，專門介紹黑人成立的美妝品牌，專欄名稱為「黑即是美」（Black is Beautiful）；黑人專用防曬品牌 Black Girl Sunscreen 的創辦人蘭蒂（Shontay Lundy）以及 Golde 的創辦人沃芙德（Trinity Mouzon Wofford）也都曾出現在專欄中。

值得關注的原因：

政治取向的消費者和多元交織型女性主義的追隨者，都在高調檢視黑人受僱率不足的議題，也對美妝品牌大聲疾呼。對品牌、零售商、出版社來說，回應多元交織議題非常重要，如此才能在消費者心中佔有一席之地。伊雯說道：「我認為消費激進主義會加速演化，大眾會持續以經濟能力來對產業及品牌施壓。」

Jeln wellness products, founded by Crystal Rowe, sold on Yard & Parish

美容

56

高級護髮產品

越來越多消費者不再使用普通的洗髮產品。

消費者開始選擇含有特殊配方且廣獲好評的護髮產品，這些配方除了能維持頭皮健康，也使用了與肌膚保養品類似的成分。

頂級護髮市場逐漸成長，《女裝日報》（WWD）報導了調查機構 NPD 集團的研究，其中廣獲好評的護髮產品在 2020 年第一季成長了 13%，這類護髮品也是美妝類別裡成長最快的品項之一。雖然 NPD 集團的數據顯示，在 2020 年艱困的第二季裡，整體美妝市場表現下降了 10%，但《Happi》雜誌也報導到髮膜和護髮品逆向成長了 30%。

不少評價高的肌膚保養品牌為了提升消費者的關注度，也開始開發這類產品，熱門的肌膚保養品牌 Drunk Elephant 在 2020 年春季推出護髮產品，其中包含頭皮磨砂膏 TLC Happi Scalp Scrub，內含植物油和果酸成分，可以溶解老廢角質和其他堆積在頭皮上的髮類產品，據該品牌所說，這款磨砂膏可以滋潤頭皮、平衡皮脂。同樣在 2020 年春季，史特姆（Barbara Sturm）博士為自有品牌推出頭皮精華 Scalp Serum，內含玻尿酸和馬齒

莧，可改善頭皮健康，因而改善髮絲狀況。就連近年進軍美妝市場的大麻二酚也開始出現在高級護髮品中。2020 年 3 月，R&Co 推出大麻二酚洗護產品系列 Super Garden，依該品牌的說法，大麻二酚可以舒緩頭皮發炎與不適。

R&Co 的創辦人霍華德·麥拉倫（Howard McLaren）告訴雜誌《Glossy》，「過去幾年來，大家開始花大錢在肌膚保養品上」，但是大家使用的護髮品，等級還是跟洗碗精差不多。他接著說到，「千禧世代開始讓品牌知道他們想要的是什麼，也願意更深入研究他們需要的護膚、護髮產品成分，這其實就是教育的成果。」

值得關注的原因：

護髮開始變得像護膚一樣重要了。消費者開始發現評價高的護髮品含有優質成分，所以護髮產品在後新冠肺炎（COVID-19）時代可能會加速成長。據調查公司 Grand View Research 的報導，2019 年高級護髮品的市場價值為 199.5 億美元，他們也預測 2020 到 2027 年間，這類產品的年複合成長率會達到 5.9%。

Left: Scalp Serum by Dr Barbara Sturm
Right: Super Garden by R&Co

美容

ck is a testing facility
open to everyone.

ces provided by Gabisa Medical, PLLC

schedule an appointment.

ENTER

健康照護＝自我照護

美容相關服務與自我照護習慣都在進化，兩者都將
健康照護納爲一環，以提高個人防護力。

自我照護這項模糊的概念，一直都被歸納在心理健康與外在美貌
兩種層面中，但現在又延伸到身體健康的領域。

水療中心不再只提供精心護理，還加入了新冠肺炎（COVID-19）
檢測服務。2020 年 5 月底，連鎖機場水療中心 XpresSpa 的服
務項目原本只包含上機前的按摩、指甲護理等等，現在他們則推
出新品牌 XpresCheck，在機場內針對新冠肺炎提供快篩鼻咽拭
子以及血清抗體快篩服務。該品牌在紐約甘迺迪國際機場初步測
試這項服務後，又迅速推廣至全美各地，其中也包含 2020 年 11
月於鳳凰城天港國際機場開張的分店。

除了休息和放鬆，西班牙的健康診所 Sha Wellness Clinic 還免
費為顧客提供新冠肺炎抗體篩檢服務，讓他們可以放下心中的大
石。2020 年 5 月底，倫敦藝文俱樂部（Arts Club）內建的奢華水
療健身會館 Lanserhof 也開始提供新冠肺炎抗體篩檢服務。

"
自我照護已經有了新的定義，接下來可以看到更多美妝、心理、醫學領域的跨界合作。
"

高端美妝品牌也在產品線中加入具有芳療功效的乾洗手產品，讓清潔衛生成為具有儀式感的活動。2020 年 5 月，獨立美妝品牌 Curie 首次推出乾洗手商品，並接著在同年 11 月於諾德斯特龍百貨公司（Nordstrom）上架同款香氛，包含經典葡萄柚香、白茶花香和橙花油香氣。高檔沐浴品牌 Noble Isle 的產品在奢華的塞爾福里奇百貨公司（Selfridges）和福南梅森百貨（Fortnum & Mason）上架，他們於 2020 年 8 月推出兩款乾洗手，其中一款富含野生海蓬子和墨角藻，帶有百里香、檸檬、杜松子的香氣，另一款則帶有大黃、杜松漿果、迷迭香味。2020 年 4 月，頂級香氛品牌 DS & Durga 推出融入品牌熱門香氣「雨後草原」（Big Sur after Rain）的乾洗手，裡面帶有嫩芽、木質調、尤加利的香味。

值得關注的原因：
自我照護已經有了新的定義，隨著乾洗手或其他新冠肺炎防護產品成為自我照護重要的一環，接下來可以看到更多美妝、心理和醫學領域的跨界合作。

58
保養網紅

新世代網紅讓肌膚保養體驗煥然一新。

大眾對保養品的關注度上升，有部分是因為 TikTok 和 YouTube 上新崛起的「保養網紅」，他們除了推薦產品，也提供產品使用教學。雜誌《Glossy》的資深美妝與心理健康記者芙蘿拉（Liz Flora）告訴偉門智威智庫：「Z 世代轉向 TikTok 保養網紅尋求產品建議，因為他們重視真實的使用心得。像是海蘭·雅柏（Hyram Yarbro）這類的保養網紅之所以成名，就是因為他們會推薦自己熱愛的產品，同時會直接批評他們不喜歡的產品。真誠讓他們在廠商贊助的紅海下成為網紅領域的權威，尤其現在 Z 世代對贊助內容（sponcon）的雷達又特別敏銳。」

TikTok 因為內容短，有著無厘頭的創意美學，以及大量的 Z 世代用戶，所以成為保養網紅愛用的工具，像是雅柏的 TikTok 帳號「Skincare by Hyram」在疫情剛爆發時原本只有 10 萬名追蹤者，但在 2020 年 9 月時已經暴增到 600 萬個追蹤；《紐約時報》

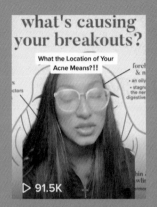

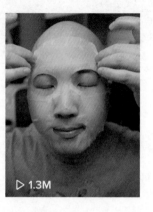

（The New York Times）當月的人物報導也包含這位 24 歲網紅的介紹文章，標題是「可以成就或毀滅一個保養品牌的內容創作者」。雅柏在產品心得中以強硬的標準看待大品牌的產品，而且他也不怕批評美妝聖品。

雅柏不是唯一一個這樣做的人，住在加拿大安大略省的 17 歲網紅凱蒂雅（Katya-Niomi Henry，帳號為 @kaytyaniomi）也是新崛起的保養網紅，在 TikTok 上有 14 萬名追蹤者。凱蒂雅讓她的粉絲不用為宣稱神奇功效的精華花太多冤枉錢，她開箱熱門開價品牌的產品成分，而且都是在好市多或沃爾瑪（Walmart）這類超市就能買到的品牌。前美妝業代劉容碩（音譯自 Young-Seok Yuh）因為真誠又幽默地分享肌膚保養知識和產品功效，所以在 TikTok 上累積超過 100 萬名粉絲，他告訴他的粉絲：「我沒有套用濾鏡。」

無論是向揭開美妝產業面紗的年輕消費者靠攏，或者和他們合作，對保養公司來說都很值回票價。據《衛報》（The Guardian）報導，Traackr 發現肌膚保養品牌適樂膚（CeraVe）在 2020 年的網紅推薦數成長了 67%，整體銷量也因此大幅提升。

值得關注的原因：

無論是歷史悠久的保養品牌抑或是後起新秀，化妝品牌需要讓更聰明且更謹慎的 Z 世代消費者感到驚艷，這個消費族群在簡短的影片當中，尋求的不再只是娛樂，他們還想要獲得正確的知識。

59
大膽的眉妝

由於現在很多國家都建議或要求民眾戴口罩，於是
彩妝師和美妝網紅把妝容重點放到眼睛上，
眉毛尤其成爲焦點。

根據 NPD 集團的調查發現，美國評價優良的眉彩產品在 2020
年 5、6 月間，銷量上升了 8%，主要原因是大家「廣泛地使用
口罩」。

2020 年 10 月，舒適牌（Schick）為宣傳舒綺（Hydro Silk）美型
刀，請來演員麥蒂森·貝利（Madison Bailey）在 Instagram 上
說明戴口罩時如何用眼妝展現自我。舒綺的品牌經理梅麗莎·蘿
西（Melissa Rossi）告訴《廣告周刊》（Adweek）：「很多女性開
始尋找可以凸顯口罩妝容的眼彩和眉彩產品。眉毛現在取代了嘴
唇的地位。」

這股趨勢也出現在伸展台上，在 2021 春夏發表的系列中，知名
彩妝師帕特·麥葛絲（Pat McGrath）為 Miu Miu 打造眉妝，她
在模特兒的眉毛上剃出精緻的線條來展現造型，而彼得·飛利浦
（Peter Philips）也為 Acne Studios 打造 90 年代的特色眉妝。

當季不少搶眼眉妝都是出自彩妝師果葛娜(Inge Grognard)之手，在德賴斯・范諾頓(Dries Van Noten)的秀場中，她在模特兒的眼睛和眉毛上方塗抹橘色色粉，並為 Blumarine 創造超自然野性眉妝。

名人和網紅也在實驗新的眉妝造型。身兼演員、導演、製作人的麥可娜・柯爾(Michaela Coel)在倫敦進行《GQ》英雄系列演講時，利用粉色眉彩來搭配髮型。譚雅・康佩斯(Tanya Compas)是倫敦青年工作者兼 LGBT 權利倡議家，她的眉妝用色多元，粉紅色、綠色、銀色等都包含在內。貝玲妃(Benefit Cosmetics)的全球眉彩專家貝里(Jared Bailey)在 2020 年 5 月時告訴《衛報》(The Guardian)：「為眉毛上色是最快也最簡單的方法，可以馬上讓你的妝容煥然一新，也更有整體感。眉彩產品現在已經取代口紅了。」

值得關注的原因：

眉毛現在取代了嘴唇的地位。搶眼的眉妝是目前彩妝師和網紅選擇的妝容重點，他們全新一季的彩妝風格會以眼妝來形塑。

#THELOOK ON @chrissy_woest, FEAT. #SkinFetish Sublime Skin Highlighter ⚡⚡💙 #makeupbypatmcgrath #patmcgrath

Left: Tanya Compas. Image courtesy of Instagram
Right: Backstage at Miu Miu SS21. Image courtesy of Instagram via Pat McGrath

60

零浪費美妝

你的垃圾可能是別人的……洗面乳？

美妝產業為環境採取行動並不新奇。宣導零浪費概念的「零廢物周」(Zero Waste Week) 在 2018 年的調查數據 (到今天還是有人引用) 顯示，全球每年製造的化妝品包裝數量超過 1,200 億個，且多數是不能回收的包材。在那之後崛起的小眾美妝品牌紛紛採取了更符合永續原則的做法來製造產品和包裝；現在，我們也在美妝產業中看到更大的推力，且有更多大品牌開始加入這個行列。

在英國發聲的品牌是 UpCircle Beauty，他們是永續美妝品牌的主力，該公司重新處理廢棄物，使其成為重要的美妝原料。UpCircle 的身體磨砂膏是他們最有名的產品之一，該產品使用的是倫敦咖啡廳不要的咖啡渣，再另外加入其他原料做成去角質成分。2020 年 9 月，該品牌把不要的海棗籽磨成粉末，做成新款身體乳液，可以減少發炎並讓肌膚更光滑。

在澳洲，美體小舖 (The Body Shop) 是最會善用格外品的品牌。2020 年 10 月，該公司推出的全新系列產品便是使用表皮腫脹的

檸檬和長歪的小黃瓜製作而成,這些都是超市不賣的「醜蔬果」。2019 年,該品牌也在英國推出類似的產品,使用的原料是別人不要的胡蘿蔔;同年 10 月,他們也為減少環境衝擊而停止生產卸妝棉。

Beauty Kitchen 讓購買美妝及個人護理用品的行為能更符合永續價值,2020 年 10 月,該品牌與聯合利華(Unilever)合作,在英格蘭里茲的阿斯達(Asda)超市推出「回收」、「填充」、「重複使用」環保站,聯合利華旗下的 Radox 沐浴膠、Simple 洗手乳、

Alberto Balsam 洗髮乳等產品,皆可以使用過的鋁罐或不鏽鋼瓶填充購買。Beauty Kitchen 表示,他們會在 2021 年推出更多商品填充站。

值得關注的原因:

零廢料運動不只與包裝有關,現在還延伸到產品配方上,因為永續價值對美妝消費者來說是一項非常重要的因素。

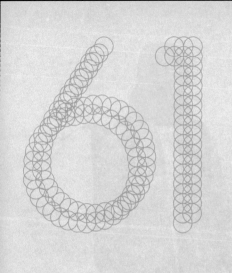

61

零售

70

61

逸境零售

虛擬衣櫃和奇幻背景激發了消費者的想像，也化解了零售業的實體疆界。

數位時尚和虛擬空間都變得更加夢幻，把消費者引領至幻境般的烏托邦。Extra Terrestrial Studio 的創辦人凱特·瑪蒂格（Kate Machitiger）告訴偉門智威智庫：「這是對 Airbnb 風格追求極簡、乾淨、時尚的反動，是一股想要回歸極致工藝的傻勁。」

2020 年 3 月，上海數位平台 Xcommons 和商家 ICY 合作，推出虛擬時裝秀。他們為新興設計師特製的沉浸式 3D 展示台讓觀眾有如置身平行宇宙，眼前所見是粉紅色的穴居房型，以及鼠尾草綠的蜿蜒小徑。

虛擬時尚品牌 The Fabricant 製作了只能在數位世界中穿戴的獨特設計款服飾。他們使用 3D 建模軟體，細膩地為顧客的虛擬角色創造服飾，讓顧客可以在社群媒體或線上遊戲等數位環境中穿搭。該品牌在各種夢幻的場景中推出作品，包括粉色沙漠和星際幻界，展現了該公司的幻想奇境工藝，而該公司的詢問度在疫情期間也顯著上升。

該品牌的共同創辦人史露檀（Amber Jae Slooten）在 2020 年10 月時告訴設計雜誌《Dezeen》：「我這輩子從來沒有幫那麼多人打扮過。」

零售

> **"**
> 這些烏托邦式的虛擬空間填補了大眾的想像，
> 也顯示出大家想離開一成不變的場景——
> 不管這些場景是真是假。
> **"**
>
> 數位設計師，夏洛克·泰勒（Charlotte Taylor）

+ WUNDERMAN
THOMPSON　Reisinger Studio

風格奇幻的數位設計品除了出現在時尚品牌的秀場中，在室內設計領域也漸趨熱門，這也指出未來的數位格式會與各類數位商家相容。

數位設計師夏洛特·泰勒（Charlotte Taylor）和一群 3D 藝術家合作，創作出柔和、烏托邦式的虛擬空間，例如有著極簡家具和家飾品的別墅。Reisinger Studio 為其作《北面陽台》（Terrace North）創作了風格古怪的戶外建築，建築體沐浴在丁香花下，還有金屬色的枕頭形物體，以及現代風格的壓克力躺椅。在《崖邊小屋》（House by the Cliff）這件作品中，跨界設計師吉亞柯梅利（Stefano Giacomello）創作了結構式客廳，裡面裝有管狀家具，搭建在鋸齒狀的岩石表面上。Loftgarten 創意總監保羅·米利斯基（Paul Milinski）在他的《夢境》（Dreamscape）系列作品中，設計了一系列風格脫俗的虛擬空間，包括明亮、充滿空氣感的〈工作派對空間〉（Work Party），裡面有著下嵌式的鮭魚粉色沙發，還有擺滿巨型圓球的籠子。

這些空間是「為引領觀眾穿越到以想像力所描繪的未來場景而設計的，讓人屏息的同時又可以帶著觀眾逃離眼前的世界。」米利斯基對《Designboom》如此說道。

值得關注的原因：

泰勒對《Dezeen》表示：「對逃離的渴望從未如此高漲，這些烏托邦式的虛擬空間填補了大眾的想像，也顯示出大家想離開一成不變的場景——不管這些場景是真是假。」這樣的渴望也引發進一步的轉變。過去幾年，實體零售商店裡的沉浸式環境與實驗型空間數量上升，這樣的趨勢現在也出現在數位世界中；不管是真實世界還是虛擬宇宙，店家已不再只是單純販售商品的地方，店內空間本身就是一種體驗，能為大眾提供風格奇幻、充滿想像的逃離逸境。

61

Left: Borders. Image courtesy of Loftgarten and Paul ......ski
Right: Work Party. Image courtesy of Loftgarten and ...... Milinski

62
瓦解經銷模式

汽車產業出現了一波破壞傳統經銷模式的風潮，
為的是回應客戶不停演變的需求。

世界各地的汽車展售間在 2020 年間的來客量都呈現下滑的跡象，
創新企業於是開始重新設計購車體驗。

2020 年 10 月，澳洲福斯（Volkswagen）導入了「福斯微型展售
方案」（Volkswagen Smallest Dealership），協助顧客在線上
購買並客製愛車；由於福斯發現線上購車的人數增加，於是決定
打造獨特的擴增實境購車體驗，推出 28 公分高的展售間微縮模
型，成為主要的虛擬展示空間，讓顧客可以在不同的情境中賞車、
開關車門、在室內空間走動，甚至可以直接在線上購車，所有流
程僅需一支手機就能搞定。

福特（Ford）把經銷服務帶到客戶的私人車道內。在美國，2020
年 8 月時福特公司推出「擴增實境車道展售體驗」（Driveway
Dealership AR），推廣 2021 新上市的 F-150 皮卡車；使用者可
以查看車輛的內裝、外型，也可以看到該車款停在自己車庫內的
模樣。

到汽車展售中心看車的好處是可以直接在現場提問，所以 Kia 決定把這些服務搬到線上，在 2020 年 7 月於中東和非洲市場推出「直播展售間」（Live Stream Showroom），客製化的虛擬賞車體驗與隨傳隨到的展示服務在卡達、沙烏地阿拉伯、巴基斯坦、科威特、巴林、南非相繼推出。

領克汽車（Lynk & Co）完全捨棄了傳統經銷策略，他們的第一個實體空間「阿姆斯特丹俱樂部」不像汽車展示中心，反倒像是會員俱樂部，此外他們也提出全新的汽車所有權概念。領克汽車由吉利汽車（Geely）與富豪汽車（Volvo）合作成立，旗下第一款車「01」（有混合動力跨界休旅車以及插電式混合動力車兩種版本）

會在 2021 年上市。領克汽車的會員可以選擇完全持有車輛或者加入共享出租計畫，讓開車成為更環保的選項；此外，他們還為出借、租用車輛的雙方提供簡單的方案，只要利用應用程式或車內面板就能輕鬆移交車輛。

值得關注的原因：

汽車經銷和其他許多產業一樣，受疫情影響而加速互動式數位轉型。由於顧客期待更順暢的購車體驗和更彈性的租車服務，車商開始大幅改變傳統的展售方式。

63

黑暗商店

實體零售店面開始出現新的型態—無顧客商店

2020 年以來，零售商的業績轉移到線上商城。據英國國家統計局報導，2020 年 5 月，網購銷量佔了全英國零售業的 32.8%，比同年 2 月增長許多（當時只有 19%）。美國人口普查局於 2020 年 11 月估計，國內電子商務在 2020 年第二季的表現比第一季增長了 31.9%，市值上漲至 2,115 億美元；與去年同期相比更是上漲了 44.5%。

為了回應這股趨勢，零售商選擇以「黑暗商店」（dark store）的形式來為網路訂單供貨。2020 年 9 月，全食超市（Whole Foods Market）在紐約市開了一家不對外開放的商店，這是該公司第一間網路限定的店面，專為線上訂單供貨或提供到店取貨服務；店裡看不到自助沙拉吧、咖啡櫃檯、吸睛的展示品，只有為了保存新鮮農作物而設計的長型走道、大冷凍櫃、冷藏冰箱。這家亞馬遜（Amazon）旗下的超市也接著將他們位於舊金山的店面改為半黑暗式店面，在下午時段不對外開放。

克羅格（Kroger）和巨鷹（Giant Eagle）等其他連鎖超市也在實驗「取貨限定」的門市，而梅西百貨公司（Macy's）則在 2020 聖誕期間將旗下兩家實體百貨公司轉型為黑暗商店，為線上訂單增添出貨人手。

沃爾瑪超市（Walmart）則將位於美國的四家實體店改成「電子商務實驗室」，用以測試不同的數位專案。2020 年 11 月，該超市宣布要將旗下 42 間原本為店面配貨的區域配送中心，轉型為網購專用的快閃配貨中心，以應付年假期間的網路訂單。

MHE 零售顧問公司（MHE Retail）的執行長喬治·瓦勒斯（George Wallace）表示，零售店家「尋求其他商業方案是正確的做法，如果可以重新分配某些店面空間，把它們當成迷你倉庫，讓顧客可以在線上下單、來店取貨或退貨，這樣就能讓你的線上商店升級。」

但瓦勒斯也提出警告，很多老牌零售商都把這些商業策略視為「短期解決方案」，藉此回應實體店面在人流減少後面臨的供給過剩問題。「20 年前，店面是越多越好，但這也為現今的企業留下一批負面資產。新冠肺炎（COVID-19）是有加劇了這個問題沒錯，但這些問題其實本來就存在了。店面應該要減少，要夠特別，也不要太大，這是未來也不會改變的。」

值得關注的原因：

隨著零售商開始調整體質、迎接電子商務時代，庫存和供貨於是成為焦點。他們將實體店面轉型，以鞏固實體業務和網購商機的共生關係。

> ❝
> 20年前，
> 店面是越多越好，
> 但這也爲現今的企業
> 留下一批負面資產。
> ❞
>
> MHE零售顧問公司執行長
> 喬治·瓦勒斯（George Wallace）

64

重置零售體驗

疫情會如何推動零售體驗的演進呢？

雖然 2021 年有望鬆綁新冠肺炎（COVID-19）的疫情限制並回歸正常社交生活，但消費者和零售商還是會盡量減少人與人之間互相接觸、親密互動的機會。店家若要吸引消費者從網路商城流向實體店面，就必須高度重視衛生標準，而這項準則也和「創造有影響力的空間」這樣的趨勢吻合。

「線上管道可以提供的東西有限」，設計工作室 Extra Terrestrial Studio 的創辦人凱特・瑪蒂格（Kate Machitiger）如此說道。這家設計工作室打造了超現實的「『深度空間』，可以連結探索和玩樂」，其創辦人也進一步表示，直接和產品互動對很多人來說是無可取代的體驗：「隨著遠距工作模式持續進行中，原本夾在工作和生活中間的『第三空間』會成為『第二空間』，可以帶人逃離混雜工作和生活的單調環境。」

+ WUNDERMAN THOMPSON   Project Earth by Selfridges. Image courtesy of Selfridges

2020 年 9 月新推出的 MAC 創新美妝概念實驗室整合了無數種的零接觸元素，且早在疫情開始以前，該公司就已擬定這項計畫，地點就定在紐約的皇后購物中心（Queens Center）內。他們規劃了「當實體遇上數位」專區，讓顧客可以在店內以虛擬的方式試用產品或套用當地彩妝師創作的妝容；想要找出完美底妝的顧客也可以使用紅外線觸控螢幕來挑選適合的底妝色號。

因應疫情，倫敦的塞爾福里奇百貨（Selfridges）在 2020 年 8 月公告了一項為期五年的環保永續計畫，名為「地球專案」（Project Earth），計畫中整合了永續原料的使用、提倡消費活動中的循環價值（例如修理、再售、租用商品）、也將長壽納為企業核心價值。塞爾福里奇百貨的集團董事長阿蘭娜・韋斯頓（Alannah Weston）表示：「受到全球疫情影響，我們開始了解到我們的系統有多脆弱、多複雜，但這也讓我們看到，如果我們能為同樣的目標採取集體行動，就能為我們自己和地球帶來什麼樣的好處。」

瑪蒂格提到未來的店面設計時說道：「雖然我們不能親手摸到店家的牆面，但我們可以打造出有重力和物質的空間，讓人產生強烈的感受，這些感受可能是興奮，也可能是平靜。」她也解釋，新型的零售體驗會更加重畫面、聲響、氣味，例如使用材質來傳遞觸覺感受，運用聲音來創造逃離或臨場感，或用氣味提示所在空間為何。「我認為大家有點過度依靠群眾創造出來的活絡氣氛了，我期待可以看到品牌將重心放在個人專屬的時刻上，而不是聚焦在熱烈的團體氣氛上。不管是遺世的桃花源還是沉浸式視覺體驗，只要設計出最好的體驗模式，就能帶來力量。」

值得關注的原因：

新冠肺炎對實體零售業來說是一大打擊，但同時也讓大家清楚地看見實體購物體驗的力量。無論是透過個人化體驗、數位型元素，或者是獨特又能啟發人心的設計，零售產業需要讓實體零售體驗變得更加突出，同時又要守護消費者的健康安全。

直播商業模式

娛樂式零售轉向線上發展，為數位優先的消費者
提供客製的互動式消費體驗。

直播銷售模式結合了線上購物的簡便與資訊型廣告的戲劇效果，
主持人或網紅在直播影片中示範產品的使用方式，並且在線上和
觀眾即時互動，這樣的模式在亞洲市場已經風行多年了，現在，這
股潮流也開始在全球各地蓬勃發展。

這個產業的龍頭霸主是中國。在 2020 年的光棍購物節期間，淘
寶直播平台上播放了 30 個串流節目，每個節目都創造了 1,530 萬
美元以上的商品交易毛額。2020 年 5 月，在連續五天的勞工節
連假中，直播平台的銷量成長了四倍之多。中國網紅與企業在這
種新型購物模式中販售的商品五花八門，從門鈴到服飾再到美
妝，應有盡有。

直播銷售早已成為中國的主流模式，目前在西方國家也逐漸茁
壯。2020 年 6 月，加拿大串流影音網購平台 Livescale 宣布要
在北美地區與小型企業愛用的 Shopify 合作；雜誌《Glossy》
在 2020 年 7 月時報導，Livescale 自同年 3 月起的企業合作量

截至當時已增加了五倍，大型美妝企業也開始在上面販售商品：Urban Decay 的 美 國 網 站、NYX Professional Makeup、契 爾 氏（Kiehl's）、IT Cosmetics，以及熱門肌膚保養品牌 Shani Darden 等，都在 2020 年間初次嘗試在 Livescale 上直播銷貨。

Shani Darden 的資深行銷總監潔蔓（Crisanta German）對雜誌《Glossy》表示：「對美妝或色彩產業來說，直播會持續成長、再成長。在觀看別人的彩妝教學時可以直接和他們互動、提問，這是 YouTube 無法做到的。」

社群媒體也在擴增零售版圖，將直播購物功能整合至平台當中。臉書公司（Facebook）在 2020 年 5 月時推出線上商城 Facebook Shop 和 Instagram Shop，更在同年夏季為美國用戶開放直播購物功能。

值得關注的原因：

直播銷售模式正在和實體店家競爭，逐漸成長的直播模式也顯示出消費者的喜好。在實體店面中整合娛樂和消費的體驗依然是觀眾目前希望的服務方式，能與品牌大使和網紅互動則是更進階的品牌互動模式，也是消費者所熱愛、卻無法在實體店家中實現的品牌策略。

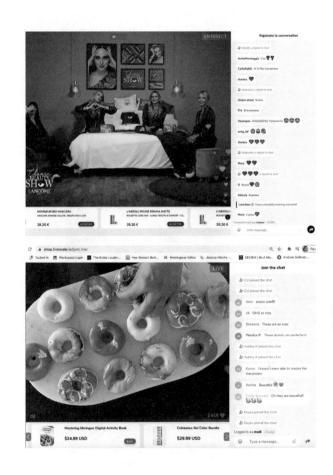

66 拿下物流生態圈

從食物到疫苗，宅配從「還不錯的服務」發展成「必要服務」，物流業可望持續成長。

過去一年間電子商務快速發展，讓大家看到以往不受重視卻相當重要的零售環節：物流服務。根據世界經濟論壇（World Economic Forum）的研究顯示，因應電商的需求成長，2030 年以前世界前百大城市的物流車數會增加 36%，送貨到府的需求更有 78% 的漲幅。

2021 年的美國消費電子用品展（CES）成為新型物流模式的展示場。威訊無線（Verizon）旗下的 Skyward 和 UPS Flight Forward 宣布要以無人機運送貨物。恆源汽車集團（Cenntro Automotive Group）也公開了電動車款 CityPorter，為城市提供宅配服務。通用汽車（General Motors）全力推出新型電動車商業物流方案 BrightDrop，希望藉由全新電動車款讓商業物流服務可以永續經營；聯邦快遞（FedEx Express）已經測試完 BrightDrop 的配送系統了，該公司也將於今年 BrightDrop 正式推出以後，成為他們的第一個客戶。

在通用汽車於美國消費電子用品展的發表會上，聯邦快遞的執行總裁理查·史密斯（Richard Smith）登台表示，疫情大幅加速了電商和宅配服務的發展。史密斯預測，這項業務還會持續成長，到 2023 年前，全美國每日運送到客戶門前的包裹量會成長到一億個，而這個數字原本是 2026 年的預估值。

其他電動車市場的競爭者也相繼在物流領域中投下資金。亞馬遜（Amazon）在 2020 年 10 月時高調發表了首款電動貨車，由加州新創公司 Rivian 協助打造而成，預計在 2021 年中開始商轉。英國公司 Arrival 在 2020 年 1 月時接到來自優比速（UPS）的訂單，要製造一萬台電動車，現代汽車（Hyundai）也有望為其投入 8,500 萬美元的資金來提升產量。2020 年 12 月，美國企業 Canoo 發表「全自動多功能貨車」，預計於 2023 年上市。

值得關注的原因：
由於商業物流蓬勃發展，許多企業紛紛為未來貨運生態系打造永續、高效、安全的服務，而這些公司之間的競爭，也正在白熱化。

抵制亞馬遜風潮

　　大眾對亞馬遜（Amazon）獨佔網購市場的反彈聲量越來越大，使得小型企業開始尋求替代方案。

IBM 表示，受疫情影響，企業的電商轉型之路提早了五年。其中，亞馬遜是最大的受益者之一，該公司 2020 年第二季的銷量與去年相比成長了 40%；於此同時，網路曝光度低的小型企業因為實體店面的客流量下滑，所以生意嚴重受創。

消費者對於亞馬遜主宰電商競技場的情況越來越反感，在 Instagram 和 推 特（Twitter）上，「#抵制亞馬遜」（#boycottamazon）甚至成為熱門標籤。為了藉機吸引這群對亞馬遜幻想破滅的消費者，網路曝光度不高的中小企業開始尋求新的合作平台，希望能夠開創新客源、新生意。

加拿大的跨國電商平台Shopify在 2020 年第二季的新用戶數量，比前一季增加了 71%。他們為各式零售商提供基礎工具，讓他們可以打造自己的線上商城、管理金流、使用禮品卡交易，若商家有需要，該平台也可協助配送。相對的，商家需支付月費以及成交

後的佣金。Shopify 也與信用卡公司 Visa 合作，為新創公司、企業家、中小企業提供免費試用方案，也為小型企業主提供網路開店的專業諮詢。

眼見在地零售業的業績衰退，新平台 DMS ShopHERE 於 2020 年 5 月在多倫多問世，他們與不同的夥伴合作，協助藝術家和小型企業提高線上曝光率，合作對象包含 Shopify、信用卡公司萬事達卡（Mastercard）、臉書（Facebook）、谷歌（Google），以及多倫多商業促進會（Toronto Association of Business improvement Areas）。

印度電商平台 Flipkart 在今年推出一項專案，協助在地小雜貨店（當地稱為「kiranas」）處理線上訂單。截至 2020 年 9 月，該平台已經協助印度全國 850 個城市裡超過 5 萬家的雜貨店成立線上商城。

值得關注的原因：

線上零售平台差異化的經營方向，為小型企業提供了出路。雖然亞馬遜這類的電商巨擘必定還是能從企業轉型至網購的趨勢中獲利，但中小企業與背後支撐他們的品牌也在變革的時代裡創新，並透過數位化的過程獲取利潤。隨著小型企業加入電商領域，消費者如果想從大品牌轉向支持在地商家，就能有更多的選擇。

"
線上零售平台差異化的經營方向，為小型企業提供了出路。
"

是網紅，也是網路店家

網紅進軍直播帶貨市場，走到哪、賣到哪，
而且還可以抽成。

截至 2021 年 1 月初，住在洛杉磯的內衣設計師阮氏（TyLynn Nguyen）在社群媒體上已經有超過 13 萬 6 千名粉絲。如果有任何一個粉絲想購買她在 Instagram 上穿著的風衣外套或是牛仔褲，他們可以直接點擊商品來購買。

阮氏在 2020 年 10 月時告訴《Vogue》：「網紅可以說是新一代的時裝目錄。如果你有靈感素材庫可以參考，那會比你走進店家購物簡單。因為店內商品琳瑯滿目，你會不知道怎麼穿搭比較好。」

直播帶貨在美國開始盛行，網紅透過直播影片銷售商品並賺取分潤，這樣的風潮只會越來越興盛。亞馬遜的直播服務 Amazon Live 於 2020 年 7 月推出，Instagram 和臉書（Facebook）也於隔月在平台上加入直播導購功能。

中國頂尖的網紅每年可以從直播帶貨賺取上百萬美元的收入，網紅的定義也已變得更加大眾化。有些中國超級網紅的粉絲數量極為龐大，可以在幾分鐘內導購大量的商品，各品牌為了和他們合作，爭相為這些網紅提供最優惠的折扣，但這些優惠可能導致削價競爭，也可能貶低品牌價值。

因此，有些品牌轉而培養點對點的銷售網路，他們也特別重視千禧世代與 Z 世代用戶，因為這兩個族群的消費者往往搶著賺取購物點數，藉此抵扣自身的消費額。舉例來說，肯德基（KFC）在微信（中國 WeChat）上推出「口袋炸雞店」（Pocket Stores），把數以千計的社群帳號變成肯德基旗下的連鎖炸雞店，上面提供客製化的菜單和裝飾，為的就是要讓每個用戶都能發揮自己的影響力。

值得關注的原因：

一個是靈感庫，一個是購物站，網紅和零售商家的界線逐漸模糊；與此同時，「誰是網紅」這件事也變得不再明確，光譜的這端是超級網紅，另一端則是社群媒體上的個人用戶。然而，這些現象其實意味著更大幅度的轉變，就像時尚新聞記者艾蜜莉·法菈（Emily Farra）在《Vogue》裡寫下的觀察：「我們想聽見的是大眾的聲音，不是企業的廣告。」

美妝貨架上的廝殺戰

隨著走道後排的商品躍升至美容保養櫃位上,
不同產品類別間的分界線正在重劃。

絲芙蘭(Sephora)和 Blume 都認為生理期護理用品應該歸類
到美妝保養貨架上。2020 年 9 月,Sephora 首次開售生理用品,
在品牌網站上賣起 Z 世代美妝及生理期護理品牌 Blume 的護墊
和棉條,目前供應的對象是加拿大的消費者。

美妝櫃位也騰出空間販售起乾洗手產品。歐洲乾洗手品牌
Touchland 於 2020 年夏季在藥妝店猶他彩妝(Ulta)上架,上架
後不到 24 小時,兩萬份商品旋即售罄;法國乾洗手品牌 Merci
Handy 也於同年 11 月在諾德斯特龍百貨(Nordstrom)和猶他
彩妝上架。

同樣地,美妝品牌也開始在產品線中加入消毒類商品。對環境
友善的個人護理品牌 By Humankind 於 2020 年 4 月推出新
款保濕型乾洗手後,24 小時內就全數賣光;純素肌膚保養品牌
Herbivore Botanicals 也在隔月推出了乾洗手商品。

居家用品也開始出現在美妝貨架上。美容織品公司 Resorè 在 2020 年 10 月發表了一款醫療等級的抗菌美容巾，可以殺死致痘的細菌。

Slip 寢具的絲質枕頭套於 2020 年在猶他彩妝上架，且被歸納在肌膚保養品的類別販售。Slip 的創辦人費歐娜・史都華（Fiona Stewart）說道：「我們一直認為 Slip 是一款美容產品，所以我們的目標一直是要上架到美妝保養區，而不是寢具用品專櫃。」猶他彩妝也售有 Kitsch 的「保濕抗老」枕套，據該品牌創辦人暨執行長薩絲薇爾（Cassandra Thurswell）的說法，這款商品在 2020 年的銷量成長了 240%。

值得關注的原因：

隨著美容產業持續擴張，其產品線逐漸與健康類產品重複，販售美妝保養用品的貨架也就跟著持續擴展。由於各品牌開始供應起抗菌美妝用品、生理期肌膚護理用品、美容巾等產品，接下來我們還會看到更多跨界商品出現在市場上。

70

虛擬與實體整合

大眾還是喜歡造訪實體店舖，只是店舖內還得要
有一些數位附加價值。

2020 年 7 月，博伯利（Burberry）在中國科技重鎮深圳成立了第
一間「社群零售店」。他們與騰訊公司合作，騰訊是社群平台暨通
訊軟體「微信」的母公司，擁有超過十億名用戶。

他們在微信上推出一個「小程序」，讓消費者可以預約參訪、預
定更衣室和咖啡廳座位（外加解鎖特別的餐點品項），同時還可
以累積社群貨幣。此外，消費者還會獲得小鹿造型的虛擬角色，
隨著使用程度不同，角色還會進化。店裡的每項商品都附有 QR
Code，掃描後就會出現商品資訊。

博伯利的執行長馬可·戈貝提（Marco Gobbetti）對英國廣播公
司（BBC）表示，「這家店展現了我們和客戶互動的全新方式。如
果要提及社群和零售方面的創新，那就一定要談到中國，因為他
們有最精通數位科技的奢侈品消費族群。」博伯利也計劃在中國
的其他分店內推出相同的企劃。

美妝品牌 MAC 也是這個領域的先驅，2019 年時，他們在上海開設了一家「新型零售」店，由偉門智威（Wunderman Thompson）協助打造而成。這家 MAC 店面也使用了微信「小程序」來為消費者連結社群媒體與線下體驗。虛擬的化妝鏡讓消費者可以試用 MAC 的唇膏；紅外線觸控螢幕可以與顧客的膚色配對，找出適合的底妝色號。另外店裡還有網紅設計的眼影盤可供選購，二樓也會舉辦網紅相關活動。

值得關注的原因：

線上與線下的零售之爭已經結束了，未來的店家會融合兩者，並提供更多服務。從社群媒體到更進階的擴增實境，你可以做的絕對不只是在更衣室裡分享自拍照而已。

71

工作

80

71

微型創業家

初試啼聲的企業家開始透過創意來打造新事業— 還有新的經濟結構。

受到疫情及經濟衰退影響,新創公司正在暴增。

在克莉莎・柯塔克(Krisha Kotak)被原本全職服務的旅遊公關公司解僱後,她認為成立自有永續時裝品牌的時機已經成熟,於是在疫情最嚴峻的時刻裡,創立了 Tūla & Tye。定居於英國的柯塔克,在疫情期間看見大眾對於家居服的需求,畢竟在家工作就是要穿著舒服的衣服。「過去幾年間我有過很多創業的點子,但在全職工作的情況下,一直沒有足夠的時間去實踐。」她接著對偉門智威智庫表示:「我覺得最重要的是,很多人突然有了時間和機會可以慢下來,好好評估什麼東西對我們來說才有價值。」

在這波新的創業潮下,柯塔克並不孤單。2020 年 9 月 12 日,麥迪森・施耐德(Madison Schneider)在堪薩斯州開了一家咖啡麵包屋,她向《華爾街日報》(The Wall Street Journal)表示,她在疫情期間開設 Lela's Bakery and Coffeehouse 的動機「只是覺得這是對的事情。」在佛羅里達州,尼克・拜倫(Nic Byron)丟掉主廚工作後,便和他的弟弟葛瑞格・拜倫(Greg Byron)一起成立了義大利麵店 Pasta Packs,將調理包遞送到

Tūla & Tye, founded by Krisha Kotak

當地顧客手中。路透社報導,里約熱內盧的瑪查朵(Valcineia Machado)先前的事業因為疫情倒閉,於是改裝了她的 1969 年款綠色福斯金龜車,成立了一家小花店。

受到全世界驚人的失業率影響,許多人都把創業當作職涯發展的下一步。根據美國人口普查局的數據統計,截至 2020 年 10 月 3 日的前一週間,美國境內提出新公司成立申請的數量比去年同期增加了 40%;專家也預估申請數量還會持續成長。

值得關注的原因:
斜槓副業以及孕育中的想法,都在隔離期間發展成展翅高飛的事業。柯塔克觀察到:「最棒的是,很多廚房都轉型了,變成一間間的紮染工廠、蠟燭製造所、藝術工作室、蛋糕店……而且還不只這些!」經濟復甦的關鍵,也許就在這些蓬勃發展的小企業中。

72

居家帝國

現在，居家空間必須要提供包山包海的功能：
從客廳到辦公室，以及這兩者之間的一切。

在家工作是傳統企業中奢侈難得的運作模式，但現在這種模式已
經成為多數人的日常，因此，居家空間設計也開始往多功能的方
向發展。

谷歌（Google）的硬體設計部副總艾維・羅斯（Ivy Ross）向雜誌
《Fast Company》表示：「住家現在已經變成辦公室或教室了。
既然如此，我們要怎麼融入最彈性的設計，讓居家環境可以應付
不同的日常模式呢？」

有些設計師選擇用可調整的創意家具來解決這個問題。2020 年
7 月，倫敦建築與設計工作室 Jak Studio 開發了一款概念沙發，
這款沙發可以調整成居家工作站，非常適合需要兼顧工作效率和
放鬆功能的小型住家空間。

「因為過去住家的設計常以開放式的空間為主，所以現在大家需要努力分隔出工作區域來提高生產力。」Jak Studio 對雜誌《Dezeen》如此表示。「現在情況很明顯，居家環境和家具都需要有所變革，才能兼顧彈性，符合每天不同的使用方式，我們也才能擁抱在家工作的全新時代。」

其他設計師則專注於永久型的解決方案。2020 年 9 月，倫敦設計工作室 Boano Prišmontas 推出組合式居家辦公室，他們宣稱這樣的設計可以在一天內組裝完畢，且「比宜家家居（IKEA）的家具更容易組裝。」挪威公司 Livit 也於 2020 年 7 月推出讀書專屬空間 Studypod，可以獨立放在後院或車庫中。Studypod 附有可拆式書桌，非辦公期間，還可以把桌子拆掉，當成瑜伽室或小客廳來使用。

這種設計回應了谷歌的想法。羅斯對《Fast Company》解釋，該品牌不只面向家具市場，他們更看重如何把其他物件也設計成多功能的型態：「是不是可以用更少的東西，來做更多的事呢？」

值得關注的原因：

居家空間快速演變成可以處理一切事物的空間，包括開會、休息等等，這是居家設計和空間功能的一大轉變。

73

工作旅行

工作旅行—結合工作與玩樂的全新旅遊型態。

富有彈性的遠距工作模式迅速成為常態，員工因此多了一份自由，可以在任何地點工作；熱門的度假景點也希望吸引這批愛好旅行的新型工作者，推出新的長期簽證並搭配長住方案。

杜拜將城市行銷成「半永居都市」，讓想要享受陽光和沙灘的外國工作者可以前往當地工作。這座阿拉伯都市在 2020 年 10 月推出新的遠距工作簽證，讓外國人最久可以在當地住上一年。

杜拜旅遊與商業行銷局的局長奧馬利（Helal Saeed Almarri）說道：「全球疫情改變了我們生活和工作的方式。因為跨國企業與全球頂尖新創公司都加快了數位轉型的速度，所以以往需要面對面才能解決的專業問題，現在已經不用如此了。」

在杜拜之前，還有其他景點也推出類似的簽證。巴貝多是首批推行這類簽證的國家之一，他們在 2020 年 7 月推出為期 12 個月的「迎賓戳章」（Welcome Stamp）；喬治亞在同月也推出「來喬治亞遠距工作」（Remotely from Georgia）計畫。愛沙尼亞和克羅埃西亞的數位遊牧簽證都在 2020 年 8 月生效；百慕達的「居留證政策」（Residency Certificate Policy）也同樣在 8 月問世。冰島則是在同年 11 月推出長期工作簽。

度假村也提供了延長住宿方案來吸引疲倦的工作者,加勒比海的尼維斯四季度假飯店(The Four Seasons Resort Nevis)在 2020 年 11 月推出新的方案,其中包含加長版的工作假期與學校假期,讓父母可以在房間或套房裡安心工作,小孩也可以參加虛擬課程和課後活動,包含體育活動、游泳課、海洋生物課程等等。

紐約五指湖區的極光旅社(Inns of Aurora)於 2020 年 5 月重新開幕後,其住客的平均住宿時間增加了 112%;馬爾地夫伐卡庫飯店(Vakkaru Maldives)自 8 月重新開放入住後,也發現加長住宿時間的住客數增加了三成。

值得關注的原因:

由於工作型態逐步轉型成遠距模式,員工不再需要綁在特定的地點上班,因此旅遊景點和躍躍欲試的旅客都想好好利用這個機會,讓數位遊牧(我們在《改變未來的 100 件事:2018 年全球百大趨勢》中提過這個趨勢)再次進化,從小眾活動提升成主流趨勢。隨著住家、辦公室、休憩場所間的界線漸趨模糊,品牌和企業都有了獨特的機會,可以重新定義奢華假期的樣貌,同時兼顧休閒與工作。

"
隨著住家、辦公室、休憩場所間的界線漸趨模糊,品牌和企業都有了獨特的機會,可以重新定義奢華假期的樣貌,同時兼顧休閒與工作。
"

員工的社會運動

員工開始對雇主咎責，要求他們遵守公司價值。

現在可以用來對企業咎責的力量已經不再只有抵制消費了，因為大眾也開始期待品牌遵守職場道德。僱員對於職場不公的忍受度降低，加上社群媒體上的抗爭渲染，許多員工於是開始發聲，要求公司要有更強的社會意識，所作所為也要公平公正。

2021 年 1 月，川普（Donald Trump）的臉書（Facebook）帳號遭到「永久」停權。早先在 2020 年 6 月時，臉書內部就曾出現嚴重的抗議聲浪，因為高層不願移除川普針對「黑人的命也是命」（Black Lives Matter）運動所寫下的挑釁貼文。該公司的員工認為，那些貼文縱容種族暴力，但公司卻認定那些貼文具有資訊價值，所以沒有違反其社群政策。據美國《消費者新聞與商業頻道》（CNBC）報導，由於當時在家工作模式已經啟動，上百位的員工於是改以虛擬抗爭表達憤怒，要求執行長馬克・祖克伯（Mark Zuckerberg）採取行動：他們以信件自動回覆的功能告知他人，他們「目前不在辦公室」，並拒絕在當天執行交辦任務。

2020 年 8 月，Pinterest 員工也於在家工作期間發起了虛擬罷工。據媒體《Verge》報導，抗爭之所以爆發，與三位備受關注的女性員工有關，她們控訴公司內的種族歧視與性別歧視；8 月 13 日當天，員工決定採取聯合行動，將他們的 Slack 平台上的大頭貼全部換成這三位女性的照片，並分享一項連署，要求公司停止在內部 Slack 頻道裡的所有歧視言論，並在當天下午罷工抗議。

媒體《Buzzfeed》也報導到，美國服飾公司 Everlane 的前僱員在 2020 年 6 月時鼓勵大家抵制公司商品，藉此控訴公司內部的職場種族歧視。這群僱員在 Instagram 上發起抗爭，創立「前妻俱樂部」（Ex-Wives Club）專頁，並使用「# 抵制 Everlane」（#BoycottEverlane）的標籤來分享她們的遭遇。該專頁的其他篇貼文也批評了公司的道歉文章，認為內容不甚真誠也缺乏行動力；還有一篇貼文甚至為粉絲介紹其他具有道德意識的品牌或店家。

值得關注的原因：

偉門智威於 2020 年 12 月發表一份報告，名為〈Z 世代：讓常態生活變得更好〉，他們為此進行調查，發現有 74% 的年輕人表示，他們不會在價值觀與他們相悖的公司裡任職。由於 Z 世代已經開始進入職場，品牌和企業若不建立明確的價值並加以遵守，可能會面臨慘淡的下場。

工作

「衛生長」位居高層

疫情迫使不同的企業先後設立了「衛生長」
（Chief Health Officer）這一全新職位。

新冠肺炎（COVID-19）來襲時，各行各業都必須做出明快的決策，
從戲院到主題公園，再到購物中心和餐廳，無一倖免，然而公司
高層中卻缺乏公衛專才來領導相關工作—幸好這種情況正在改
善。

2020 年 6 月，泰森食品（Tyson Foods）宣布他們設立了醫療長
一職，並計畫聘僱 200 名護理師及其他人員來防範新冠肺炎。
一個月後，皇家加勒比集團（Royal Caribbean Group）也公布
了該公司的首位全球健康與醫療總監，將為顧客和船上的員工
把關，監管健康相關的防護措施。奢侈品網購平台 Farfetch 也
於 2020 年底開始招聘健康總長。

在此之前，如此受關注的職務只存在於醫院、藥廠、保險公司等
機構。摩根士丹利（Morgan Stanley）於 2018 年聘用了公司的第
一位醫療長，此舉在當時被認為相當不尋常；該投資銀行聘任醫
療長的目的是為了控制員工的健保開銷。

WUNDERMAN
THOMPSON　　Viking cruises has hired retired vice admiral Raquel C Bono MD as its chief
health officer

"
未來，「衛生長」
是否將成爲領導階層中
不可或缺的一員？
"

受到新冠肺炎影響，有更多不同類型的公司開始考慮增設這些職務，且還會取代人資（例如員工健保相關業務）以及安全衛生管理人員（通常只負責當地或該區域的業務）的部分工作。

2020 年 6 月，在哈佛公衛學院的虛擬論壇上，愛德曼公關公司的執行長理查德·愛德曼（Richard Edelman）對企業表示，他們應該要招募公衛總長，且擔任這個職位的人會在高層技術人員中享有「搖滾明星般的地位」。

在全球企業重新開始運轉後，這些職務更顯重要。2020 年 11 月，維京遊輪（Viking）雇用拉奎爾·波諾（Raquel C Bono）任職衛生長，她是華盛頓州的新冠肺炎醫療指揮官，而且擁有出色的軍旅生涯。在郵輪復航前，她為公司制定相關措施。維京遊輪表示，他們已開始在海洋郵輪上設立 PCR 檢測實驗室，也為停靠在河邊的船隻開發岸邊實驗室。

值得關注的原因：
對企業來說，疫情讓大家清楚地看到，公衛以及財務部門不能分頭獨立運作。未來，「衛生長」是否將成為領導階層中不可或缺的一員？

76

虛擬優先的企業總部

虛擬優先的辦公室昭示了未來「去中心化」
的工作模式。

「在家工作」已成為全球常態。歐洲某些國家甚至導入相關規範，
來保護在家工作者的權利。2020 年 9 月，德國推出一項法案，規
定在許可的情況下，需保障員工在家工作的權利，並對工時加以
規範。在此之前，西班牙已經通過類似的法案，愛爾蘭也開始考
慮立法。

德國勞動部長胡貝圖斯·海爾（Hubertus Heil）告訴《金融時報》
（Financial Times）：「我們無法阻止工作模式持續演進，而且
我們也不打算這麼做。現在的問題在於，我們要怎麼把這些科技
方面的發展、新型的商業模式、更高的工作效率帶給大眾，而不
只是侷限在少數人身上。」

科技公司扮演領頭羊的角色，利用創新的數位方案來把短期措施
變成長久的營運模式，並為未來彈性且虛擬的工作模式鋪路。

這當中最著名的案例是 Dropbox，他們大幅改動了公司的工作
架構。2020 年 10 月 13 日，這家科技公司宣布他們將成為一家

「虛擬優先」的企業，把全球各地的辦公室都改造成 Dropbox Studios，讓在裡面工作的人可以彼此合作、成立社群，不必單打獨鬥。由於該公司在 2017 年簽下舊金山史上最大的租約，這項調整對他們來說是非常重大的轉變，他們總部大樓的四棟建築佔地共 73 萬平方英尺，現在多數的空間都將出租出去。

其他公司也採取有創意的作法，將實體辦公室打造成虛擬場景，讓員工可以聚在裡面互動、工作。WeTransfer 在 2020 年 5 月開設了虛擬辦公室，把公司荷蘭總部的辦公室數位化，員工可以創造虛擬角色在裡面走動、開會，或到酒吧一起喝一杯。

2020 年 4 月，Sine Wave Entertainment 為遠距工作模式設計了虛擬產品 Breakroom，為維珍集團（Virgin Group）、電競公司 Torque Esports 等企業提供 3D 辦公室。義大利國家電力

公司（Enel）在過去一年間也和 Spatial Systems 合作，透過擴增實境與虛擬實境技術製作場景，讓員工可以使用虛擬角色進入虛擬會議室裡開會。

值得關注的原因：

《紐約雜誌》旗下的 Podcast 節目《Pivot》的主持人卡拉·史威許（Kara Swisher）預測：「科技公司在這方面是佼佼者，我想大型辦公室應該已經成為過去式了」，取而代之的是越來越多的虛擬優先辦公室。由於員工散布各地，且工作模式開始朝向數位發展，辦公室的定位也因介於虛擬和實體之間而變得更加模糊，與此同時，這也為全新的合作模式和工作分配方式開啟了另一扇大門。

Z世代職涯發展

疫情打亂了Z世代的遠大志向，除了受到目前經濟衰退、家庭財務緊縮的影響外，職缺列表也反映出截然不同的局勢。

年輕一代開始重新思考他們的工作動機，包含熱情、興趣、自由、賺錢等面向，除了思考如何從工作中獲得安全感，他們也想要貢獻社會。很早就有跡象顯示，他們有興趣的領域包含社會服務、健康、科學、物流、電商或其他數位服務。據《紐約時報》（The New York Times）報導，光是亞馬遜（Amazon）一家公司就在2020年1月至10月間，在全球雇用了42萬7,300名員工。

在美國，諮詢公司 Civis Analytics 在 2020 年 6 月為偉門智威智庫做的獨家研究發現，有39% 的大專院校或是職業學校在學生表示，疫情影響了他們的職涯選擇，有28% 的人決定轉換科系或領域。

當這群人被問到疫情對經濟產生的影響時，有31% 的人說他們現在比較想往科學、科技、工程、數學領域發展，只有21% 的人表示他們想往社會科學發展，而人文領域更只有18%。另外，有少

> 美國Z世代被問到疫情對經濟產生的影響時，有31%的人說他們現在比較想往科學、科技、工程、數學領域發展

部分的人（13%）表示，他們比較傾向循技職體系來發展他們的志向與理想。

為了將失業的年輕人媒合至社會需要的職務上，開始有人呼籲國家推出青年服務計畫。紐約大學的行銷系教授史考特・蓋洛威（Scott Galloway）建議成立「新冠工作團」（Corona Corps），其概念有如現代版的「和平工作團」（Peace Corps）。他在一篇《華盛頓郵報》（The Washington Post）的文章裡解釋道，這種新型機構會招募 18 到 24 歲的失業青年，以基本工資聘雇他們從事防疫電話客服工作，也會教導他們寶貴的知識，包含流行病學、社工服務、作業管理技巧等等。

值得關注的原因：

疫情大幅地改變了 Z 世代對世界的期待，現在他們即將進入的成人社會，出現了和以往不同的需求與機會，而且大學學歷的價值也越來越不受重視。與失業相關的負面聯想也逐漸減弱；美國年輕人發揮創意，在國際版抖音（TikTok）上記錄他們的求職過程，也試圖藉機吸引雇主的目光。

78

氣候相關職涯

氣候變遷開始出現在課綱上，為新興世代的氣候專家奠定基礎。

根據《紐約時報》(The New York Times) 報導，2020 年 9 月，義大利成為第一個把氣候變遷列入公立學校必修課程的國家，每個年級的學生都必須修習氣候變遷與環保永續課程，每年總時數需達到 33 小時。

大學也調整了課程，加入氣候變遷議題。2025 年前，英國雪菲爾大學所有科系的學生都必須修習永續課程，校方請所有系所重新調整課綱，讓各系學生都可以從永續發展的視角來檢視自己領域的專業知識。

紐約的綠點圖書館與環境教育中心 (Greenpoint Library and Environmental Education) 於 2020 年 10 月開張，這也宣告了培養氣候識讀的能力將成為未來趨勢。該圖書館與教育中心「讓有志者可以實際動手做，藉此了解我們脆弱的地球系統中相對難以掌握的面向。」這棟建築由景觀建築公司 Scape 打造，其設計總監吉娜‧沃斯 (Gena Wirth) 對《Fast Company》雜誌如此說道。

"
Z世代已經佔了全球勞動人口的
四分之一,他們也開始把對於氣候
行動的理想帶進職場。
"

隨著教育出現變化,畢業生的能力和專長也有所改變,美國人口普查局的研究發現,環境科學越來越受學生歡迎,主攻自然資源與保育的畢業生在 2017 到 2018 年間增加了 4.59%;未來十年,這股成長動能將會帶動就業市場轉型。美國勞工部勞動統計局發現,環境科學專家的就業率在 2019 到 2029 年間會成長 8%,比所有職業加總後平均的成長速率還要快。

值得關注的原因:

Z 世代把氣候變遷列為首要的全球議題,根據國際特赦組織的調查,全世界每 10 位 Z 世代人口中,就有 4 位表示氣候變遷是世界上最重要的議題之一。Z 世代已經佔了全球勞動總人口的四分之一,也開始把他們對氣候行動的理想帶進職場,在未來的幾年內,將對企業結構產生影響。

需求導向的辦公室

**觀光旅遊業正在轉型迎接新型旅客：
朝九晚五的上班族。**

由於以往的客群不復存在，飯店與餐廳開始把空間改成出租型辦公室。

從精品住宿品牌到連鎖飯店，飯店業者重新將房間改造成半永久型的辦公室，為遠距工作者提供全新的日間費率方案。2020年7月，布魯克林的威思飯店（Wythe Hotel）和共同工作空間經營者 Industrious 合作，把某層樓 13 間的客房全部改成出租型空間，他們把房裡的家具換成辦公桌椅和檯燈，每日 200 美元的租金包含 Wi-Fi 使用費、無限閱讀《紐約時報》（The New York Times）電子報，還有免費的咖啡和點心。2020年9月，Industrious 與飯店集團 Proper Hospitality 合作，把這個概念推廣到該飯店集團旗下位於奧斯汀、舊金山、聖塔莫尼卡的飯店，客戶可自行選擇日租、週租或月租方案。

2020年10月，希爾頓集團（Hilton）在北美和英國推出希爾頓工作空間（WorkSpaces by Hilton）。該集團旗下位於曼哈頓的康萊德（Conrad）飯店，日租方案從美金 300 元起跳，會將早餐、午餐、調酒送到客房，還會提供鄰近健康生活館 Clean Market 的禪修盒以及療程優惠券。

萬豪旅享家會員計畫（Marriott Bonvoy）也把目標放在個人辦公室業務上，他們的「辦公無界計畫」（Work Anywhere）於 2020 年 10 月啟動，讓會員可以在早上 6 點到晚間 6 點之間自由刷進刷出，但不能過夜。

萬豪的全球客戶體驗專員蘿依（Peggy Fan Roe）提到，「過去長時間以來提高空房住宿率的方式，現在可能會有所改變，我們看到越來越多的旅客來休息，但不是每天都有，而且也沒辦法把空房時段都補滿。」

餐廳也開始有所調整，2020 年 7 月，星巴克（Starbucks）在東京推出專為遠距工作者設計的分店，他們和 Think Lab 合作，把咖啡廳的二樓改造成商務中心，有包廂式的單人工作區，還有比較大型的會議空間。消費者可以預定單人工作區（以 15 分鐘為計時單位），並使用應用程式付款和解鎖工作區的門禁系統。

值得關注的原因：

短期出租辦公室市場在疫情期間的快速成長有目共睹，按需求租用的工作空間越來越多，這也彰顯了未來的趨勢——餐廳、飯店等場所的經營模式將會變得更富彈性。威思飯店的老闆彼得·羅倫斯（Peter Lawrence）對《Fast Company》表示：「可以應付多種需求的空間以現在來說特別重要。我不覺得是因為新冠肺炎（COVID-19）才造成這種現象；我覺得這樣的重大轉變會一直持續下去，讓員工可以在任何地方辦公。」

79

80

防止女性成為經濟弱勢

經濟衰退造成的影響，對女性來說首當其衝，
因此目前有新的計畫開始提倡職場性別平等。

美國全國經濟研究所表示，女性失業率比男性還高。

女性政策研究機構（Institute for Women's Policy Research）的主席暨執行長 C·妮可·梅森（C Nicole Mason）告訴《紐約時報》（The New York Times）：「我們應該要直接把這種現象稱為『女性成為經濟弱勢』（shecession）」，她認為 2020 年經濟衰退對女性造成的影響過於龐大。麥肯錫（McKinsey）的研究也顯示，從全球的角度來看，女性丟掉工作的機會比男性多 1.8 倍。美國勞工部勞動統計局的數據指出，2020 年 4 月的失業總人數有 2,050 萬人，而女性就佔其中的 55%。

因此企業現在也開始尋找可以支持女性員工的做法。美國運通（American Express）和資助女性有色人種的機構 IFund Women of Color 合作，在 2020 年 11 月推出「雙百計畫」（100 for 100），要為 100 位女性黑人企業家提供 25,000 美元的資金，加上可以免費使用 100 天的企業資源。亞馬遜（Amazon）和優比速（UPS）決定使用他們的平台來推廣由女性成立的

企業。在美國，女性企業全國協會（the Women's Business Enterprise National Council）推出「女性企業」（Women Owned）計畫，提高大眾對女性企業的關注。

雖然有很多計畫都在支持女性企業，但對女性員工的關注度卻仍顯不足。在美國，軟體公司 Qualtrics 與線上商城 The Boardlist 在 2020 年 8 月做了一項調查，結果顯示男性在疫情期間的升遷機會比女性高了 3 倍。

值得關注的原因：

「女性成為經濟弱勢」會讓職場中的女權再次倒退，聯合國婦女署（UN Women）的副執行總監艾妮塔·巴蒂亞（Anita Bhatia）認為，這樣的走勢會對經濟造成危害，她在 2020 年 11 月時告訴《BBC》：「這不只是權力的問題，這還影響到經濟的面向，讓女性完整參與經濟活動，才符合經濟常理。」

醫療保健

健康免疫力

健康品牌開始擴張事業版圖,為想要提升病毒抵抗
力的消費者推出可增強免疫力的商品。

「免疫力」在全球保健產業中,成為熱門詞彙,2020 年 3 月,這
個詞在谷歌(Google)上的搜尋排行上升到五年來的新高,健康
照護品牌也因此調整了服務內容。

六善水療中心(Six Senses)的紐約分店預計於 2021 年在曼哈
頓開張,這是該品牌在北美設立的第一家分館,他們把健康護理
服務聚焦在免疫層面上,整合了忠實顧客期待的各類服務,包含
阿育吠陀療程以及中藥療法,主要目標是要提升免疫力,讓身體
更健康。該中心透過飲食控制、生活習慣調整來預防疾病,也以
生物駭客計畫來協助顧客改善健康狀況。六善水療中心在疫情後
開始轉型,透過調整服務項目來回應此刻大眾對於預防醫療以及
免疫力提升的需求。

> "
> 增強免疫力的產品
> 以往被歸類在醫療領域
> 使用，但現在健康品牌
> 也開始推出這類產品，
> 來拓展其事業版圖。
> "

2020 年 10 月，曼哈頓奢華會員俱樂部 Spring Place 舉辦了戶外健康活動「防疫早點名」(Immunity Morning)，活動由精品健身工作室 The Ness 的共同創辦人布莉亞·墨菲 (Dria Murphhy) 主導，活動選用的課程、飲食、產品等，每個環節都以增強免疫力為目的。

其他公司也在轉移經營重心。2020 年 12 月，奠基在營養基因體學上的健康品牌 Caligenix 推出營養食品 Immunotype，該產品以基因資料庫研究為基礎，從基因層面解決人類的免疫系統問題，同時也是該公司跨足營養品領域的首發之作。機能飲品公司 So Good So You 在 11 月的融資中募集到 1,450 萬美元的資金，該公司預計利用這筆經費來研發與免疫力相關的新產品，藉此應付日漸成長的客戶需求。機能健康品牌 Remedy Organics 也在 10 月時推出增強免疫力的植物蛋白飲「免疫莓果」(Berry Immunity)。

值得關注的原因：
增強免疫力的產品以往被歸類在醫療領域使用，但現在健康品牌也開始推出這類產品，來拓展其事業版圖。接下來可以還可以看到更多產品和服務，會將免疫力與預防治療功效收編其中。

Stay Home
If Sick

82
健康圖像學

重新設計與健康相關的視覺語彙來傳達新的規範。

健康相關考量持續改變我們在公共空間中的活動方式，企業也為此徵召設計師來創作圖像，鼓勵大眾遵守安全守則。設計公司 Base 是這方面的領頭羊，2020 年 7 月，他們受到建設公司 Hastings Architecture 委託，推出設計相關標誌的計畫 Way Forward Signage Co。這些經過簡化的室內專用標誌，看起來就像現代版的交通號誌一樣，提示大家往來移動以及行為互動的準則。

該計畫的目的是要創造清晰、明確、所有人都能辨識的視覺語彙，讓大眾能在疫情期間遵守適當的行為標準，同時又不會產生恐慌。Base 的合夥人傑夫·庫克（Geoff Cook）對偉門智威智庫表示：「我們做了個重大的決定，不只要讓視覺語彙和圖像看起來非常簡單、易懂，也要傳遞樂觀正向的情緒。」

醫療保健

Exit Only

Wipe Area Clean After Use

Mask Required

Washing Hands Stops the Spread

Mask Required

...se ...Distance

Mask Required

Temperature Check

Max Capacity: 3 Please Social Distance

Max Capacity: 5 Please Social Distance

Stay Home If Sick

...hat was Last Thing Touched?

Going Down? Use This Stairway

Max Elevator Capacity:1 Mask Required

在新冠肺炎（COVID-19）期間，這個計畫也推動業界創造出更多風格一致的企業標誌。庫克說道，因為辦公室與公共空間都重新敞開大門，「對於這類號誌系統的需求只會越來越多。」

除了建築空間以外，設計師也開始想像，高度重視衛生的未來生活會是什麼模樣。中國設計師周宸宸（Frank Chou）和陳旻（Chen Min）在 2020 年 3 月展開了「創造治愈」（Create Cures）計畫，成為 9 月「設計中國北京」（Design China Beijing）的展覽焦點之一，這項計畫邀請世界各地的設計師一起來分享解決公衛問題的方式。

倫敦設計工作室 Bompas & Parr 在 2020 年 3 月初推出了一項競賽，參賽設計師需要重新設計給皂機，並構思「更有創意的衛生清潔方式」，藉此鼓勵大眾多多洗手。這項計畫名為「衛生之泉」（The Fountain of Hygiene），他們鼓勵設計師嘗試新的造型與功能，針對洗手這個簡單的動作來思考，看看有哪些作法可以改善大眾的行為模式。

值得關注的原因：

設計思考可以用來鼓勵並加強大眾的衛生習慣。設計博物館（Design Museum）的總監暨總執行提姆·馬洛（Tim Marlow）說道：「設計有個很重要的功能，它可以解決我們每天面對的許多挑戰。」由於疫情期間的新規範慢慢成為文化的一部份，接下來可以看到更多品牌和設計師繼續為健康相關的視覺圖像努力。

數位養分

使用社群媒體和吸收數位內容,都開始和憂鬱、焦躁、孤獨產生關聯,然而,數位內容有沒有可能讓你心情變好,不讓情緒變得負面呢?

「數位養分是讓人類邁向繁榮的全新第六支柱。」AeBeZe Labs 的創辦人暨執行長、同時也是「數位營養學家」的麥可·莫斯柯維茨(Michael Moskowitz)對偉門智威智庫如此表示。莫斯柯維茨相信數位內容若吸收得宜,可以增強抗壓力、對抗失神問題,還能增進健康、提升潛能、帶來快樂。他解釋到,「內容不等於故事;內容其實就像化學反應,它以敘事方式為稜鏡,而且有很大的發揮空間。」

AeBeZe Labs 製作了幾樣工具,包括數位營養元素表、數位營養標示、個人化數位營養計畫,為的就是要讓大眾找出均衡、營養的數位養分,並且在接收到媒體內容的時候,可以培養「更強大的心理素質」。此外,網站《商業內幕》(Business Insider)也在 2020 年 2 月報導,該公司正在大規模測試此一概念,同時也在測試他們為美軍研發的「數位藥品」。

莫斯柯維茨告訴偉門智威智庫,他們還計劃在 2021 年 1 月推出兩項新產品,其中一項是神經傳導分析工具,另一項是營養追蹤數位平台。

AeBeZe Labs 的工具旨在解決兩個和數位養分有關的問題,也就是數位衛生和數位識讀能力。莫斯柯維茨解釋道:「大眾需要知道他們接收的內容裡面含有哪些內容,並理解特定數位行為的風險與報酬,以及特定的視聽資源與經驗會帶來哪些影響,接著,他們還要了解哪時候能拒絕特定類型的數位媒體,或為何要拒讀這些媒體,藉此提升抗壓力。」

> **"**
> ## 數位養分是讓人類邁向繁榮的全新第六支柱。
> **"**
>
> AeBeZe Labs 的創辦人暨執行長
> 邁克爾·莫斯柯維茨(Michael Moskowitz)

值得關注的原因:
大眾開始重新衡量數位內容的營養價值。接下來可以看到更多為特定目的所設計的「科技藥品」(需要從螢幕攝取),還有更多促進心理健康的數位產品。

84

禮賓照護

日常照護服務再升級，整合了禮賓服務以及精心
設計的舒適環境與空間美感。

醫療業者把經營重心轉向禮賓級的護理服務，讓客戶再也不必浪
費時間等待。The Lanby 是位於紐約的全新初級照護會員俱樂
部，預定在 2021 年秋季開幕，結合醫療照護服務與奢華旅宿般
的高級環境，會員每年支付 3,500 美元的會費，便可無限使用館
內設施，且每項都是「最受喜愛的紐約飯店和餐廳裡會看到的設
施」。

此外，會員權益還包含以手機應用程式預約全年無休 24 小時的
遠距護理服務，也能預約使用次日的空間。每位病患都會由一
個專門的照護團隊負責照料，團隊成員包含醫師、營養師、健康
顧問，還有負責管理個人健康計畫的禮賓管家。除了醫療護理服
務，該俱樂部還提供定期演講、討論會、客座講座，以及免費的咖
啡廳。

> "
> 創新的健康護理服務從高級觀光旅宿業者身上得到靈感，為客戶提供升級版的護理服務。
> "

在倫敦，自稱「世界第一座醫療健身房」的 Lanserhof 在 2020 年 8 月慶祝開幕滿一週年。Lanserhof 是倫敦藝文俱樂部（Arts Club）的附屬設施，結合了有健康認證的頂級德國醫學水療池，以及光鮮亮麗的倫敦私人俱樂部招牌。六層樓的 Lanserhof 除了提供預防醫療及再生醫療服務，還有最先進的的健康與運動訓練設施供會員使用。一年 6,500 歐元（約台幣 22 萬）的會費，讓會員可以享有健康檢查、健檢顧問、客製訓練計畫、使用貴賓室等服務，甚至還有管家為你清洗與整理運動裝備。

The Soke 於 2020 年 10 月在倫敦的南肯辛頓區開張，他們專為個人心理健康設計的新型服務概念提供了諮商和引導訓練。創

辦人馬揚·梅丁（Maryam Meddin）特別在住宅區開設這家諮商所，使其與眾不同。寧靜且充滿時尚氣息的空間設計為病患提供了優雅的氛圍，而且還能增強心理健康，不會像一般診所那樣讓病患聯想到身心疾病。

值得關注的原因：

創新的健康護理服務從高級觀光旅宿業者身上得到靈感，為客戶提供升級版的護理服務。OneMedical Group 提供的禮賓護理服務只向顧客收取 200 美元的年費，他們的業務成長，證明了服務導向的護理服務很有潛力成為主流。無論所在產業為何，各品牌都應把精力轉向絕佳的顧客體驗與服務上。

84

85
未來的健身方式

沈浸式體驗搭配上更優異的技術，開啓了
嶄新的遊戲健身時代

電動遊戲原本被視為缺乏身體活動的行為，但在虛擬實境遊戲與相關系統開發完成以後，電動便開始成為增加身體活動量的項目之一。2020 年 4 月，Oculus 和虛擬實境工作室 Within 共同推出全新健身應用程式「超自然」（Supernatural），該程式採取訂閱制服務，在讓人驚嘆的虛擬實境美景中，為玩家提供客製的健身課表和教練服務。

運動類遊戲 The Beat Saber 於 2019 年推出，玩家使用遊戲搖桿來當做光劍，在虛擬環境中砍擊飛向自身的色塊。2020 年以來，他們推出多款全新資料片，包含新的遊戲曲目，例如鼓勵玩家多多運動的「健身節奏歌」（Fitbeat）。

除了頭戴式裝置，Virtuix 也將於 2021 年開始販售虛擬實境跑步機 Virtuix Omni One，該設施配備齊全，內建大約 30 款遊戲。

隨機台附贈的頭戴式裝置會以安全帶固定在跑步機上,玩家戴上以後,便可以在機台上跑動、跳躍、跪站,是目前最具活動力也最符合沈浸式體驗的機台系統。

值得關注的原因:

這些新款遊戲和應用程式的沈浸式設計,讓用戶以為他們只是在玩遊戲,忘記他們其實是在運動。有了互動式運動遊戲以後,正常的伏地挺身和仰臥起坐可能都要被歸類到類比世代的運動項目裡了。

資訊健康

管理個人資訊使人耗盡力氣，而新型自我照護方案的出現，正是要為大眾舒緩這樣的情緒壓力

一般人可能不認為違法個資會影響心理健康，但消費者體驗卻為此提供了證據。Pew Research Center 的研究指出，面對個資議題時，美國人會感到擔憂、困惑、脆弱，而偉門智威數據服務也顯示，當受試者得知個資會有安全問題後，有 55% 的美國人覺得迷失，48% 的人覺得受到侮辱，37% 的人則感到害怕。

這些真誠的想法讓大眾對個資的焦慮持續上升。提升道德與消費者滿意度的機構 Better Ethics and Consumer Outcomes Network 簡稱「Beacon」，其創辦人暨願景總監喬・托斯卡尼（Joe Toscano）告訴偉門智威智庫：「隱私問題是大眾心中揮之不去的煩惱之一，長期下來，可能會對心智造成類似焦慮抑或者更甚於焦慮爆發時所帶來的創傷。」

由於資料安全會影響大眾的心理健康，企業與機構於是紛紛開始設計產品和平台，來協助大眾達成數位自我照護，也為數位資訊場景鋪設出一條更健康的道路。

2020 年 7 月，臉書公司（Facebook）與印度中央政府中等教育委員會合作，推出與數位產品安全和健全網路使用相關的認證課程。該年度早前還有謀智（Mozilla）和策略科技（Tactical Tech）合作推出的「資料排毒套裝」（Data Detox Kit），裡面有提升數位健康的指南，例如：如何從讓人困惑的設計中找到清楚的指示、如何執行應用程式清理工作、如何「鎖上你的數位門戶」、如何保護虛擬資產。透過療癒的自然景觀插圖，資料排毒套裝這一平台結合了資料隱私與現代生活風格，也把數位安全當作整體身心健康的重要核心。

值得關注的原因：

在面對資訊安全問題時，大家通常不會多做思考，而是會去感受。托斯卡尼說道：「隱私問題帶來的影響並未出現清楚的定義，但我們卻能從痛苦和恐懼中真切感受到它的存在。」由於和資料隱私相關的討論漸趨成熟，接下來還可以看到更多數位避難所、資訊清理工具、資料隱私產品的誕生，為大眾帶來心靈的平靜。

87

抗病毒布料

衣著正在朝著「眞·機能」的方向邁進，它們開始變成大眾的鎧甲，穿上後就可以對抗疾病、提升健康、加強能力，甚至保護我們免受氣候變遷的衝擊

全金屬夾克 The Full Metal Jacket 是一款抗病毒衣著，由英國新創時尚科技公司 Vollebak 推出，該公司致力發展未來的衣著。這件夾克在 2020 年 5 月上市，其中有 65% 是由銅所構成，銅本身就有對抗有害微生物的功能，可以殺死細菌及病毒。該產品的設計目的是為了證明把金屬加到衣料中是可行的，也證明這種做法有潛力成為未來創新衣著的基礎。

瑞士織品公司 HeiQ 和巴基斯坦的丹寧廠 Artistic Denim Mills 合作，在 2020 年 6 月推出「世界第一件抗病毒牛仔褲」。這款褲裝以 HeiQ 的抗病毒技術 Viroblock 製成，在布料上塗上一層隱形抗病毒薄膜，可以在 30 分鐘內有效對抗細菌。該技術保證褲子可以耐受至少 30 次的溫水（60°C）清洗，且在 2020 年 5 月經過實驗室測試，證明可以有效對抗導致新冠肺炎（COVID-19）的病原體 SARS-CoV-2。在 2020 年 7 月，迪賽（Diesel）也和瑞士化學公司 Polygiene 合作，推出一款抗病毒牛仔褲。

Full Metal Jacket. Image courtesy of Vollebak and Sun Lee.

"

**你穿的衣服會讓你的身體更加強健，
就像吃藥一樣。**

"

Vollebak 的共同創辦人
史蒂夫·蒂德博爾（Steve Tidball）

我們在 2020 年時終於真正體認到人類的脆弱之處。由於我們即將邁入不可預測的未來，氣候變遷造成了極端的氣候現象，疫情的潛在發展也仍未有所定論，這些都讓我們的生存環境變得更具挑戰，服裝設計師也因此有了新的任務，要讓人類變得無堅不摧。

值得關注的原因：

設計師開始推動時尚布料的演進，加入智慧、直覺、具防護力的材質。Vollebak 的共同創辦人史蒂夫·蒂德博爾（Steve Tidball）在一場《衛報》（The Guardian）專訪中解釋道：「衣著與科技會開始互相結合，你穿的衣服會讓你的身體更加強健，就像吃藥一樣。」

88

超淨化

淨化標準再升級，開始往客廳、公共空間發展。

飯店開始提升清潔衛生的標準來讓客人安心。萬豪酒店（Marriott）的「潔淨承諾宣言」於 2020 年 4 月公布，他們成立萬豪國際全球衛生清潔委員會，採納食品微生物學、公共衛生學、傳染病學等專家的意見，重新改寫該集團的工作準則。該飯店集團也推行了新的清潔衛生規範，包含需使用紫外線和類似落葉吹除器的裝置來噴灑抗菌液。萬豪的美洲地區營運暨客戶體驗副總斯科特·麥考伊（Scott McCoy）在 2020 年 9 月時告訴《旅遊者雜誌》（Condé Nast Traveler）:「突然之間，安全變得很吸引人，清潔也變得很新潮。」

希爾頓（Hilton）和英國來舒（Lysol）製造商合作改進其清潔規範，並向診所梅奧醫院（Mayo Clinic）諮詢，藉以提升員工訓練效果。四季酒店（Four Seasons）在 2020 年 5 月成立了新冠肺炎（COVID-19）顧問團，集結來自約翰霍普金斯國際醫療集團的專家來修訂衛生清潔程序。

三星（Samsung）的智慧魔衣櫥（AirDresser）於 2020 年 7 月在美國正式推出。他們首次發表這件產品的地點是 2018 年的歐

洲,當時只用作居家乾洗機使用,但現在這款產品已經變成健康清潔專用衣櫃了,三星宣稱這台機器可以為各種衣料消滅 99.9% 的細菌。

義大利設計師卡爾洛·拉帝(Carlo Ratti)認為,衣著滅菌這一特色會持續扮演重要角色,即便新冠肺炎的限制鬆綁、社交生活恢復後也還是一樣。他的同名設計工作室 Carlo Ratti Associati 在 2020 年 4 月發表了除汙衣櫃 Pura-Case 的概念,他們也於同年 7 月開始打造商品原型,希望在募資平台 Kickstarter 上推出這款產品。該裝置會使用一小時的臭氧淨化程序來清潔布料。

值得關注的原因:

因為除汙淨化一直都是重要的議題,所以清潔認證開始成為主要賣點。淨化程序在未來幾個月甚至幾年內,都還是有可能持續扮演左右顧客決策的關鍵。

89

哀傷治療

為了解決這波文化創傷，健康服務開始整合悲傷
管理療程，成為整體健康護理服務的一環

失去的痛苦在疫情期間更為強烈，因為實體互動、社交往來都在疫情期間受到限制。無論是失去所愛、丟掉工作，或者從媒體報導中得知社會不公不義的事因而產生間接的失落感，對很多人來說，排解強烈的痛苦都是一個人無法負荷的沈重負擔，更不要提大眾已經隔離與失落了好幾季度了。為了回應這項問題，具備前瞻思考的健康從業人員開始利用嶄新的方式來管理悲傷的情緒。

2020 年 7 月，全面健康管理工作室 HealHaus 舉辦了「在悲傷中呼吸」（Breakwork for Grief）工作坊，並表示「我們正身處在一個集體創傷、集體悲痛的時代」。瑜伽老師兼直覺治療師蜜雪兒·強森（Michelle Johnson）把悲傷療程加入她 2020 年 6 月的線上靜養空間 Healing in Community : A Space for Collective Grief and Liberation 當中。蕾森解釋到，該空間旨在「提供一個正視悲傷的環境」，並檢視「為何未經處理的悲痛會導致更強大的痛苦」。

Goop 和 Well & Good 等線上健康平台也邀請了悲傷治療師來寫作文章，講述如何處理不安和失落的情緒。治療師克萊爾·史密斯（Claire Bidwell Smith）告訴 Goop，大家展現悲傷的方式正在改變，「苦難隨處可見，所以我認為我們戴上面具來面對世界的動機也不盡相同，因為全世界都受傷了。然而，我們還是有其他的方式可以一起走過這段創傷。」

值得關注的原因：

過去從業人員把焦點放在健康與治療上，但現在他們開始提供哀傷治療，將個人文化背景也納入考量。無論是為大眾打造可以安全抒發情緒的空間，或者推廣充滿正念的體能活動，這些都是很好的商業點子。新世代悲傷療法於此開展，且對所有人來說，都能有所助益。

沉靜娛樂

娛樂平台開始把觀眾導向寧靜的世界。

內容創作者開始鼓勵大眾練習冥想、正念、自我照護，把這些練習當作新的娛樂。

串流影音巨擘網飛（Netflix）推出一部可以連續追很久的全新「解毒」影集——《冥想正念指南》（Headspace Guide to Meditation），該動畫於 2021 年 1 月 1 日在網飛上首播，為觀眾提供新的冥想指南和正念技巧，並傳授觀眾每日練習這些技巧的好處。冥想應用程式頂空（Headspace）的共同創辦人安迪·帕帝康（Andy Puddicombe）告訴《Vulture》：「在一天當中的任何階段，我們都能用正念來面對生活。因此我們希望藉由這樣的影集來讓觀眾知道，這不只是冥想而已，而是『學習用更正向的心態來面對生活的大小事』。」

正念相關製作橫掃娛樂產業，而《冥想正念指南》是這串相關名單上最新出現的項目；但在 2020 年 10 月，HBO Max 也和一款正念應用程式 Calm 合作，共同推出《寧靜的世界》（A World of Calm），他們宣稱這部片是「現代生活的即時解毒良方」。這部作品每集的片長是 30 分鐘，特色是有藝人參與講述輕鬆的小故事，藝人名單包含馬赫夏拉·阿里（Mahershala Ali）、伊卓瑞斯·艾巴（Idris Elba）、基努·李維（Keanu Reeves）、妮可·基嫚（Nicole Kidman）、凱特·溫斯蕾（Kate Winslet）等等，並以「讓人陶醉的音樂、以科學為基礎而精心設計的敘事方式、讓人震驚的影片，來轉化你的情緒」。

迪士尼（Disney）也想幫助觀眾找回內心的平靜。2020 年 5 月，該公司在 Disney+ 上推出《禪意動畫》（暫譯自 Zenimation），該影集剪接經典迪士尼動畫片段，包含《阿拉丁》、《小飛俠》、《小美人魚》、《冰雪奇緣》等，再為它們配上寧靜的音樂，「以求帶來片刻的心靈沉靜」，該品牌表示。這個「動畫聲景體驗」包含來自海浪的噪音、柔和的空氣流動，幫助觀眾「關機、放鬆、重新整理心境」。

HBO 頻道則開始鼓勵觀眾建立自我療癒習慣。2020 年 11 月，該公司在推出奇幻影集《黑暗元素》（His Dark Materials）第二季之前，搶先上架了同名應用程式《His Dark Materials: My Daemon》，使用者可以在上面進行人格測驗，決定自己的動物類型和個性，進而創造出屬於自己的惡魔，該頻道也把這個成果稱為「個人靈魂的動畫版形象」。製作完成以後，惡魔會鼓勵用戶練習自我照護技巧，例如外出散步、跑步、跟朋友聯絡，或者讓自己好好放鬆一下。

值得關注的原因：

正念相關事業在疫情期間迅速飛漲。Calm 在最新一輪的募資結束後，在 2020 年 12 月的市值衝到 20 億美元，而頂空也在 2020 年多募到 1 億美元的資金。由於對正念資源的需求上升，娛樂產業也讓自我照護再次升級，把獨特的沈浸式體驗整合至其中。

91

金融

100

公正的銀行服務

金融服務升級,變得更具包容力。

只有線上服務而沒有實體分行的新型銀行開始增加,解決了常受忽視的弱勢族群需求。

美國饒舌歌手「殺手麥克」(Killer Mike,本名 Michael Render)加入前亞特蘭大市長楊恩(Andrew Young)與美國頻道 Bounce TV 創辦人萊恩·葛洛佛(Ryan Glover)的行列,在 2020 年 10 月推出名為 Greenwood 的銀行服務。這款數位金融應用程式以黑人與拉丁裔消費者為優先服務對象,並將服務重點放在較難從傳統銀行獲得貸款的企業家上。

Simba 是專為不具美國國籍的美國移民服務的新型銀行,於 2020 年夏天在美國成立。Simba 和其他銀行不同,他們是「由新移民打造,且專為新移民服務」的銀行,不要求申辦人持有社會安全碼或稅籍編號,只要具備有效護照和美國住址就能申請開戶。

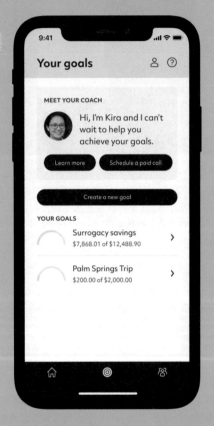

Simba 不收取開戶費用，並且提供較低的海外匯款手續費，希望可以支持新移民家庭，讓他們擁有比較好的財務狀況。該銀行甚至還為金融教育計畫和社區機構提供資金。

LGBTQ+ 社群的成員也能享有專屬的新型金融服務。Daylight 於 2020 年 11 月推出，隸屬在信用卡公司 Visa 旗下的金融科技快速追蹤計畫（Fintech Fast Track Program）之下。Daylight 希望能在 LGBTQ+ 社群成員的各階段人生中，為他們提供教育並予以支持，其金融顧問接受的訓練中，還包含了處理該社群專屬財務議題的方式，例如變性手術等等。該服務讓使用者能在金融卡上使用自己喜歡的稱號，不需要再額外花大錢申請改名。花旗銀行（Citi）也發現了這項需求，他們也在 11 月開始與萬事達卡（Mastercard）合作，共同推出「正名」（True Name）服務。

值得關注的原因：

在各個服務業當中，為不同族群解決特殊需求是未來的必要趨勢，金融科技即是下個要拓展服務和擁抱多元價值的部門。這些小眾銀行比傳統銀行更支持顧客，在相關意識提高的狀況下，這類新型服務會吸引到更多需求。往後，我們可能可以看到一波新型銀行應用程式與服務，把目標鎖定在邊緣社群上。

92

保險科技

保險科技再掀金融科技新浪潮。

以往，保險公司通常會推出各式各樣的工具來囊括不同的風險；「保險科技」則透過資料分析、人工智慧來改善保險市場，開發大量的新款利基型商品，保障探險、單車運動等特殊活動，甚至可能出現駕駛特斯拉（Tesla）的相關保險。

綜觀全球，疾病險和壽險的條約內容都在疫情期間大幅增加；傳統保險公司以外的新創企業，則趁此刻動身進入市場。

伊隆・馬斯克（Elon Musk）在 2020 年 7 月表示，特斯拉將推出一家「大型保險公司」，利用旗下電動車收集到的數據，做精確的風險分析，為安全駕駛提供較實惠的保險。

英國腳踏車險的先驅 Laka 是一間新創公司，專門提供單車騎士需要的保險產品，包含意外、受傷、車體毀損或遺失等項目。特別的是，這間公司並不是一家營利機構，而是一個集體社群，他們不收取固定保費，而是由顧客平均分攤該年度的賠償金，並根據投保設備價值不同而訂定不同的賠償上限，Laka 只從中收取理賠協商的費用。

此機制背後的信念，與美國新創公司 Lemonade 喊出的「創造附加價值」不謀而合——Lemonade 照常收取固定費用、支付賠償金，而理賠後的盈餘，則會捐給會員指定的慈善機構。Laka 和 Lemonade 雖在作法上有所差異，但都聰明地簡化了協商理賠的程序。

香港第一家數位保險公司保泰人壽（Bowtie），也以同樣的做法來吸引精通數位科技的年輕客群。他們推出這麼一支廣告：雙手和單腳都打上石膏的顧客，在輪椅上用一根腳指打字，且輕輕鬆鬆就完成理賠申請，同時搭配上超洗腦的廣告詞：「線上索賠超easy！」

值得關注的原因：

如同金融科技撼動古板的銀行業一樣，保險科技也提供了大量的商品，撼動傳統保險業，其中包含利基型與非利基型的產品，且價格通常較實惠。新進業者善用科技，讓理賠流程變得簡明快速！

財經網紅

財經網紅（finfluencer）讓金融成為年輕人之間的新潮話題。

Z 世代除了跟單網紅推薦的保養品，也開始在 TikTok（國際版抖音）和 YouTube 平台上學習個人理財知識，並樂見更多財經網紅出道。

杭弗瑞·楊（Humphrey Yang）、托里·唐拉普（Tori Dunlap）、萊恩·法蘭斯（Ryan Francis）等財經網紅都擁有好幾十萬名粉絲；楊在 TikTok 上的粉絲數甚至突破百萬。這些網紅提供的理財建議包括信用管理、稅務、預算規劃，還有金融領域的相關問答，例如「年輕人如何投資？」、「買車 vs. 租車，哪個划算？」。

疫情助長了這股趨勢。截至 2021 年 1 月，財經 YouTuber 萊恩·史克里布納（Ryan Scribner）已擁有 68 萬名粉絲；他在 2020 年 4 月告訴《女裝日報》（WWD），在他的所有影片中，和新冠疫情相關的創作，觀看數是其他影片的四倍。剛從商管學校畢業的潔咪·范可豪瑟（Jamie Fankhauser）在 2020 年 5 月創立了自

Credit Unions vs Banks

▷ 371.6K

己的 TikTok 帳號，同年 12 月，該帳號突破 3 萬人追蹤，總讚數也來到 11 萬以上；她的影片涵蓋各式金融議題，包含股市、儲蓄、創業等等。

2020 年 4 月，Instagram 網紅「道瓊小姐」（Mrs Dow Jones，本名 Haley Sacks），喊出一項為期八週的計劃：幫助 Z 世代在疫情期間好好理財，每週主題包含工作、個人財務規劃、健康護理、稅務等。道瓊小姐說：「對平常沒有特別關注金融資訊的人來說，這個話題很吸引他們。很多人對未來職涯充滿疑問，也不知道該如何賺錢或者管理現有資產。」

值得關注的原因：

失業人數暴增。2020 年 4 月，美國的失業率飆升到 14.7%，達近年 (1948-2020) 新高。經濟衰退之下，年輕人首當其衝——2020 年春季，25 歲以下美國人的失業率為 24.4%，而 25 歲以上的勞動人口失業率則是 11.3%。英國智庫「決議基金會」（Resolution Foundation）2020 年 10 月的公開報告顯示，英國 18 歲至 29 歲的失業率將達到 17%，與 1984 年金融危機時相去不遠。Z 世代的觀眾正在自我提升，希望能在財務安排上更具韌性，同時也把新一代理財型網紅推上寶座。

WUNDERMAN
THOMPSON

Top: @humphreytalks. Images courtesy of Humphrey Yang and TikTok
Bottom: @herfirst100k. Images courtesy of Tory Dunlap and TikTok

無條件基本收入實驗

政府重擬實施無條件基本收入計劃。

幾十年來，政壇上無論左派或右派人士，都曾提出某種形式的無條件基本收入方案。如今，新冠肺炎（COVID-19）為社會經濟帶來的負面影響，促使政府正面回應對於這類重大國家政策的呼聲。

加州康普頓市長艾賈・布朗（Aja Brown）在 2020 年 10 月公布了「康普頓承諾」（Compton Pledge）。這項為期兩年的實驗計劃，保障了當地特定居民的最低收入（金額未定），且每月皆以現金支付。布朗說：「市民正經歷艱困的時刻。確保一定的收入，能讓大眾有時間思考他們的處境，騰出一些喘息空間，可以重回校園、探索新職業涯、共度親子時光，或者改善身心狀況。」

回望疫情，日益加劇的社會不公，加上人工智慧和自動化科技可能衍生的失業問題，再再強化了無條件基本收入的需求。各國中央與地方政府，紛紛開始測試無條件基本收入計劃，若試行成效卓越，往後可能擴大實施。根據 2017 至 2018 年間，芬蘭某地區政府實驗的結果顯示：參與實驗的群眾當中，憂鬱症人口下降了 37%，受試者對未來的信心也上升了 22%。

"
緊接在2020年的經濟困頓與暴增的失業率後，與無條件基本收入相關的新論點，有望成為國家復原的契機。
"

在歐洲，西班牙推動了一項 30 億歐元的計劃，確保每位公民都有 462 歐元以上的基本月收入；款項可全額支付，或在未達基本收入門檻時作為加給。該計劃初期的服務對象，涵蓋了 250 萬名符合該計劃定義的「弱勢條件」公民，是目前最大的無條件基本收入實驗計劃之一。

韓國立法人員也提出多項無條件基本收入法案，其中，有一個道廳提出擴大防疫補助計畫，讓當地居民以「區域貨幣」領取每月薪資，有效期限最長三個月。

官方主導的計劃在全球爭議百出；目前還在開發階段的美國應用程式 Comingle 卻承諾會以線上社群的形式，為成員提供保證收入。該平台要求會員將 7% 的週收入提撥至共有基金，資金在經過平台重新分配以後，每週會再匯入成員的帳戶當中。

值得關注的原因：

皮尤研究中心（Pew Research Center）在 2020 年 8 月的一份調查報告顯示，多數（54%）美國人反對為所有成年公民提供每月 1,000 美元的無條件基本收入；但某些人還是對此興致勃勃，包括 18-29 歲的年輕人、民主黨支持者、經濟弱勢族群。加拿大政治人物和公民之間也出現類似的辯論，該國議會的預算辦公室在 2020 年夏季發布了一系列保障最低收入的潛在計畫。緊接在 2020 年的經濟困頓與暴增的失業率後，與無條件基本收入相關的新論點，有望成為國家復原的契機。

中國金融科技

投顧市場漸熱，中國線上平台也想分一杯羹。

騰訊控股公司自 2020 年 8 月起，開始透過旗下基金分配平台「騰安基金」來為顧客提供基金諮詢服務，並將服務擴展至旗下通訊軟體「微信」的用戶上（該軟體擁有超過 10 億名用戶）。無獨有偶，「螞蟻集團」先前也與美國合資公司「領航投資」（Vanguard）共同推出客製化投資方案；該集團的行動支付程式「支付寶」擁有 10 億用戶，他們和領航投資的合作案從 2019 年 12 月就已啟動。「螞蟻金服」是騰訊競爭對手「阿里巴巴」麾下的金融科技機構，他們原計於 2020 年首度公開發行（IPO），豈料新的借貸法規上路，因而延宕了時程。

彭博智庫（Bloomberg Intelligence）負責亞洲網路業務的高級分析師凌薇瑟（音譯自 Vey-Sern Ling）表示，此舉很符合科技巨頭的作風，他們一直努力尋求新的方式，從龐大的用戶流量中獲利。凌薇瑟告訴偉門智威智庫：「最典型的做法就是推出遊戲、

投放廣告或導購；『流量重導』或『推薦流量』也是獲利管道。我認為，網路公司中所有與財務相關的業務，都可納入這個類別，無論是基金諮詢、貨幣市場基金、理財商品、證券經紀，甚至網路銀行也不例外。」

這些科技公司握有深度數據和分析能力，能鎖定金融科技使用者。此外，疫情更推升了基金經理人的數位行銷策略，在新冠肺炎（COVID-19）隔離期間，中國內部投資類型的研討會直播，吸引了成千上萬名觀眾一同收看，熱門程度可見一斑。

值得關注的原因：

中國的基金管理公司可能還無法和西方國家並駕齊驅，但其成長指日可待，且有望呈現指數型飆升。儘管螞蟻集團目前遭遇監管問題，但凌薇瑟認為，線上投資和網銀「在未來幾年內仍會成為結構性趨勢」。未來，金融科技公司終將面對與傳統銀行相同的監管約束。

影響力投資

以價值觀爲核心的銀行服務將成爲正道。

《紐約時報》（The New York Times）在 2020 年 8 月的一篇文章中宣稱：「投資社會公益事業，將變得有利可圖。」他們引用的是 RBC 資本市場（RBC Capital Markets）的研究，該研究指出，那些為促進環境或社會發展而進行的「影響力投資」，在疫情期間的表現其實優於傳統投資項目。基於這樣的動能，投資者和金融機構正積極行動，讓大眾能更輕易地投資這類具有環境意識和社會道德的公司。

理財機器人 Betterment 協助大眾投資「改善氣候變遷和社會衝擊」的企業。2020 年 10 月，該公司推出新的投資組合，其中涵蓋了承擔社會責任的企業，讓客戶加以識別並投資，例如：碳足跡最少的公司、經全國有色人種促進協會認定的多元價值企業。

據《華爾街日報》（The Wall Street Journal）報導，摩根大通（JPMorgan）在同月宣布他們與義大利國家電力公司（Enel）達成新協議，「強調金融業的綠色轉型」。其交易條款以雙方的永續實踐為基礎，若其中一方未達成協議上的環保目標，另一方則可以提高價碼。

2020 年 9 月，「聯合國全球契約首席財務官特別工作組」為各企業的「影響力投資」建立了一套架構，呼籲其他公司高管共同制定投資決策，達成聯合國的永續發展目標，其中包含終結貧困、對氣候變遷採取行動等。該工作小組成員來自全球各行各業，總共有超過 30 家公司的資深財務長；他們表示，該小組已計劃為企業永續財務發展提出相關指南、案例研究與相關報告。

2020 年 6 月，投資公司 Robasciotti & Philipson 製作了一份「種族正義名單」，供大眾免費使用。該公司內部另有一份行徑不軌的公司名單，而這份「種族正義名單」則列出所有不在前一份名單上的公司。同月，洛克菲勒兄弟基金會（Rockefeller Brothers Fund）宣布，他們將開始積極投資更多由少數族群掌權的公司，並從 2020 年起對外公開其投資組合的多元價值。該基金會總裁暨執行長史蒂芬·海因茲（Stephen B Heintz）對《紐約時報》表示：「為改變而生的槓桿，本身就是資本的一環。」

Betterment 的資深副總裁波里斯·肯托夫（Boris Khentov）說道：「受價值觀驅動的投資動能與其迫切程度都持續增長。投資者不必再去猜測他們的投資標的是否與自身價值觀相左，也無須再在社會公益和低成本之間做出選擇。」

值得關注的原因：

金融服務是最新一個為消費者價值觀調整結構的行業。為了回應日益提高的消費意識，銀行和財務顧問開始改變他們的服務，讓投資者可以更輕易地善用資金，也讓具有社會責任的公司從中獲利。

97

社群媒體信用

社群媒體的排行即將成為調高信用額度的依據。

在 YouTube、Instagram、推趣（Twitch）這些平台上的內容創作產業，受到 Karat 公司的高度重視；其共同創辦人魏輝（Eric Wei）和威爾‧金（Will Kim）以前分別受僱於 Instagram 和高盛（Goldman Sachs）。他們想根據社群媒體上的信用排名來為用戶提供獎勵，而排名則以社群媒體上的統計數據和收入來源為基礎。

Karat 意圖挑戰傳統銀行經營模式。傳統銀行很晚才將網紅的「社群媒體信用」視為穩定的商業模式，而 Karat 想建立一個新的市場金流模式。其共同創辦人金告訴雜誌《連線》（Wired）：「傳統銀行體系混亂不堪，忽略了這些資料不齊全的廣大族群需求，所以我們就想，『欸，這是個很好的機會。』」

克拉黑卡（The Karat Black Card）是該公司發行的第一張信用卡，目前正由一小群創作者進行測試。該卡與支付公司 Stripe 合作發行，目前並未收取手續費，也不用支付利息，目的是要拓展市占率，如此才能擴大經營，將觸角伸入更多金融服務項目，例如房屋貸款。

值得關注的原因：

人工智慧驅動的分析平台 HypeAuditor 指出，2019 年光是 Instagram 網紅的市值就達 52.4 億美元，且有超過 300 萬則貼文標上了「#贊助」（#sponspred）標籤。越來越多內容創作者、品牌、行銷人員，將社群媒體視為核心業務之一，因此形塑了這類新的度量系統，為無法取得傳統銀行金援的人員和機構，提供財務支援。

98

危機儲蓄

**財務狀況不明朗的未來，大眾的消費與儲蓄習慣
正在改變。**

失業率上升、股市動盪、經濟衰退的止血點遙遙無期，消費者正勒
緊褲帶生活。根據 TD Ameritrade 在 2020 年 5 月底的一項調查
指出，超過三分之二的美國人表示，疫情讓他們找到降低開銷的全
新方式。多數人都提到食品和生活用品的開銷劇增，但同時也省下
了外食、旅行和治裝的費用。

如同 TD Ameritrade 的報告顯示，多數人的金錢觀變得更加謹
慎，仔細追蹤每一筆開銷，並儲備生活應用金。2020 年 9 月，哈里
斯民調（Harris Poll）為 CIT 銀行展開一項調查：他們針對 2,000
名成人進行研究，結果顯示，53% 的美國人在當年 6 月至 9 月存
下的錢高於以往同期，就連失業的人口裡，也有 41% 的人持相同
看法；另外還有 76% 的人計劃要在往後每月都存下更多錢。

儲蓄率也為這樣的說法提供佐證。美國經濟分析局表示，疫情前
的儲蓄率（每戶家庭從每月收入中提撥的儲蓄比例）是 7.5%；而
西北互惠（Northwestern Mutual）的研究也顯示，2020 年 4 月
的儲蓄率飆升至 33.7%，達歷史新高，且其後數月都保持在 20%
上下。

年輕消費者也緊守錢包。2020 年 10 月，偉門智威數據服務
為其智庫所做的研究指出，70% 的 Z 世代人口表示，新冠肺炎
（COVID-19）改變了他們的消費習慣。富國銀行（Wells Fargo）
的數據也顯示，超過 16% 的 Z 世代人口以及 18% 的千禧世代人
口，都在疫情後開始決定為退休生活存下更多財富。

他們的態度說明這個轉變並非稍縱即逝。偉門智威的研究顯示，
65% 的 Z 世代人口認為自己傾向儲蓄而非花錢，80% 的人同意
聰明消費比賺大錢更重要，還有 77% 的人每次收到款項後一定
都會預先存下其中的一部分。疫情期間養成的理財習慣，形塑了
Z 世代的身份認同，甚至可能影響他們的一生；也許此後，年輕人
會比上一輩更擅長管理財務。

值得關注的原因：
根據 TD Ameritrade 的調查，64% 的美國人表示，其消費習慣因
疫情而從此改變。品牌需要為接下來的保守消費做好準備，調整
行銷語彙和手段。

電子錢包大亂鬥

全球都在尋找現金的替代品,且跳過信用卡,
直接使用電子支付與電子錢包。

電子錢包的選項不計其數,母公司類型也包羅萬象:從電子叫車
服務公司(例如新加坡的 Grab 提供了 GrabPay、印尼的 Gojek
提供 GoPay),到電信公司(印度的 Jio Platforms 旗下有
JioMoney),再到線上雜貨(印度的 Flipkart 握有 PhonePe),
又或是電商市場(新加坡的蝦皮有蝦皮支付)。馬來西亞的
Touch'n Go 最初是智慧卡片,用來支付高速公路過路費和停車
費,如今也推出 Touch'n Go 電子錢包。

相關風險很高,因為和電子錢包合作,是把消費者導流至商家的
關鍵,讓攤商和市集透過優惠來吸引消費者,並確保顧客忠誠
度——因為大眾會忠於固定的電子錢包,就像他們會選擇固定的
銀行一樣。

想了解市場有多零碎,看看印尼就對了。根據 2020 年 10 月益普
索(Ipso)的一項調查顯示,印尼市場的領導品牌為蝦皮支付,其
滲透率為為 48%,其次是 OVO(46%)、GoPay(35%)、Dana

ONLINE PAYMENTS

Buy movie tickets, shop online, book flights and more!

> 因爲大衆會忠於固定的電子錢包，就像他們會選擇固定的銀行一樣。

（26%），再來是 LinkAja（16%）。據貝恩管理顧問公司（Bain & Co）統計，在整個東南亞區域內，使用現金付款的比例從 48% 降至 2020 年的 37%；電子錢包的交易量也從 18% 升至 25%。

如果這樣還不夠競爭？中國和西方的大型科技公司，也想來搶攻東南亞市場。臉書（Facebook）和谷歌（Google）都投資了印度的 Jio；微信支付於 2020 年進入印尼市場；在撰文之際，支付寶也打算透過和曼迪利銀行（Bank Mandiri）、印尼人民銀行（Bank Rakyat）合作，正式入主印尼。支付寶和微信支付早期在全球各地的拓展計劃，主要是為迎合在各地旅遊的中國遊客，但近期已轉而鎖定當地市場。

值得關注的原因：
疫情加速了數位支付轉型，政府剛好也在鼓勵社會邁向無現金交易。然而，在某些國家，電子錢包的數量可能已經趨近飽和了。

沙發型理財顧問

財務管理是一道難題，但新型的沙發型理專正在改寫此事。

全球各地都感受到新冠肺炎（COVID-19）造成的經濟衝擊，對財務的焦慮也漸升。美國國家公共廣播電台於 2020 年 9 月的統計指出，美國四大城市皆有至少半數的家庭面臨重大財務危機：芝加哥 50%、紐約 53%、洛杉磯 56%、休士頓 63%。2020 年 10 月來自西北互惠（Northwestern Mutual）的調查顯示，美國有近三分之一（31%）的成年人，每個月至少會有一次因財務焦慮而感到沮喪。

西北互惠的執行副總暨客戶關係總長克里斯蒂安·米歇爾（Christian Mitchell）說道：「大眾為此感到焦慮是正常的。」但他也指出，有問題的不只是壓力—不知道如何控制自己的財務狀況也會引發焦慮。「壓力可能會癱瘓你的生活，尤其在不確定要採取什麼具體措施的情況下更是如此。這裡的關鍵是要取得控制權、參考他人觀點，並付諸行動。」

大眾開始向朋友尋求相關建議。

愛爾·郭德菈朵（Ale Cuadrado）於 2020 年 7 月開始在 TikTok 上發布理財相關影片，分享她在疫情期間求職的沮喪經驗；此內容受到矚目，她自己也相當驚訝。其中一支影片提及她在紐約失業後的理財習慣，觀看數超過 34 萬，她認為其中的賣點是坦率—從同儕中獲得的觀點較為真實、易懂，和正規的金融教育途徑有所不同。郭德菈朵對《i-D》說道：「這是非常重要的事，特別是對年輕一代而言。我們大多數人都面臨失業或工作不穩定，所以當大家知道自己並不孤單，其實會覺得很欣慰。」

肯德基大學的疼痛醫學研究員惠特洛博士（Dr Bryan T Whitlow）也持相同論調。他告訴《紐約時報》（The New York Times）：「聽到有人的處境和你相同時，他們對你的影響力會更大，因為你知道他們原本也和你一樣。」他自己也是人數不斷成長的「理財練習生」之一，而這波成長主要是來自大眾開始轉向朋友和同事尋求理財指導。

據《紐約時報》在 2020 年 7 月報導，麻醉師布拉德博士（Dr Ty L Bullard）為北卡羅來納大學的醫學系住院醫師創辦了個人理財學習計劃，鼓勵住院醫師在職涯早期就開始預備退休生活。他們在講座和研討會中討論投資計劃，並分享自己的理財決策和失誤。

"
財務焦慮叢生，理財顧問的角色因而變得更加多元。
"

國際貿易規範顧問妮可翡丁（Alannah NicPhaidin）現居科羅拉多州，她「在無意間成為朋友的顧問」。她從個人生活出發，談論自己為葡萄酒和巧克力制訂的預算規劃，隨後才進入相關表單。「如果你很喜歡和朋友討論財務保障，而且有辦法讓他們知道財務規劃的重要和好處，那他們也會感到很開心。」妮可翡丁對《紐約時報》接著說道：「而且這不只是老年人的陳腔濫調：『你要做好財務規劃』；因為你可以做的不只是這樣。」

值得關注的原因：

財務焦慮叢生，理財顧問的角色因而變得更加多元。大眾想要掌握自己的財務狀況，並轉向信任的人尋求指導，讓財務導師生態呈現新的樣貌。

專家的話

產業領導者如何預測2021年的趨勢呢?我們詢問了21位專家,請他們分享對2021年的看法。從旅遊、科技、行銷,到美妝領域,涵蓋的主題有:如多重宇宙般的內容產業正在擴張;消費者行動主義仍持續推進,品牌需具備更大的社會責任;科技無所不在,加上混合不同實境技術日趨成熟;對大自然的敬仰加倍成長;居家飲食再升級。

品牌&行銷

「冠狀病毒在 2020 年發生的衝擊造成了極大的損失。健康成為優先考量，由於科學進展我們得以放寬許多限制，現在品牌的第一順位會是心理和身體健康。全世界都在重新定義健康對居家和職場生活來說究竟是什麼，而社群、大眾、使命感會成為企業高層的優先考量。」

WPP執行長，Mark Read

「2020 年發生的種種事件，都讓消費者對於新聞事件的反應變得特別敏銳，也更願意發聲、起身對抗他們認為不道德的品牌。2021 年，若有品牌說的和做的不同，將會面對更加激烈的危機。品牌需要表明自己的立場，並制定社群媒體回覆策略，遇到社會、經濟、種族正義等議題時，務必在最短的時間內於社群媒體上做出回應。」

Check My Ads 共同創辦人
潔米（Nandini Jammi）

「人們希望品牌承擔更多責任，使命感也因此有了新的定義。大家終於有時間坐下來仔細想想，究竟什麼對我們來說才是重要的。至 2021 年年底，品牌責任對銷售量將會和行銷一樣重要。」

Did They Help? 創辦人
摩爾加利艾（Pooj Morjaria）

「內容創作者不僅成為焦點，並且有大量的需求，這是目前觀察到的現象。創意行銷公司開始僱用創作者，即便是高中生也無所謂；透過教育訓練，讓他們活躍於不同的產業當中，因為各行各業將會需要內容創作者。」

Uplab創辦人暨品牌成長總監
Fabian Ouwehand

「我認為『復原力』會成為明年主要的品牌選圖主題。雖然每個人的 2020 年都過得很辛苦，整個社會充滿了那股想要跨過這些挑戰的決心，讓消費者聚焦於培養在地和全球的復原力。」

Adobe圖庫創意與消費者洞見主管
米莉絲（Brenda Milis）

科技&創新

「就算一月份沒有好萊塢新片上映，多重宇宙般的內容產業還是
會持續發光發熱，而且不只是加速發展而已，連種類也變得更加
多元。除了電影、劇集、實境節目、體育賽事、音樂、播客節目、
遊戲、其他惡搞類的作品之外，也有融合敘事方式和參與式娛樂
的全新內容型態。」
**AeBeZe Labs創辦人暨執行長
莫斯柯維茨（Michael Moskowitz）**

「虛擬實境是把遠端聚會帶到全新階段的關鍵。臉書
（Facebook）剛出現時，他們在網路、電腦大流行，之後是
iPhone，臉書成功地轉移到手機平台上。我覺得接下來從手機轉
移到頭戴式裝置的過程也會如此，未來五年間，最大的發展契機，
就是頭戴式裝置的流行。」
Teooh執行長暨創辦人，Don Stein

「未來我們不會看到單一『實境』（擴增實境、虛擬實境、
延展實境、現實生活、網路世界等等）躍升至主流，而是會在全新
領域中，看到他們華麗地整合在一起。Coachella 音樂節會回歸，
其他大型節目也是，同時提供虛擬的體驗模式。
火人祭今年會更賣力地呈現開創性的多重宇宙面貌，讓無法
來到沙漠盆地的人們也可以感同身受。最後，我們會
分不清眼前使用的究竟是哪種實境，他們會完美地結合在一起。
未來不是只有現實或模擬，而是兩者都要，
只是看怎麼結合而已。」
Meta創辦人暨執行長，Justin Bolognino

「產品遊戲化、數位會議、串流服務等日趨普及，預計 2021 年會
看到互動數位內容平台持續爆炸地成長。虛擬實境、
擴增實境、混合實境、音控裝置都會回歸，我期待看到
B2C 類型的公司開始量產虛擬實境和擴增實境裝置，藉此回應
這些需求，例如蘋果（Apple）和亞馬遜（Amazon）。」
**Soho House Group全球內容總監
Nelly Gocheva**

旅遊&觀光

「緩慢、充滿意義的旅行和體驗，會受到越來越多的關注，特別是那些有一大群人湧入，就會干擾到當地環境的地方。我們觀察到這個現象，是因為攝影師開始關閉定位服務，防止有一大群人跑去破壞當地的生態，那些地方可能不適合大量的旅客造訪。」

Tentrr創意總監
克里斯荷姆（Gareth Chisholm）

「過度觀光、氣候變遷，加上新冠肺炎，這些都成為催化劑，讓人們開始好好省思旅遊的目的、價值、風險。後設旅遊（教你如何聰明旅行的旅遊方式）會慢慢成形，接下來可以看到更多注意力放到旅行帶來的療效，旅遊顧問不再只想快速推銷行程，還會分享新領域的知識，像是心靈健康、快樂、潮流、創意、玩樂、轉型等等。」

旅遊顧問與旅遊網站
《Revisit: The New Art of Luxury Travel》作者
Philippe Brown

醫療保健

「我預測在 2021 年會看到更多科學與科技的整合，科技公司會把輔助型護理目的加在他們的使命與營運。傳統醫學模式會改變，使用數位科技來結合感應器並且提供直接的互動回饋，讓健康護理從診間服務延伸到居家和工作環境當中。」

Lanserhof醫療總監，Sebastain Kunz

金融

「金融科技持續演變成更符合個人化需求，由於消費者和企業都在尋找量身定做的產品。我們思考的是專為自由工作者、移民、電商商家、房東所設計的銀行產品，而不是為所有人都提供一樣的服務。」

Karat共同創辦人，魏辉

食品&飲品

「未來我們可能還是會減少在外用餐的次數,但是有更多機會吃到別人為我們準備的餐點,我覺得這是未來五年會出現的最大轉變,所以特別想談到這點。如果在 20 世紀,是把餐點打包好、送到路程 10 分鐘內的顧客手中,那我想代表 21 世紀的就是把料理好的餐點一鍵送到任何顧客手中。」
**歐睿國際(Euromonitor)飲食服務研究部全球主管
沙非(Michael Schaefer)**

「吃早餐越來越像在參與盛會。等限制鬆綁以後,大家會想要體驗新的事物,我預期接下來會看到更多值得關注的特殊用餐體驗。」
**《倫敦早餐:正港倫敦人吃什麼?》(暫譯自 *Breakfast London: Where Real Londoners Eat*)作者
布莉基(Bianca Bridges)**

「我們預測近期會出現不同的烘焙趨勢,口感奢華、閃閃發亮、搖搖晃晃的果凍,開始佔有一席之地。過去 13 年來,我們一直在做果凍,現在我們終於可以期待看到果凍的黃金年代來臨。」
Bompas & Parr共同創辦人,Sam Bompas

「人們在家用餐的機會變高,但這不代表他們不想去餐廳、酒吧或者咖啡廳。因此,我們未來會看到很多創意居家飲食企劃,許多餐飲都是以往不會在家享用的品項。」
**The Food People資深編輯
希賈茲(Shokofeh Hejazi)**

美容

「我們發現種族話題成為主流趨勢，這和以往不太一樣，雖然這個現象也已經持續滿多年了。過去十年內，『購買黑人產品』（#BuyBlack）的標籤慢慢取得了一席之地，所以美妝產業也開始受到這樣的多元文化對話所啟發。消費者和員工會持續推進這股從 2020 年開始的趨勢，在 2021 年勇敢發聲，透過日常消費與工作實踐，要求在工作氛圍上站不住腳、仍然存有種族歧視的企業出來面對。」

Geenie創辦人暨執行長
伊雯（Chana Ginelle Ewing）

「對很多美妝品牌來說，永續發展仍然會是重要的考量，因為永續已經不再只是稀有小眾的任務，而是美妝和個人護理品牌的未來。」

Cocokind創辦人暨執行長，Priscilla Tsai

零售

「（我預期接下來會看到）越來越多的零售業者把便利納入考量，有些業者會使用類似諾德斯特龍百貨（Nordstrom）的『在地 Nordstrom』概念，把重點放在網路訂單的取貨和退換貨服務上。」

《Glossy》總編，Jill Manoff

「線上平台變得越來越重要。在 2021 年，企業需要破除枯燥的作法，把重點放在數位平台上，思考如何用更吸引人的方式，正確地傳遞品牌價值。對於促進情感連結和鋪設銷售管道這兩件事情，企業需要同樣的重視。」

Base設計工作室合夥人，庫克（Geoff Cook）

關於偉門智威智庫 (Wunderman Thompson Intelligence)

偉門智威智庫是智威湯遜面向未來思考的研究和創新單位，負責觀察剛興起的現象以及未來的全球趨勢、消費型態變化、創新發展模式，並在進一步解讀這些趨勢後，將其見解提供給品牌參考。偉門智威智庫提供一系列諮詢服務，包含客製化研究、簡報、聯名品牌報告與工作坊，且本智庫也勇於創新，與品牌合作，在品牌既有框架下引領未來趨勢，並執行新產品與概念。本單位由偉門智威智庫的全球總監 Emma Chiu 所帶領。

如欲瞭解更多資訊，請造訪：

intelligence.wundermanthompson.com

關於《改變未來的 100 件事：2021 年全球百大趨勢》

偉門智威智庫的年度預測呈現了未來一年的面貌，並指出最引人注目的趨勢，讓你的雷達保持敏銳。這份報告點出了 10 個產業當中的 100 個趨勢，包括文化、科技與創新、旅遊與觀光、品牌與行銷、食品與飲品、美容、零售、工作、健康、金融。

+ WUNDERMAN
THOMPSON

聯絡人：

Emma Chiu
偉門智威智庫 | 全球總監
emma.chiu@wundermanthompson.com
台灣偉門智威
wt.taipei@wundermanthompson.com

總編輯
Emma Chiu

編輯
Emily Safian-Demers

撰稿人
Chen May Yee, Marie Stafford, Elizabeth Cherian, Sarah Tilley, Maeve Prendergast, Nina Jones, Jessica Rapp

副編輯
Hester Lacey, Katie Myers

翻譯
林庭如（Rye Lin Ting-Ru）

創意總監
Shazia Chaudhry

封面圖片
Paul Milinski（圖片來源：Loftgarten）